D1097747

The Novelist's Responsibility

NATHANIEL HAWTHORNE
From the photograph by Matthew Brady

The Novelist's Responsibility

BY

L. P. HARTLEY

HAMISH HAMILTON
LONDON

First published in Great Britain, 1967
by Hamish Hamilton Ltd
90 Great Russell Street, London, W.C.1
Copyright © 1967 by L. P. Hartley

Printed in Great Britain by
Western Printing Services Ltd, Bristol

ACKNOWLEDGMENTS

'The Novelist's Responsibility' first appeared in *Essays by Divers Hands*, published by the Royal Society of Literature; the essays on Jane Austen and Emily Brontë were written for the Jane Austen Society and for the Brontë Society. 'Nathaniel Hawthorne' comprised the Clark Lectures given at the invitation of Trinity College, Cambridge. 'The Near and the Far' was the introduction to the Reprint Society's edition of L. H. Myers' tetralogy. 'The Novels of C. H. B. Kitchin' appeared in the *London Magazine*, 'The Novelist and his Material' in *The Times Literary Supplement*, and 'Remembering Venice' in the *Geographical Magazine*. I am grateful to these institutions and publications for permission to reprint the material contained in this book, also to Messrs. William Heinemann and the executors of the D. H. Lawrence estate for permission to reprint, in 'Nathaniel Hawthorne', extracts from Lawrence's *Studies in Classic American Literature*. If I have overlooked any other due acknowledgments, it is because I have no record of where some of the shorter essays first appeared.

L.P.H.

To
PATRICK

CONTENTS

CONTENTS

I

THE NOVELIST'S RESPONSIBILITY

A T THE outset I wanted to leave the title of this paper rather vague, for the novel is a large subject and I didn't quite know from what angle to approach it. So I called it 'Some Thoughts on the Novel'. And then this title struck me as not only vague but also pretentious. Some *thoughts* on the novel. I don't know if anyone still remembers the poetry of Ella Wheeler Wilcox. She was well known in her day and wrote one immortal line, as well as many that were not immortal. Well, she wrote one poem called *The Legacies* or *The Gifts*. I've never read it, but I understand that in the poem she makes gifts or legacies to three of her friends. I can't remember what the first two presents were, so I speak subject to correction, but I fancy they were concrete keepsakes of some sentimental but no great monetary value. But to the third friend she gave something different, something that might be more welcome today, an *abstract* gift. She bequeathed him a thought, just a thought. And someone wrote in the margin of the book, 'How like our dear generous Ella to give what she could least spare, a *thought*.'

So I took warning from this and decided to call my paper 'The Novelist's Responsibility'. But then I felt uneasy about this title too. A little while ago I was in Paris when a book of mine came out, and some reporters interviewed me. They asked me for details of my life and I longed to be able to say: 'I have been a lumberjack', or 'I served with the North-West Mounted Police', or 'I once lived with the gipsies', but the most romantic thing I could think of was that I had once been an amateur gondolier. But that didn't seem to cut much ice, and at last in desperation I said: 'I am a moralist!' and the effect of this announcement was quite electrifying. But no sooner had I seen it going down in the man's notebook than I was overcome with shame, and cried, 'Please cross that out! Of course I'm not a moralist! What *would* my friends say?' But the reporter said soothingly, 'You needn't worry. It means something quite different in French!' What the difference is I still don't know, but the sentence duly appeared in the paper—'Je suis un moraliste.'

Well, I felt rather the same when writing about the novelist's responsibility. The words 'moral' and 'morality' seemed to appear in every line, and moral as I am I began to fear I was doing the subject to death and should end by giving morality itself a bad name. So I thought that before discussing the novelist's responsibility I would try to say something about the novelist's sensibility. Sensibility is a word much used in contemporary fiction criticism. What does it mean? It means, for one thing, the ability to feel what one is writing about. There is no recipe for it: it is like feeling in real life—one either has it or one has not. It has been said that a novelist will never be any good until he has learnt to exteriorize himself and to write about characters who are in no way like him. He must learn to objectify. There is a certain truth in this. A novelist must give the impression of a world of external reality existing outside himself: if he mentions a table it must be a real table, and not an unsubstantial dream-table. And he must create a world which the reader can accept and live in, without feeling that it would dissolve like Prospero's if the author was not somehow behind it. It must exist independently of the author's testimony, but not of his sensibility, not of his feeling for it, which must be as strong as, or stronger than, the feeling he has for his own life.

And to be that it must, in some degree, be an extension of his own life; its fundamental problems must be his problems, its preoccupations his preoccupations—or something allied to them. As Mr. D. S. Savage has said, it must be an analogue of his own life. The reason why so many first novels are good novels is simply this: the author has an impulse to communicate his own experience, and his first attempt has a freshness which none of his later work, though it may have gained in literary skill, can show. *Castle Rackrent* was Maria Edgeworth's first novel, and also her best; *Evelina* was Fanny Burney's first novel, and also her best. Some of the best novels have been single novels—*Les Liaisons Dangereuses*, *Adolphe*, *Dominique*, *Wuthering Heights*, *Vathek*, *I Promessi Sposi*. Their authors achieved perfection, or something near it, without practice, because they were writing about something that was essential to their thoughts and feelings.

Wish-fulfilment is a despised term, but it describes a universal experience. And if it has been the dynamo of many bad novels, it has also been the inspiration of many good ones. It can be, and generally is, combined with autobiography; but seldom with pure autobiography. The novelist presents his experience— sometimes in a rosy light, sometimes in a gloomy light, sometimes hoping to arouse his reader's admiration, sometimes hoping to arouse his pity. (In even the most austere novels there is generally a kind of flirtation between the author and his reader: and when he seems to be flouting him on purpose, for instance devising an unhappy ending that will disappoint or horrify him, he is really trying to win the reader to his side.) Tolstoy, who is usually considered one of the most objective of novelists, drew many of his characters from people he knew, hardly bothering to change their names. He put himself into *War and Peace* as Pierre, and into *Anna Karenina* as Levine—a puzzled, clumsy, worried, well-meaning sort of character, at sea in the world, anxious to achieve happiness and goodness through farming and family life. He did not idealize himself, however, in the way that Stendhal did in his novels. Stendhal is the *locus classicus* of a wish-fulfilment novelist; is it significant, I wonder, that he has never been more highly thought of than he is today? He was, in fact, a fat, ugly little man, devoted to women, with whom he had apparently only moderate success; in his novels, whether he appears as Julien in *Le Rouge et le Noir*, or as Fabrice in the *Chartreuse de Parme*, or as Lucien in *Lucien Leuwen*, he is brilliantly good-looking and greatly beloved. In *Lucien Leuwen* he presses his suit unsuccessfully with Mme de Chasteller, but she loves him all the same; she can hardly bear to resist him; and he has the compensation of being richer, cleverer, better-looking, and a better horseman than all his fellow officers in the garrison at Nancy. For all their factuality and realism his books are daydreams in which one sees him quite shamelessly compensating himself for his personal handicaps and for the dullness and boredom of his life as a consul in Italy. 'Boredom', he wrote, 'is the only unhappiness', and his novels are the first, I believe, in which the characters suffer consciously from boredom, as from an illness. He was a man of extreme but disarming vanity—he extolled and belittled himself in the same breath. In spite of his vein of charlatanism (he used 200 aliases when writing) and in spite of being the hero of his own opera, so to speak, he was a prophet of our modern consciousness; there is no novelist of his time whose psychology has dated so little. And one reason for this is that, allowing for the idealizations, he put himself raw into his books. He knew what a driving force vanity is. He understood that everybody's ego needs a great deal of support. He also understood that every man has an idea of himself, as a pillar of society, it may be, or a lover, or a rogue—an idea of himself to which he is determined to live up. He understood the feelings and above all the fluctuations of the feelings, better than almost any novelist has. The practising novelist knows how terribly difficult and risky it is to represent a character as changing his mind or his mood. The character can do it once or twice, just as a politician may change his party once or twice; but if he does it oftener the thread of personality is broken. The ordinary novelist cannot afford to let his characters be as inconsistent as people are in real life. Stendhal's characters may be grossly inconsistent half a dozen times in a page, be in love, out of love, happy or unhappy, bored or interested, but never for a moment does one feel they are not the same person.

Forgive this digression on the theme of the novelist in his own novels. There are many instances of it. Charlotte Brontë drew her own portrait in *Jane Eyre*, but she did not idealize herself: she makes Jane look in the glass and say, 'Portrait of a governess, without connections, poor and plain.' But Flaubert went much further than that in self-depreciation. *Madame Bovary* is not a wish-fulfilment but a fear-fulfilment novel. It seems a far cry from Flaubert, the blond Norman who looked like a Viking, and was a friend of most of the great writers of his day, to Emma, the wife of a very stupid provincial doctor, eating her heart out in a small town, dreaming dreams of grandeur and trying to implement them by furtive and unsatisfying intrigues. And yet we have his word for it that Emma was a projection of himself: 'Madame Bovary', he said, 'c'est moi.'

Even such an objectifying novelist as George Eliot was far more at home with her art when she could identify herself with her characters—with Maggie Tulliver, or Dorothea Brooke, for instance—than when she left herself out, as she did in *Romola*. *Romola* was a task she set herself: she approached it from outside with a history of Florence at her elbow, just as Flaubert approached *Salammbô* with a history of Carthage at his—and both novels are comparative failures, dead, in spite or because of the pains their authors lavished on them.

The conclusion is, that it is safer for a novelist to choose as his subject something he feels about than something he knows about, or has got to know about by study and conscious observation. And if not something he feels about—since feeling is at a rather low ebb just at present—then something he thinks about, for feeling and thinking are not easy to disentangle.

The value of egotism, said Goethe, depends on the value of the egotist. It is a truism, I suppose, but it contains a truth one is apt to overlook when one gets irritated with egotists. Nearly all writers are egotists because, even if they are not writing of themselves, their work is an extension of themselves, to a degree to which a non-artist's work is not. 'All the things that I have written', Goethe said, 'are but fragments of a long confession.'

Many novelists who do not make a personal appearance in their books are haunted by a particular idea or situation which embodies what they feel about life and enables them to apply their sensibility to it, and to choose what elements in it nourish their gifts, just as surely as if they were writing about themselves. This idea or situation goes on in them like a kind of murmur; it is what their thoughts turn to when they are by themselves. Most of us, writers or not writers, have some orientation of that kind, a magnetic north for our private musings. Cervantes was everlastingly fascinated by the idea of three realities—he distinguished many more than three, but there were three chief ones: the world as it appeared to Don Quixote, the world as it appeared to Sancho Panza, and the world as in fact it was (the last a cruel world, which laughed at both Knight and Squire, and tossed poor Sancho Panza in a blanket). Most of the episodes in *Don Quixote* illustrate the discrepancies between these rival realities. Henry James was haunted by a situation: the situation of the *naïf*, simple American, man or woman, coming to Europe and being taken in and exploited by the unscrupulous, often penniless, and generally good-looking representatives of our corrupt, older civilization. Over and over again this situation repeats itself in his novels: he is always balancing the innocence and virtue of the New World against the beauty, charm, and unscrupulousness of the Old. Hawthorne, from whom James borrowed so much, is haunted (according to one account he was literally haunted) by the idea of the sins of the fathers being visited on their descendants. He himself had a witch-hanger among his ancestors. Joseph Conrad was concerned with honour; he saw life in terms of faithfulness, as a trust; the fidelity a man owed to himself, the fidelity he owed to his employers—the Company, it might be, for example, to whom his ship belonged. The Servant of the Company: what dignity, what grandeur he gets into this simple phrase. He is concerned with the problem of how a man is to keep his self-respect; and how, when he loses it, the mainspring of his life is broken. After thirty years I can still remember those two words in *Lord Jim*, which recur so heartbreakingly—'I jumped.' There is a life's tragedy in them. Apropos the novelist in his own novels, Joseph Conrad, as we all know, was a Pole, and when he was 17 or 18 he went to live as a sailor in the South of France, after which he settled in England. There was no overwhelming reason, as far as I know, why he should *not* have left Poland, but he regarded it as a desertion, almost as a betrayal. Lord Jim was first or second mate (I can't remember which!) of his ship, and he could not afterwards forgive himself for leaving it to sink, with the pilgrims on it—against all the traditions of seamanship. Nor could Conrad forgive himself for leaving Poland, which was another sinking ship. The feeling of guilt he had about it, and the fact that he could not help identifying himself with Lord Jim, make the novel one of his best.

Well, these are all writers of the past. How does the novelist of today fare when he tries to interpret his age through the medium of his sensibility?

To try to answer that question I must again return to the past; and it may be a useful guide to the present if we ask ourselves what the attitude of novelists has been towards their human material in general and how it has changed during the last two hundred years. Two hundred years ago their attitude to their human material was highly critical and governessy. With the exception of Sterne—who is an exception to all generalizations—and perhaps I should add, in some of his books, Defoe, the novelists of the eighteenth century were not at all indulgent towards human frailties. They considered it to be their mission to reform the public. Fielding, I believe, said in so many words that he wrote to reform morals. It is an ironical reflection that for nearly a hundred years *Tom Jones* was thought to be a book unfit to put into the hands of a young person. He thought that there was a danger of the public admiring criminals as heroes; so he wrote *The History of Jonathan Wild the Great* to castigate at once the criminals and the public. It is the story of a gangster's progress (and as such very applicable to modern times). 'Greatness' means eminence in crime. What then have I to do', asks Wild, 'in the pursuit of greatness, but to procure a gang and make the use of this gang centre in myself? . . . Out of this gang I will prefer to my favour the boldest and most iniquitous . . . the rest I will . . . as I see occasion . . . transport and hang at my pleasure; and thus convert those laws which are made for the benefit and protection of society for my single use.' Richardson was a less declared satirist than Fielding, but he was even more intent on moral uplift. He called his first novel *Pamela, or Virtue Rewarded*, and he expressed the hope that it might 'turn young people into a course of reading different from the pomp and parade of romance-writing . . . and tend to promote the cause of religion and virtue'.

As for Swift, we know what he thought about the human race; he has told us in *Gulliver's Travels*. He wrote to show humanity up, not to reform it. He was a misanthrope; and there is, or may be, all the difference between a misanthrope and a satirist. Fielding was a lover of humanity as Dickens was, but he was sharply aware of its shortcomings and thought they needed pointing out. And so did Jane Austen, who wrote in the nineteenth century, but who spiritually and morally belonged to the eighteenth. She, too, was a satirist. She kept her satire within the bounds of the convention of comedy; but sometimes, as in the characters of Miss Bates and Mrs. Norris, it runs away with her. On the whole she was very just to her creations; but she was a severe moralist; it would never have occurred to her that she ought to be indulgent to, still less to justify, their faults.

With the Victorian Age there came a change. It was the age of humanism and humanitarianism—the second the child of the first. Humanism was to become a religion to many people, and no wonder: see what progress Science had made in the material world! And what progress enlightenment had made in the moral sphere! Man was sufficient unto himself. Belief in progress was one of the strongest of Victorian beliefs; and it entailed belief in the perfectibility of man. But meanwhile there were many abuses and injustices to put right, and the more generous-minded and socially conscious of the Victorian novelists threw themselves into this task with a will. Dickens was a vigilant champion of the underdog; the passion that other novelists have kept for the emotion of love he put into delineating the sufferings of little boys at school, into the sufferings of the oppressed everywhere: the Court of Chancery, which oppressed its victims with its eternal delays, the Circumlocution Office, which did the same, came in for the most tremendous trouncing from Dickens. And that is one reason why his novels have a universal appeal— because most of us believe ourselves to be oppressed. Other novelists achieved fame through their passion for putting right injustices. Charles Reade attacked prison systems and private lunatic asylums; Charles Kingsley exposed the wrongs of little boys who were made to sweep chimneys, in *Water Babies*— though it doesn't live for that reason. Last and most glorious in the company of reformers, Harriet Beecher Stowe attacked the Slave Trade and undoubtedly helped to abolish it—though again it is perhaps not so much her reforming zeal that has made *Uncle Tom's Cabin* live, but the appeal of its characters—the terrifying wickedness of Simon Legree, the engaging naughtiness of Topsy, and the angelic goodness of Eva.

All this is too well known, perhaps, to be worth mentioning; but my point is that the attitude of the Victorian novelists towards humanity in general differed radically from that of their eighteenth-century predecessors. Their predecessors thought that all mankind, more or less, was in need of a scolding (there are exceptions to this, of course—Squire Allworthy in *Tom Jones* is one), whereas the Victorians thought that some people, perhaps most, were all right, and beyond the need for criticism, whereas others needed chastising. They supported one section of the community against another. They were partisans in the moral sphere: they distinguished sheep from goats. The bad were very bad but the good were very good, and capable of perfection if they had not already attained it. And to match this, their heroes and heroines tended to be good-looking as well as good, and their villains (though not always their villainesses) bad-looking as well as bad.

This was the second phase in the evolution of the English novelist's attitude towards our moral state. But among the Victorian novelists was one, a lonely giant, who did not subscribe to the views of his colleagues, and that was Thomas Hardy. Hardy was one of the most revolutionary novelists, from the moral standpoint, in the history of fiction. He was a great lover of humanity and if he did not actually think that human beings could do no wrong, he thought that the wrong they did was *not their fault*. He drew moral distinctions: there are good and less good characters in his novels. There are rich, charming, idle ladies who lead young men astray. There are sensual women like Arabella, who are contrasted with loving women like Sue Bridehead. There are weak men like Angel Clare; there are flashy, unreliable types like Alec Durberville and Sergeant Troy. There are patterns of faithful patient goodness like Giles Winterbourne and Marty South. (Some form of faithfulness was the chief virtue in Hardy's eyes, as it was in Conrad's.) But whatever evil men do, he insists, it is not their fault. It is the fault of Destiny; Destiny is malevolent, Destiny is to blame. One remembers the famous closing words of *Tess of the D'Urbervilles*: 'the President of the Immortals had ended his sport with Tess'. And one remembers, too, the quotation on the title-page: 'Poor wounded name, my bosom as a bed Shall lodge thee.' Hardy, as Mr. Edwin Muir has admirably said, 'lifted the burden of sin off the shoulders of humanity and laid it on the Universe'.

For some reason, Hardy's view of the human predicament, that human nature was fundamentally good and Destiny fundamentally bad, did not catch on. As far as I know, no subsequent novelist has adopted it. Perhaps it is because we are secretly too proud of our misdeeds to wish to ascribe them to any outside cause. But another novelist, whose view of the problem of Evil has some of the implications of Hardy's, has had a greater influence on the spirit of the novel, as distinct from its form or technique, than any other writer, and that is Dostoevsky. It is Dostoevsky whose work sometimes gives the impression that evil deeds do not matter greatly because one's actions are no indication of one's spiritual state in a word that the tree is not known by its fruit. Dostoevsky was a Christian, and he may have felt that the essence of Christianity is contained in the parables of the Lost Sheep and the Prodigal Son, and in Christ's words to the Good Thief on the Cross. He was a writer of great spiritual insight, and he certainly exalted the spiritual above the moral: to my mind a most dangerous proceeding, for morality is a fact capable of being demonstrated whereas spirituality is a matter of guesswork. A murder is a fact;

the spiritual state of the murderer at the time he does it is beyond finding out, and must remain an opinion.

D. H. Lawrence described Dostoevsky's characters as 'sinning their way to Jesus', and if the phrase is an exaggeration it is also a near-truth. Turgenev said that Dostoevsky was the most evil Christian he had ever known. There is a story that when Turgenev went to Oxford to receive a degree Jowett asked him what he thought of Dostoevsky, to which Turgenev replied: 'Mish-mash, flim-flam, what you would call Broad Church.'

The influence of Dostoevsky has been enormous, and it has been reinforced by the influence of two writers of whom he would probably not have approved—Marx and Freud. Different as they are, the doctrines of Marx and Freud have combined to undermine the individual's sense of personal responsibility. Marx held that our actions are conditioned by the class of society to which we belong; and Freud held that our actions are subject to influences—pre-natal and juvenile—over which we have no control. Marx (I imagine) thought that the evil in man's nature could be cured by political action; Freud thought that when a man had been properly psycho-analysed, properly integrated, and adjusted to his surroundings, he would automatically lose his anti-social tendencies.

So far neither of these doctrines has been proved right. The countries ruled by the Soviet are not morally impeccable, while in countries where modern methods of psychiatry are having a good trial the figures for delinquency go up and up.

Freud and Marx have been perhaps the strongest single influences on contemporary moral ideas. But there is another, more insidious, though it hasn't the force of a dogma behind it. Many of us remember how the idea of the Little Man grew up in the thirties—and indeed before that, with H. G. Wells and Charlie Chaplin. He was a cousin of the Common Man, and had much in common with him, except that the emphasis was laid on 'little'—perhaps in reaction against Nietzsche's Super Man, who had been deservedly discredited. The Little Man was a poor, puzzled creature, pushed around by everyone, and he became almost a symbol of man in the modern world; a nondescript person, and essentially *little*: nothing much, either good or bad, could be expected of him. Well, the novelists, or some of them, got hold of him and he became their hero—he was not good-looking, he was not clever, he was not brave—like the heroes of old: his point was that he had no heroic qualities in the accepted sense at all. And the heroic qualities thereupon became unfashionable; to have them was to be as unpopular, as anti-social, as to be rich when other people were poor.

The Victorian hero and heroine forsook the pages of serious fiction and joined their fellows on the screen, where they flourished exceedingly.

One of the difficulties, perhaps the chief difficulty, that the novelist of today has to face is that the individual has been devalued, like the pound. As individuals we can only expect about half of the interest and sympathy that the public would have given us before the First World War. If you or I, gentle reader, had been crossed in love, which isn't the worst disaster that can befall, but it's a very painful one, I don't think many people would weep with us: they would tell us to pull our socks up and snap out of it.

After the war, the devaluation of the individual in fiction, as in life, went still further, and his stature shrunk. Various factors contributed to this. One was the sufferings and inconveniences that most people, even those who had not been in the services, went through in the war years. The standard of suffering went up, or down, as you like to look at it, for everybody in every country. People ceased to expect a happy, easy, or even a physi-cally safe life: and this had, perforce, an effect on the novelist's outlook. With stories of the atom bomb and the concentration camp, and the appalling sufferings they involved, fresh in people's minds, how could the novelist claim sympathy for a character who had, say, lost his money or his job or his wife, or even his life? What was one broken heart when so many millions of hearts had been broken? I remember telling a woman novelist, a friend of mine, about a story I was writing, and I said, perhaps with too much awe in my voice, 'Hilda is going to be seduced', and I inferred that this would be a tragedy. I shall never forget how my friend laughed. She laughed and laughed and could not stop: and I decided that my heroine must be not only seduced, but paralysed into the bargain, if she was to expect any sym-pathy from the public.

When one remembers the tears that were shed over Little Em'ly, when one remembers how Samuel Richardson in the eighteenth century (quite a tough period in its way, bear-bait-ing, cock-fighting, and so on) was besieged with letters from the

public begging him to 'spare Clarissa' Harlowe from death or
from a fate worse than death—and when one remembers how,
in *Les Liaisons Dangereuses* (a novel considered so wicked that
Marie Antoinette kept it on her bookshelves under a blank
cover), the crowning act of wickedness was the seduction of a
girl of fifteen—one realizes how public taste has toughened.
There is certainly a deficiency of feeling nowadays. If one sets
out to shock one's readers (perhaps not a very praiseworthy
aim) one almost has to *stun* them. And novelists are trying that
method.

*

The other day a friend said to me: 'I get some satisfaction in my
old age from watching the moral standards of my friends decline.'
Looking at me defiantly, he gave me an example of his turpitude,
which I won't repeat. 'Quite right', I said, not wanting to seem
a prig. Priggishness is now a deadly sin, for it suggests superiority, and superiority is taboo. There is, as a writer in *The Listener*
said, 'a general frightened tittering at excellence'. Any form of
excellence is suspect, for it is liable to arouse envy, and a leading authority on aesthetics has recently observed that the human
race must be made safe from envy.

To be interesting the characters in a novel must have a certain
freedom of action and self-expression. Even if the author's theme
is frustration (it is a very common one and no wonder) and he
means to thwart his characters at every turn he should, I think,
suggest (*a*) that they want to be free; (*b*) that there exists a
freedom that they might attain to. But if no such freedom exists,
the desire for it gradually atrophies: in self-defence we adapt
ourselves to circumstances, we are content to lie down under
such Juggernauts as pass over us. In the reign of George III
Mr. Dunning put forward his famous resolution that 'the
influence of the crown has increased, is increasing, and ought to
be diminished'. Well, no one could make that criticism of our
present sovereign; but there are other powers which have increased, are increasing, and ought to be diminished. Perhaps I
may be allowed to relate a personal experience in illustration of
this. Soon after I went to live in Bath I received an official
notification that certain authorities intended to use their powers
to erect an electric transformer in my garden. No explanation;
no by your leave; no sorry you will be troubled; just a bare

official intimation, such as might be served on a felon. I rushed to my solicitor; was there no power *I* could invoke to resist the project? No, he said, there is nothing you can do. So there it stands, a white, glaring object like a deconsecrated chapel, with two medieval arrow-slits let into it, though why an electric transformer should need these antiquated methods of defence I fail to see. And soon after arrived another official notification, also unaccompanied by any explanation, apology, or request for permission. This time the authorities announced that they were going to use their powers to lay a sewer through my garden. A plan of my garden obligingly was enclosed showing that all unknown to me they had been busy staking out their claim, marking where the sewer was to go. Again I consulted my solicitor; I consulted three solicitors: 'No,' they all said, 'there is nothing you can do.'

And now I come to a point which I shall return to. Persons connected with the sewer—if I may put it so—three times made appointments to see me. They chose their own times and dates, and I naturally waited for them. The first time they failed to keep the appointment; but they came, without making an appointment, a fortnight later. When I said, 'But I expected you a fortnight ago', they stared at me, blankly. The other times, they did arrive; but on each occasion nearly two hours late. Once they had got held up by a fog; once they had gone to the wrong house. The third time they apologized. And not only did they go to the wrong house, they came, in a sense, to the wrong person. I well remember our conversation as, almost ankle-deep in mud, we tramped round the doomed garden. 'We can leave you this apple tree, Mr. Hart, but we shall have to take this cherry tree down. The sewer will run through this lawn, Mr. Hart, then through these flowerbeds, then through these blackcurrant bushes, Mr. Hart, and then through these cabbages.' At last I convinced them that my name was not Hart, but it made no difference: Hart or Hartley, it was all one to them. I was just someone through whose premises a sewer was to be laid. Walt Whitman was right to complain of 'the unending audacity of elected persons'.

Brian de Bois Guilbert said in *Ivanhoe*, 'Many a law, many a commandment have I broken, but my own word, never', and going further back we find Coriolanus (not altogether a sympathetic character, I admit) saying to Aufidius: 'I do hate thee worse than a promise-breaker.' I don't say a promise is no longer binding but it is less binding than it used to be. Many people use a promise as a conversational gambit with no intention of keeping it . . . A speaker might say to his audience: 'If I, ladies and gentlemen, had failed to turn up tonight (it would have been worse for me if you had failed to turn up, but then you were under no obligation to come), you might have felt, mingling with your relief, a momentary sense of irritation. But if you had thought it worth while to ask me, 'Why didn't you come when you said you would?' I might have stared at you blankly; I might not have deigned to answer; I might have said I got held up in a fog, or 'I came to the wrong place', or I might have said simply, 'I didn't feel like it', or to be more in the fashion I might have said I was suffering from a state of diminished responsibility. This excuse is now enshrined in the Statute Book, and will enable you to get away with anything, from failing to turn up at a lecture to committing a murder, and in the present state of public opinion I think you would have had to accept that as a sufficient answer. I didn't feel like it, and, as the lawyers say, there is nothing you can do about it.'

But of course there is something we can do, however much we are crushed by bureaucratic controls and the other restrictions of modern life: however much we are being devalued as individuals. We have only to look at the newspapers, the less squeamish newspapers, to see what some of these things are and they don't always make pleasant reading. And the danger is, that from tolerating something it is a short step to admiring it and imitating it. Well, what is the novelist of today to do, faced by this swing-over in public opinion? Is he to accept it, or is he, as the eighteenth-century novelists did, to take up a governessy attitude?

I think that in most cases novelists are accepting it. The other day I had a letter from a friend, a novelist, who had managed to excuse himself from serving on a jury. 'I am rather shocked', he wrote, 'to find in how many crimes my sympathies are instinctively with the criminal and not with so-called justice.' And this attitude is not confined to writers with no religious convictions. M. Mauriac, one of the most admired novelists of our day and a devout Christian, recently wrote an essay on the art of fiction and his own view of it; and in it he says that he likes the bad characters in his books (and they can be very bad:

see the *Nest of Vipers*, for instance) better than the good ones.
He didn't say he enjoyed writing about them more, which would
be understandable, for good people are notoriously difficult to
portray; he said he liked them better. Milton has been accused
of having had a partiality for Satan, but I am sure he would never
have admitted to it. And there are religious novelists in our
country whose writing suggests that a life of crime doesn't
matter much, if it closes with an act of faith. One has always
supposed that faith and morals were of equal importance in the
Christian life. Nowadays morals is regarded as a poor relation
of faith, hardly a relation at all. Yet we have all seen how disastrous to the world faith without morals can be. Nearly all our
present troubles are owing to it; it is the state of mind that
produced the Nazi régime and the Communist régime and it is
the most dangerous state of mind a human being can get into.

Whatever happens, it seems, we mustn't blame human beings,
and this is a comfortable doctrine, for then we needn't blame
ourselves. I once asked a psycho-analyst if he thought one could
improve one's character by trying, and after some hesitation he
answered, 'No.' So that's that: we are excused personal responsibility but at the cost of being denied Free Will. The new
humanism differs from the more confident nineteenth-century
variety. We no longer say with Swinburne, 'Glory to man in
the highest, for man is the master of things.' We take a more
subdued tone; we say we shall be better when we are all Com-
munists or when we have all been psycho-analysed; if religious,
we throw ourselves on the mercy of God, saying, in effect, like
the dying Heine, *'Dieu me pardonnera, c'est son métier'*: 'God
will forgive me because it's His job to.' You must have noticed
how many characters in modern novels feel themselves cast for
the roles of the Lost Sheep and the Prodigal Son.

If *Jonathan Wild the Great* had been written today, I think he
would have been the hero of it, not the villain, and we should
have been expected to feel sorry for him. For compassion is the
order of the day. The highest praise that a reviewer can give
a novelist is to say that he writes with compassion. I had a letter
from a stranger the other day in which he said he was sure my
books came from an unusually compassionate heart. Well, I have
nothing against compassion, far from it: if one considered only
a millionth of the sufferings of mankind, not to mention one's
own, one's tears would never be dry. But the reviewers mean

another sort of compassion, compassion for men's misdeeds, and with that I'm not so sure I am altogether in sympathy. What becomes of justice? Is it to be completely drowned in compassion? Is not justice a fundamental need of the soul, just as much as compassion is? And there is a risk lest compassion, flowing in this new direction, should leave dry the areas it used to irrigate; we shall feel sorry for the criminal, but not for the victim of his crime. Detective stories have helped to bring this about, and the convention that the murderee is always an unpleasant person, better out of the way. A little while ago there was a case of a young woman who was telephoning from a public call-box (she was a dentist's secretary, but that is nothing against her). And two youths who had possessed themselves of some firearms and were crawling about on the roofs nearby, shot her. I don't know how seriously she was injured, but some of the comments, I was told, ran like this: 'Why did she choose that moment to telephone, when two high-spirited lads were crawling about the roofs, armed with guns? What more natural than that they should shoot her? It was a provocative act on her part. There she was, provocatively telephoning, a natural target for any boy of spirit; you wouldn't expect them not to shoot her: it was madly provocative of her.' In their eyes the boys were to be pitied much more than the girl. There are a great many people, and some very good people, who are more shocked by punishment than by crime.

I am sorry to have laboured this at such length, and to have preached a sermon which I'm not at all qualified to do. And I must make it clear that when I speak of novelists I mean those novelists who are trying to interpret the spirit of the age—not the novelists deplored by Mr. E. M. Forster, and there are many good ones, who content themselves with telling a story, unaffected by the ethical outlook round them. But they will not be able always to remain unaffected by it, for nothing is so catching as a fashion in thought. The novelist—at least I think so—must believe that *something matters*, or at any rate his characters must believe that something matters. The popular catchwords of today or yesterday—'It's just too bad', or 'I couldn't care less', or 'You've had it'—all suggest ironical acceptance of the inevitable, with the corollary that nothing really matters. I don't think that a novel *can* be written in that frame of mind, or any art worthy of the name be born from it.

Something must matter, either as an object of attainment or avoidance, and what is it to be? If the question 'Whither Fiction?' is raised, the novelist will have to make up his mind which side he is on. Is he to write: 'She was a beautiful woman, witty, clever, cultivated, sympathetic, charming, *but*, alas, she was a murderess'? Or is he to write: 'She was a beautiful woman, witty, clever, etc., *and* to crown it all, she was a murderess'?

II

JANE AUSTEN

WHEN THE Secretary of the Jane Austen Society did me the honour of asking me to give the address at their annual meeting, I accepted without too much misgiving, for I remembered a saying which my father was fond of quoting, and which he attributed, I believe mistakenly, to Lord Melbourne, to the effect that 'every man has the ability to do a job he has the ability to get'.

This consoling dictum sustained me for some time, but as the zero hour drew nearer it began to lose its hold. Someone said 'Culture is the sediment of things forgotten.' If that is so, no one could be more cultured than I am about Jane Austen. But merely to have forgotten something is not enough; and what could I possibly say about Jane Austen that has not been said, and said better, before? The discouraging epigram, 'What is true is not new, and what is new is not true', began to ring in my ears. At last I consulted a friend who told me, 'Jane Austen knew nothing about the Abyss.'

I pondered over this, and the question at once arose, what exactly *is* the Abyss? How does one define it? The term was vaguely familiar, but it was a modern conception and susceptible of more than one interpretation. If it was a collective Abyss, the Abyss that the Atom Bomb has dug in our consciousness, even whether we are aware of it or not, the threat of universal extinction, then it was historically impossible for Jane Austen to know about it. Such a threat was not implicit in the French Revolution or the Napoleonic War. Careless readers have made the sweeping assertion that Jane Austen never mentioned the latter, which is quite untrue. There is a reference in *Persuasion* to Trafalgar, and to the action of San Domingo in 1806, and there are many other indirect allusions: the prize-money won by sailors—by Captain Wentworth, for instance. And even if she did tend to disregard it, the Napoleonic War was not the international catastrophe that the two world wars of our century have been, still less the catastrophe that a third world war would be. One cannot imagine a Duchess of Richmond giving a ball on the eve of the descent of the hydrogen bomb, supposing we had been given warning of it.

No, that kind of Abyss could not have been known to Jane Austen. It has been suggested that she had an intuition of coming calamity and for that very reason kept her pen and her thoughts away from it. I do not find this argument convincing, for the pen no less than the tongue goes to the sore place. But most of the Janeites I consulted said, 'Nonsense, of course she knew nothing about the Abyss, if there is one, and thank goodness she didn't. Thank goodness we can bask in the sunshine of her mind and the inspiration which commonsense and confidence in the social order helped to give her, without indulging in such dark preoccupations.'

But supposing the Abyss represented not a cosmic but a personal catastrophe? As far as I know Jane Austen only uses the word abyss once, when she puts it into the mouth of Henry Tilney, perhaps the most amiable and attractive of her heroes. Catherine Morland says that in Bath she sees a variety of people in every street but at home in the country she can only go and call on Mrs. Allen. Mr. Tilney, we are told, was much amused. 'Only go and call on Mrs. Allen!' he repeated. 'What a picture of intellectual poverty! However, when you sink into this abyss again, you will have more to say. You will be able to talk of Bath and of all that you did here.' So the Abyss was, for Henry Tilney, the intellectual void represented by a social call on Mrs. Allen.

But I think there are much stronger evidences of its existence in Jane Austen's novels, even if the word itself is not used. I first read them in 1913, when I was at school, and she at once became my favourite novelist. I preferred her immeasurably to Dickens. She wielded a much finer pen than he did; as regards style and construction, she was infinitely his superior; her characters were portraits, not caricatures, and the subtlety of her humour made his seem obvious and exaggerated. Her world was real to me, and his the world of make-believe. Not that I didn't enjoy Dickens, but I felt that he used his genius as a conjurer might, to create illusions, whereas she used hers to irradiate the unchanging surface and texture of life; by her selectiveness she enhanced its meaning and by her humour she banished its humdrumness. It was her humour that especially appealed to me, for I felt it was a kind of universal solvent, that could be applied to any experience and, by making it comic, could make it comprehensible and even enjoyable. One only had to look at things the Jane Austen way and all would be well. Life at a public school was not always easy or pleasant. I felt unconsciously that had Jane Austen chosen to describe it she could have made it a subject for comedy without romanticizing or distorting it, but simply by seeing its comic side, as she had seen the comic side of *The Mysteries of Udolpho*, whose terrors I could never take seriously after I had read *Northanger Abbey*. Public schools do not come much into Jane Austen's books—Eton and Westminster are mentioned—but I felt she would have understood them by her unrivalled knowledge of the strains and stresses of a stable and conventional society—and what more stable and conventional (as it seemed then) was there than public school life? It did not occur to me that Jane Austen who was self-educated, except for one year's schooling at the gatehouse of Reading Abbey, which ended when she was nine, would not have written a school-story. I didn't then know about the two inches of ivory to which she (perhaps mistakenly) confined herself. I thought that her attitude of mind—her prevailing sense of life as a subject for comedy—could be applied to *any* set of circumstances. I did not realize that it implied respect for certain social rules and regulations—for civilized living, in fact —and if she had doubted these values, moral and social, her exquisite art might have fluttered with a broken wing. As Blake said,

If the sun and moon should doubt,
They'd immediately go out,

and it is the same with the artist, if he loses his fundamental conviction.

The War came, and as Gunner Hartley I went into the Army, which had its rules and regulations, indeed, but not such as I understood, nor do I think Jane Austen would have understood them, for civilized living had gone by the board. Although I never went overseas, Army life did seem at the beginning a kind of Abyss; a chaos without signposts or landmarks, in which dread and bewilderment reigned. I think that during that time my confidence in Jane Austen as an interpreter of life must have been severely shaken, and though I read some escapist literature, I did not return to her. Instead, I read *The Brothers Karamazov* with intense excitement, for it seemed to show what life was like in the raw—the kind of life into which I had been pitchforked, though I never experienced its ultimate horrors.

After the war my taste in fiction inclined, or declined, to the romantic. I returned to the Brontës, who had been an early love of mine, and it was then that I read Charlotte Brontë's letter to her publisher, W. S. Williams, dated 1850, about Jane Austen. Had I read it before the First World War I should have dismissed it with indignation or irritation or perhaps with a smile, but in the light of my more recent experience it impressed me deeply. I am sure that everyone knows it, but I will read it again, for it puts Charlotte Brontë's case against Jane Austen with incomparable force.

I have also read one of Miss Austen's works—*Emma,* read it with interest and with just the degree of admiration which Miss Austen herself would have thought sensible and suitable. Anything like warmth or enthusiasm, anything energetic, poignant, heartfelt, is utterly out of place in commending these works; all such demonstration the authoress would have met with a wellbred sneer, would have calmly scorned as outré and extravagant. She does her business of delineating the surface of the lives of genteel English people curiously well. There is a Chinese fidelity, a miniature delicacy in the painting. She ruffles her reader by nothing vehement, disturbs him by nothing profound. The passions are perfectly unknown to her, she rejects even a speaking acquaintance with that stormy sisterhood. Even to the feelings she vouchsafes no more than an occasional graceful but distant recognition—too frequent converse with them would ruffle the smooth elegance of her progress. Her business is not half so much with the human heart as with the human eyes, mouth, hands and feet. What sees keenly, speaks aptly, moves flexibly, it suits her to study; but what throbs fast and full, though hidden, what the blood rushes through, what is the unseen seat of life and the sentient target of death—this Miss Austen ignores. She no more, with her mind's eye, beholds the heart of her race than each man, with bodily vision, sees the heart in his heaving breast. Jane Austen was a complete and most sensible lady, but a very incomplete and rather insensible (*not* senseless) woman. If this is heresy, I cannot help it.

Well, this diatribe had a disturbing effect on me, as it may
have had on other devotees of Jane Austen, and it certainly
strengthens the case of those who think that she knew nothing
about the Abyss. But great novelists are apt to underrate each
other (did not Henry James speak of 'poor little Hardy'?) and to
imagine that an intention that differs from their own must be
misguided.

Writing to G. H. Lewes, in January 1848, Charlotte Brontë
says:

> What a strange lecture comes next in your letter! You say I must
> familiarise my mind with the fact that Miss Austen is not a poetess,
> has no 'sentiment', you scornfully enclose the word in inverted
> commas, no eloquence, none of the ravishing enthusiasm of poetry!
> And then you add I *must* learn to acknowledge her as one of *the
> greatest of artists, of the greatest painters of human characters,* and one
> of the writers with the nicest sense of means to an end that ever
> lived—the last point only will I ever acknowledge.
> Can there be a great artist without poetry?

Charlotte Brontë was in her way a fair-minded woman; but
she was critical and censorious, as witness the passage in her
introduction to *Wuthering Heights*, in which she wonders if it is
wise to create human beings like Heathcliff. Except for the Duke
of Wellington, in whom she could find no fault, her armour
of partisanship was by no means flawless.

In a letter to W. S. Williams she writes:

> I had a letter the other day announcing that a lady of some note,
> who had always determined that whenever she married, her husband
> should be the counterpart of Mr. Knightley in Miss Austen's *Emma*
> had now changed her mind, and vowed that she would either find
> the duplicate of Professor Emanuel [in *Villette*] or remain for ever
> single!

At another time she asked him,

> Whenever you send me a new supply of books, may I request that
> you will have the goodness to include one or two of Miss Austen's?
> I am often asked if I have read them, and I excite amazement by
> replying in the negative. I have read none except *Pride and Prejudice.*
> Miss Martineau mentioned *Persuasion* as the best.

In January 1848 she wrote to G. H. Lewes:

> If ever I do write another book I think I will have nothing of what
> you call melodrama, I *think* so, but I am not sure. I *think* also, I will

endeavour to follow the counsel which shines out of Miss Austen's 'mild eyes' 'to finish more and be more subdued'.

Why do you like Miss Austen so very much? I am puzzled on that point. What induced you to say that you would have rather written *Pride and Prejudice* and *Tom Jones* than any of the Waverley novels?

I had not seen *Pride and Prejudice* since I read that sentence of yours and then I got the book. And what did I find? An accurate, daguerreotype portrait of a commonplace face; a carefully fenced, highly cultivated garden, with neat borders and delicate flowers, but no glance of a bright vivid physiognomy, no fresh air, no blue hill, no bonny beck.

Granted that any novelist, of lesser stature than Charlotte Brontë, would have been annoyed to be told to study the works of another novelist, especially another woman novelist, her verdict on Jane Austen's is still surprising.

Of some forgotten novelist of the day she writes that she is 'as shrewd as Miss Austen but not so shrewish'.

I think that the explanation must be that Charlotte had only read *Emma* and *Pride and Prejudice*, the two novels of Jane Austen in which the sunlight much exceeds the shadow. Had she read *Sense and Sensibility*, or *Mansfield Park*, or *Persuasion*, her opinion would surely had been different.

Pride and Prejudice and *Emma* are favourites with Jane Austen's readers, perhaps because in them she realizes most fully her gift for comedy and approaches most nearly to the perfection at which, as Flaubert did, she always aimed. She kept within her range of experience, or of the experience which she could best translate into art.

But re-reading her novels after so many years, I rather wonder if this perfection has not been achieved by the exclusion of other qualities that would have jarred on or even imperilled it. Perfection is, one would think, an absolute quality: there cannot be degrees of perfection. Yet no one would say that an object by Fabergé, however perfect, could be compared, in artistic value, to a painting by Rembrandt, however faulty. *Madame Bovary* is a great novel, one of the greatest and perhaps the most perfect; but its perfection depends on rigid exclusion of some of the most precious (and incidentally the commonest) human qualities. There is only one nice character (I apologize to the shade of Henry Tilney, who was justly critical of it, for using the word 'nice'), there is nothing in *Madame Bovary*, as Matthew Arnold said, to rejoice or console us. Perfect it may be, as a work of art, but it takes a one-sided view of life. And it might be argued that the perfection of *Emma* is partly due to the absence, or at any rate the rare appearance, of anything that might *not* rejoice or console us.

> *Faultily faultless, icily regular, splendidly null,*
> *Dead perfection, no more—*

this is not true of *Emma*, whose life-enhancing qualities will never cease to delight, but it is a warning against the dangers of perfection—or the quest for it. I have been told, but do not vouch for its truth, that Persian rug-makers (those of the Mahometan faith) always leave some part of the pattern flawed or incomplete, so as not to challenge comparison with Allah, in whom alone perfection lies. I don't say this to belittle *Emma*, the most perfect of Jane Austen's works (and, incidentally, the one most vulnerable to Charlotte Brontë's criticism), but as a plea for those that are sometimes considered less good, *Sense and Sensibility*, *Mansfield Park*, and *Persuasion*.

Revisiting the world of Jane Austen in 1965, I got a very different impression of it from the one I had in 1913. Then I rejoiced in the comedy; Mrs. Norris could not be too grasping and disagreeable, or Miss Bates too garrulous and fatuous, for me. I longed for their reappearances. Mrs. Charles Musgrove, in *Persuasion*, was another of my favourites, and her complaint that her sore throats were worse than other people's, has delighted me down the years, because I thought (perhaps with more reason than she had) that mine were worse, too. The tribulation of the lovers (of the heroines, I should say, for they suffered much more than the heroes), I didn't take very seriously, for I knew that all would come right for them in the end, and the social background I took for granted, as I took for granted the map of Europe; it had been, was, and always would be, just the same as Jane Austen painted it.

I re-read the books with different feelings. They did not seem so funny as they had seemed. The change was not in Jane Austen, it was in me; my sense of humour had dwindled, and I could no longer see human life in the aspect of comedy. Nor, I think, am I alone in this. It is said that human nature doesn't change, but I think it does, and has, and not least in its sense of humour. I remember a friend of mine, a novelist, saying to me, 'There is no sort of joke now except a bad-taste joke', and she was no mean exponent of jokes of that kind. 'Sick' humour is the order of the day. Jane Austen was quite capable of sick humour; she had been condemned as unfeeling because of a joke in a letter to Cassandra about a miscarriage which anyone might have made if they had the wit to make it; and who would escape the charge of ill-nature if it was founded on some malicious remark in a letter to a close relation?

But if I didn't find Mrs. Norris and Miss Bates and Mr. Collins as funny as I once had, I marvelled anew at the cleverness, the subtlety, and the economy of the means by which Jane Austen makes her effects—the beauty of single sentences and the wonderful chapter-endings, which miraculously combine a faint note of finality with a stirring of expectation for what is to come. And I found many more instances than I expected to find of visual images and feeling for Nature—the 'March that was more like April', and so on. And if I could not look at Pemberley with the rapt excitement of Elizabeth Bennet, I could still see, with my mind's eye, what she saw. Those shrubberies! What a nostalgia they evoke! I should like to plant one myself, if my age and the size of my garden did not make the project what Jane Austen might have called 'imprudent'.

But what struck me most (and this brings me back to the edge of the Abyss), is the sadness to be found in all the novels, except perhaps in *Emma*. There is more sunshine than shadow, of course, but there is more shadow than I remembered from my confident pre-war days. Many, many years ago an artist told me that every picture should have a passage in it 'as black as paint can make it'—otherwise (I suppose he meant), the colours would lose their relative value. I don't know if this rule still holds but it seemed to hold then. I studied a great many pictures, and always seemed to find a black patch somewhere. Indeed, I have seen a modern painting which was *entirely* black. Is the presence of a black spot essential to serious fiction?—for Jane Austen is a serious novelist. She cannot be likened, say, to Shakespeare or Thomas Hardy, without their tragedies. The two inches of ivory included much more than that.

As Lord David Cecil has said, there are no deaths, or deaths that matter, in her novels. (There are eight in *Wuthering Heights*.) What deaths there are have mostly taken place beforehand, and left only a legacy (sometimes a disappointing one) of *money*, to influence the story.

Money is discussed much more openly in Jane Austen's novels than it would be now. Mr. Rushworth had 12,000 pounds a year, Mr. Darcy 10,000, Mr. Bingley 4,000, and the Bennets, I think, a mere 2,000, which were anyhow entailed on Mr. Collins. Multiplied by ten, as I suppose they should be to bring them in line with the value of money today, and being more or less tax-free (though Jane Austen does once refer, I think, to some tax-problem), these figures represent a great deal of money and money plays a great part in the marriages of Jane Austen's heroines.

How was it that she herself never married? Someone, I think it was Miss Mitford, described her as a 'husband-hunting butterfly', and she cannot have been a dull woman. We hear of attachments to various men, Mr. Blackall (ominous name) was one, but none which is properly authenticated, and both she and her sister Cassandra died unmarried. The most obvious explanation is that neither had a large enough dot to tempt a suitor, for Jane Austen's father, who had seven (or was it eight?) children, had, I think, only £750 a year to bring them up on and provide for their futures.

Did Jane Austen really *want* to marry? All her novels are about *getting* married, and marriage might be thought the be-all and end-all of her heroines' existence; but as someone has pointed out, despite this strong emphasis on the bliss of *getting* married, there are few completely happy marriages in Jane Austen's novels: Mr. Bennet certainly did not enjoy being married to Mrs. Bennet.

'Oh dear, let him stand his chance and be taken in. It will do just as well. Everybody is taken in at some period or other.'

'Not always in marriage, dear Mary.'

'In marriage especially. With all due respect to such of the present company as chance to be married, my dear Mrs. Grant, there is not one in a hundred of either sex who is not taken in when they marry. Look where I will, I see that it *is* so.'

Perhaps Jane Austen, whose mind was so fully occupied with other things, did distrust the married state; perhaps, like Fanny Price, she would not marry someone she did not love; but I can't help thinking that lack of money and the 'consequence' that money brings, may have been at the bottom of it.

Why, otherwise, are there so many Cinderellas in the novels? Fanny Price, Catherine Morland, even Elizabeth Bennet, are handicapped, matrimonially and emotionally, by mixing with people much better off than themselves. To be a man was a great advantage; to be a rich man was a still greater advantage, compared with the lot of the unmarried woman. Not all novelists project themselves into their novels, but the majority do, either from the wishful or fearful-thinking which, more than any other single factor, enables a novelist to unite his material with his sensibility.

These heroines, then, or some of them, suffered from an inferiority complex which made Elizabeth Bennet pert, Catherine Morland gauche, Fanny Price submissive, Anne Elliot resigned. It did not embitter them, however, still less did it make them delinquents. I saw a case the other day in which some teenage malefactor pleaded (I think successfully) in his defence that as a child he had suffered tortures from a sense of social inferiority. Jane Austen would have thought this nonsense. A friend of mine said she lacked compassion—which is not true, she had plenty of compassion, and although she generally withheld it from evildoers, she sometimes extended it to them. Wickham gets off more lightly than he deserves, and as for that odious General Tilney! I cannot forgive Catherine Morland, or Henry Tilney, for forgiving *him*, on the grounds that his daughter's marriage to a peer had put him into a better temper.

On Jane Austen's monument in Winchester Cathedral (a favourite building with her, we are told) is quoted from the Book of Proverbs, 'In her mouth was the law of kindness.' Someone said that you cannot expect truth from a lapidary inscription, and I think this one went rather far, as regards Jane Austen the author, if not as regards Jane Austen the woman. As an author she was not particularly kind, but was just: justice is a quality that shines out of her works. She was a stern moralist—perhaps of all novelists the most moral. She makes it quite clear if she dislikes this or that character, but in company with Shakespeare, who put so many *bons mots* into the mouth of (say) Iago, she allows the most unpleasant or the most stupid of them to say a good thing now and then.

But I am wandering from my point, which was the element of sadness in several of Jane Austen's books. She did not write about Belsen and Buchenwald; she did not, like Dostoevsky, depict a human soul in the last stages of despair and dissolution, but she was acutely aware of suffering and sorrow; and sometimes, I think, in portraying them, she overruns the two inches of ivory which was the limit she set herself. Suffering, of course, is relative; but how acutely one feels for Catherine Morland, so cruelly turned out of Northanger Abbey without the money to pay her fare. Catherine expected something horrid to happen at Northanger Abbey, and she finds it, though not in the guise she expected. With consummate skill Jane Austen plays on the reader's apprehensions, just as she plays on Catherine's; now allaying them with the discovery of a laundry-list, now renewing them with partial but disquieting revelations of her host's sinister nature; and when the catastrophe comes, it comes, as always in Jane Austen, with dramatic suddenness. The evil in Northanger Abbey was not a supernatural matter of cabinets and tapestries and long-forgotten documents. It was quite natural, a rather frightening middle-aged man, who caused her more suffering than any phantom would have. Of which of Jane Austen's characters is it said, 'He is black, black, black'? I can't remember, but how flat *Northanger Abbey* would be without this sudden irruption of blackness at the end.

'Happiness,' Jane Austen is credited with saying, 'is a dull thing to write about.' For myself, in my later years, I find the darker passages often more satisfying than the social chit-chat, the Court Guide to Bath, the references to money, the importance of 'consequence' and precedence—all of which were so well within her range that she could do them on her head, without always avoiding the danger of self-imitation. The irony which shimmers over her books is one of the most delightful qualities, but it can pall—it can suggest that we need take nothing seriously as long as we see it in the aspect of comedy; and no one, however vigilant his sense of humour, can see life like that, as if all experience was something that could be laughed or shrugged off. Charlotte Brontë's gibe, that Jane Austen ignored the 'unseen seat of life', is untenable; nearly all her characters (Lady Russell in *Persuasion* is one of the exceptions) are very much alive, even if it isn't the kind of life with which Charlotte Brontë had most sympathy. The charge of 'nothing heartfelt' would be easier to sustain. I fancy that Jane Austen would have thought that to unbosom oneself to the public, even in a work of fiction, would be a breach of good manners. But there are times when she discards the mantle of irony—in the passage in *Northanger Abbey*, for instance, where she defends the novel against the charge of triviality. In this (though irony is present) she commits herself to what she is saying; we hear the true voice of feeling, the voice of personal conviction, as we hear it, still more clearly, in the famous conversation between Anne Elliot and Captain Harville, as to the relative fidelity, in emotional relationships, of men and women.

'God forbid', says Anne (and it is one of the few times when the word God is mentioned in Jane Austen's novels),

> God forbid that I should undervalue the warm and faithful feelings of any of my fellow-creatures! I should deserve utter contempt if I dared to suppose that true attachment and constancy were known only by women . . . All the privilege I claim for my own sex (it is not a very enviable one, you need not covet it) is that of loving longest when existence, or when hope, is gone.

With Jane Austen, almost less than with any other writer except Shakespeare, can one assume that her characters voice her own opinions; but one feels that Anne is speaking for Jane Austen here.

At the end of *Mansfield Park* occurs another, equally famous passage, and this time Jane Austen is speaking with her own voice. 'Let other pens dwell on guilt and misery. I quit such odious subjects as soon as I can, impatient to restore everybody not greatly in fault themselves, to tolerable comfort and to have done with all the rest.'

This is all very well, but Jane Austen's pen has been dwelling on guilt and misery for a great many pages, and prior to the Crawford episode there has been what Mr. R. W. Chapman has called the 'long-drawn agony of Fanny Price'.

> That great black word *miserable*! ... Her mind was all disorder. The past, present, future, everything was terrible. But her uncle's anger gave her the severest pain of all. Selfish and ungrateful! To have appeared so to him. She was miserable for ever. She had no one to take her part, to counsel, to speak for her. Her only friend was absent. He might have softened his father; but all, perhaps all, would think her selfish and ungrateful. She might have to endure the reproach again and again; she might hear it, or see it, or know it to exist, for ever, in every connection about her. She could not but feel some resentment against Mr. Crawford; yet, if he really loved her, and were unhappy too!—it was all wretchedness together.

Surely this passage gives us a glimpse of the Abyss, if it does not take us into the Abyss itself.

In its physical aspect Jane Austen's world was much safer than ours. There was very little danger to life and limb from accidental causes. Motor-cars did not run over people; aeroplanes did not crash; and as far as I can remember, even horses did not run away. Yet there are moments when the outside world shows its teeth, and how vividly Jane Austen describes them! The Cobb at Lyme Regis: I have often negotiated those few unperilous steps, and wondered how Louisa Musgrove could have fallen down them, though I had no one to 'jump' me. Yet what a tremendous experience Jane Austen makes of it—just as she does of the incident of the gipsies in *Emma*, another irruption of the irrational and dangerous into Jane Austen's well-ordered world. Here was a group of juvenile delinquents, 'half a dozen children headed by a stout woman and a great boy, all clamorous and impertinent, in look though not absolutely in word'. Poor Harriet could not follow Miss Bickerton, 'who had given a great scream', because she suffered from cramp after dancing. Frank Churchill arrives in the nick of time to save her and escort her back to Hartfield, where she immediately fainted away.

The phenomenon of violence, so familiar to us, hardly came into Jane Austen's purview at all; but it is clear that she knew how to describe it when she wanted to. Her world was ruled by reason, by moral considerations; when anything goes wrong, it is somebody's *fault*; they have acted, to use a familiar phrase, without due care and attention—not to the dangers of the roads but to the dictates of prudence, reason, conscience and religion —and for that they are punished.

Most people would agree with G. H. Lewes that her novels are deficient in poetry, though there is much more of it than she is given credit for. A more serious lack, I think, is that she makes almost no allowance for the *irrationalism* of much of human behaviour, an element of which *we* are only too painfully aware, and should be, even if Freud had not emphasized it, and perhaps encouraged it. Nor does she recognize the existence of evil as something to be reckoned with; there are a few villains in her novels, but very few villainesses, except that very black one, Lady Susan, who might have come out of the pages of *Les Liaisons Dangereuses*, via *Clarissa Harlowe*, which we know Jane Austen read; or at any rate, we know that she bought it, for the bill exists. All the great novelists, except Jane Austen, have recognized the importance of the irrational as a factor in human behaviour, and the greatest of all, Cervantes, made it his subject; for what is *Don Quixote* but a study in unreason?

Sense and Sensibility is sometimes regarded as the least successful of Jane Austen's novels, but to me it is one of the most satisfying, simply because it does recognize, however distantly and disapprovingly, the force of unreason in human life. Marianne Dashwood is one of my favourite characters in fiction. I like her for herself (she was nice to her mother and had many other amiable qualities besides), and I like her because she does *not* act from prudential considerations. She does not feel (in the beginning, at any rate) that money should be the *sine qua non* of marriage, or that love must be founded on esteem (an idea Jane Austen seems to have held, though it is, and always has been, unsupported by experience). 'I have never yet known', Mrs. Dashwood says, 'what it was to separate esteem from love.' It is generally thought that Jane Austen was on Elinor's side, the side of sense, against Marianne's side, the side of sensibility. But I wonder. Her mind may have condemned Marianne, but her feelings did not: Marianne, with all her faults, her disregard of public opinion, her anti-social tendencies (playing the piano whether other people wanted her to, or not), her determination to go her own way and be herself—all these things endear her to me. I cannot think that when Charlotte Brontë wrote the letter about *Emma* she had read *Sense and Sensibility*. For surely here the 'unseen seat of life' is defined as clearly as it ever can be, and the 'sentient target of death' (though it never gets a shot in the bull's-eye) is *not* ignored; it is present throughout Marianne's illness, the wonderful account of which, with its harrowing alternation of hopes and fears, its complete lack of sentimentality, its insistence on the medical and mental aspects of the case, would give it a high place in any anthology of sick-bed scenes.

In her last illness, Jane Austen was asked if she wanted anything, and she replied 'Only death.' That was in 1817, a year before the birth of Emily Brontë, who also died young and who also, apparently, at the end wanted only death. As women, and as novelists, the two might be thought the antitheses of each other, the one loving society, the other solitude. Someone said to me, 'If Jane Austen knew nothing about the Abyss, Emily Brontë knew nothing about anything else.' The social background which meant so much to Jane Austen meant nothing to Emily Brontë. Only Mr. Lockwood ever called at Wuthering Heights, no one ever called at Thrushcross Grange, unless Heathcliff can be regarded as a visitor, when he spent the night in the garden knocking his head against a tree and howling like an animal. The only concession, the only recognition, that *Wuthering Heights* vouchsafes to society is when Catherine Earnshaw tells Nelly Dean that one reason for marrying Edgar Linton is that she would then be the 'greatest woman of the neighbourhood'. One has to laugh, for what neighbourhood, in the social sense, was there round Wuthering Heights? Some ghosts, no doubt. But all the same, there are many points of resemblance between Marianne Dashwood and Catherine Earnshaw, apart from the fact that the one nearly dies of love and the other dies of it. Each was determined to be herself, cost what it might to herself and those who loved her; many of their remarks would, *mutatis mutandis*, be interchangeable. Marianne recants, and apologizes to Elinor, to society, and to God, for her errors, whereas Catherine dies impenitent, only asking Heathcliff for forgiveness. Yet they both hold our sympathy, or at least they hold mine, by each possessing a quality of incorruptibility which can be summed up in one of Emily Brontë's few recorded remarks, 'I want to be what God made me.'

Catherine was not happy with her dull husband, Edgar Linton. Was Marianne likely to be happy with her dull husband, Colonel Brandon? He was fairly well-off no doubt, but as Marianne (in her unregenerate stage) said to Elinor, 'What have wealth and grandeur to do with happiness?'

Northanger Abbey is a satire on one aspect of the Romantic Movement; *Sense and Sensibility* is a much more subtle and serious criticism of it. Even if we sometimes suspect that Jane Austen is trying to convince herself, she means to convince the reader.

To Emily Brontë as to Marianne, autumn was a season rich with romantic yearning. Emily shows it in a poem, Marianne in a conversation between herself and Elinor. Emily writes, as always, from the heart, and Jane Austen seems to make fun of Marianne's feelings—but they are none the less moving. The subject is falling leaves, and Emily's poem reads:

> *Fall, leaves, fall; die, flowers, away;*
> *Lengthen night and shorten day.*

Every leaf speaks bliss to me
Fluttering from the autumn tree.

I shall smile when wreaths of snow
Blossom where the rose should grow;
I shall sing when night's decay
Ushers in a drearier day.

'And how does dear, dear Norland look?' cried Marianne.

'Dear, dear Norland,' said Elinor, 'probably looks much as it always does at this time of year. The woods and walks thickly covered with dead leaves.'

'Oh!' cried Marianne, 'with what transporting sensations have I formerly seen them fall! How have I delighted, as I walked, to see them driven in showers about me by the wind! What feelings have they, the seasons, the air, altogether inspired! Now there is no one to regard them. They are seen only as a nuisance, swept hastily off, and driven as much as possible from the sight.'

'It is not everyone,' said Elinor, 'who has your passion for dead leaves.'

'No, my feelings are not often shared, not often understood, but *sometimes they* are.'

There is no doubt that Elinor gets the better of this encounter, but it is Marianne's words which, at any rate for me, linger longest, however exaggerated their sentiment may be.

I feel that Marianne was a tragic character and (with all respect) that *Sense and Sensibility* should have been a tragic novel. That Jane Austen could have made it one, had she wished, I have no doubt; the ingredients are all there, and she had nothing to do but change the emphasis at the end. The danger for a novelist of straying outside his range is really no greater, if in a different way, than when he sticks inside it. Who would have prophesied that Dickens would have made such a success of *A Tale of Two Cities*, a novel that was quite outside his ordinary beat? To experiment in fiction may be disastrous, but it may open up veins of imagination that the author did not know of.

But before I fail to prove my point that Jane Austen might have been a tragic novelist, may I quote a letter that I recently received on this very subject?

I found *Adam Bede* a tragic book, and poor Hetty Sorrell had all my sympathy, but *Sense and Sensibility* unearthed too vividly that awful period of desolation, rejection, and humiliation ... It is extraordinary. I have wept reading this book, and I thought my tears had dried up years ago.

III

EMILY BRONTË
IN GONDAL AND GAALDINE

ONCE AT a dinner party, speaking of literary reputations, A. E. Housman mentioned three that in his opinion were grossly overrated. Perhaps you know which they were. I don't think anyone could guess, for the three writers had little in common, so little indeed that their names reveal nothing of Housman's own literary taste except that it was eclectic. They were Homer, Charles Lamb and Emily Brontë.

What were the reasons on which he based his judgment I do not know. Homer is one of the most impersonal of all writers and the least mannered; I fail to see how he could arouse any extreme antipathy except among humanitarians and pacifists, and schoolboys who are compelled to read his works against their will. He nods, we are told. But that is rather endearing; no one was ever disliked for making a mistake. With Lamb, the case is different. He is a buttonholing, rib-nudging writer, who wears his personality on his sleeve. He was also, by his own admission, or boast, a man of imperfect sympathies, and if one does not like him it is scarcely possible to enjoy his work.

Emily Brontë is a personal writer too, but in another way. She is a spell-binder, stealing one's judgment and perhaps one's heart. Her work does not lend itself to comparison or analysis. The desire for the absolute ruled her thoughts and feelings, and the reader who is infected by this longing soon comes to regard her as a priestess rather than a writer. Moreover, she is a figure —perhaps now the central figure—in the Brontë legend, which draws its strength as much from the tragic circumstances of their lives as from their contribution to literature. The Brontës are perhaps a literary taste of the unliterary, just as P. G. Wodehouse is an unliterary taste among the literary; and fastidious people with a dry light in their minds (of whom Housman was one, though his poems are sentimental enough) may easily feel they are being hoodwinked and bamboozled by an emotional, esoteric cult. Emily does not parade her personality or court the reader's friendship, but she has gathered around her a company of passionate partisans who have only to hear her name mentioned to feel in themselves an intoxicating dilation of their egos, a capacity for spiritual experience denied to ordinary mortals. She was not apparently a friendly person. 'As friendless after eighteen years, as lone as on my native day', she wrote in 1837, when she had twice been to school and had had the same opportunities as Charlotte for discovering an Ellen Nussey or a Mary Taylor. She did not want friendship, she wanted love.

Having said she is a personal writer, I must qualify my statement. Her novel is one of the most impersonal of novels; she never speaks in *propria persona*, never steps outside the page to make a generalization or a comment, still less to address the reader. Her poems are among the most personal of poems. They seem as much the expression of personal experience as does an exclamation when you have run a pin into yourself. (Not all of them, of course; the Gondal poems are to some extent objective, but more of that later.) The novel was written for publication: the poetry to satisfy a private need; it was not meant to be seen by any eye but hers. Even Anne, Emily's collaborator in the Gondal chronicles, did not always know what Emily's poems were about and Charlotte had never set eyes on them until she accidentally discovered them, to Emily's fury and dismay. This may partly account for the difference in outlook between the poems and *Wuthering Heights*. But both the poems and the novel were personal in the sense that they have the same strong, almost obsessive, appeal for certain people, while others are untouched or even repelled by them. It is not only their literary quality that attracts. *Wuthering Heights* is an acknowledged masterpiece and one by one the criticisms levelled against it have been silenced or demolished. The reviewers of one hundred years ago recognized its originality and many of its qualities. They were far from being completely hostile and gave Emily what now would be thought good measure indeed, five reviews averaging 3,000 words each. But they were shocked by the book's brutality. Let us peer into Emily's desk where she kept her newspaper cuttings. Here is a quotation from one review:

Wuthering Heights is a strange inartistic story. There are evidences in every chapter of a sort of rugged power—an unconscious strength—which the possessor never seems to think of turning to the best advantage. The general effect is inexpressibly painful. We know nothing in the whole range of our fictitious literature which presents such shocking pictures of the worst forms of humanity. *Jane Eyre* is a book which affects the reader to tears: it touches the most hidden sources of emotion. *Wuthering Heights* casts a gloom over the mind not easily to be dispelled. It does not soften, it harasses . . . it is a sprawling story, carrying us, with no mitigation of anguish, through two generations of sufferers— though one presiding evil genius casts a grim shadow over the whole and imparts a singleness of malignity to the somewhat disjointed tale.

A more natural unnatural story we do not remember to have read. The reality of unreality has never been so aptly illustrated as in the scenes of almost savage life which Ellis Bell has brought so vividly before us. The book sadly wants relief. There is not in the entire *dramatis personæ* a single character which is not utterly hateful or thoroughly contemptible. If you do not detest the person you despise him; and if you do not despise him you detest him with your whole heart. Hindley, the brutal degraded sot, Linton Heathcliff, the miserable, drivelling coward, and Heathcliff himself, the presiding evil genius of the piece, the tyrant father of an imbecile son, a creature in whom every passion seems to have reached a gigantic excess—form a group of deformities such as we have rarely seen gathered together on the same canvas.

So wrote the critic of the *Atlas*, two centuries after the close of the Thirty Years War. We, with the memory of the atom bomb and the concentration camp fresh in our minds, cannot pretend to be shocked by the pinchings, hair-pulling, puppy-hangings, slappings—by the elementary brutality of *Wuthering Heights*, itself an embryo concentration camp, and must respectfully agree with the author, who said that people who called it brutal must be affected. It is a book which will always offend the conventional, by whom I do not mean philistines or blimps, but those who think that fiction should be based on the evidence of the senses, directed by an intelligent, highly trained mind; that it should be satisfied with imitating the surface of life and should not attempt a transcendental interpretation. What lies beneath the surface can be inferred; to try to dig it out will probably lead to a greater distortion of truth than to leave it covered.

This is a rational view and accounts for the evergreen popularity of Jane Austen and Anthony Trollope; but we live in an age of unreason and cannot, after what has recently happened in the world, and may happen again on a greater scale, refrain from inquiring what it is in human nature that makes such convulsions possible. The only English novelist, it seems to me, whose characters could be guilty of such enormities, if pressed far enough, is Emily Brontë. But though her characters are destructive (the inmates of Wuthering Heights, I mean, not those of Thrushcross Grange), destruction is not their aim, any more I suppose than it is our aim today, though we do so much of it. Their aim (Heathcliff's and Catherine's) is a union of spirit so complete as to fuse their two identities: 'Nelly, I *am* Heathcliff', Catherine says. And this corresponds, I think, to a perpetual need of the spirit—perhaps its deepest need—a need which it will do anything to satisfy.

Herein lies, I think, one of the secrets of the book's increasing hold on the public: it presents the dilemma of the soul in the most naked and uncompromising fashion. Had humanity progressed, as the nineteenth-century believed it would, with an ever-developing civility of life, then *Wuthering Heights* might have become a literary curiosity, justifying Sir Leslie Stephen's stricture: 'Emily Brontë's feeble grasp of eternal facts makes her book a kind of baseless nightmare.' But it has not. Experiences that have been real to us would have seemed utterly unreal to most eminent Victorians; but not to Emily Brontë. The critic of the *Atlas* hit on a happy phrase when he wrote of an unnatural natural story, illustrating the reality of unreality. We are bewildered by the threatening aspect of humanity today; Emily Brontë, who realized how little reason could restrain those human instincts which are outside its reach, was not. She wrote as a rebel (all the Brontës, except possibly Anne, were rebels against society, they saw it as a conspiracy of corrupt worldlings against the goodness and integrity of the individual), her heart was with Heathcliff and Cathy in their Paradise Lost to which pride and ungovernable passions had exiled them.

I shall return to *Wuthering Heights*, but the purpose of this preamble was to show that its position as a classic seems to be at the moment unassailed, in spite of Housman's judgment. Even its construction—once regarded as a weak point even by its admirers—now commands praise. Percy Sanger's little pamphlet shows how deliberately and carefully Emily had thought out her scheme; and the device of putting the story into the mouths of two narrators—one of whom starts almost at the end—once thought so clumsy, is now applauded for its originality. The indirect narration has another justification too, which Sir Leslie Stephen might have noticed: it bathes the whole fantastic story in the clear cool light of Mrs. Dean's commonsense; no one knew better than Emily that the passions that ruled at Wuthering Heights were a deviation from the normal, from the kindly and charitable feelings, the ordered and civilized routine of life that prevailed at Thrushcross Grange.

One need not apologize for claiming *Wuthering Heights* as a masterpiece; but what of the poems? They are, except for a handful that are in all anthologies, much less well known. Nor is opinion as to the poems' artistic merit at all unanimous. They have had warm supporters, among them Robert Bridges, but his delightful essay quotes as Emily's—and indeed singles out for special praise—poems which the sleuthing of Mr. Hatfield now ascribes to Branwell, which slightly shakes our faith in his critical judgment. Another woman poet whose opinion carries much weight, Edith Sitwell, once said to me of Emily Brontë, 'I reverence that great woman, I genuflect at the mention of her name, but I do not care for her poetry, nor do I think that the emotions expressed in it [she instanced 'Cold in the Earth'] are genuine.'

One must be careful how one differs from such an authority, and I can only say that to me the emotions do seem genuine, that is, genuinely felt; whether they are the emotions Emily actually experienced, in her own life, in circumstances similar to those which the poems so tantalizingly outline, and whether they were the key with which she unlocked her heart, is another matter. They are the emotions of a rather weak, fearful, clinging, mood- and nerve-ridden personality, striving for unity of outlook. Certainly they are not the emotions that dominate *Wuthering Heights*.

Emily Brontë has been called the sphinx of Literature. Let us look at her portrait for a moment—her portraits, for there are several, and they do not all agree.

'Stronger than a man, simpler than a child,' wrote Charlotte, 'her nature stood alone.' This is the Emily Brontë we first think of, the one who arises from the letters Charlotte wrote about her in her last illness, and from the introduction and biographical note to *Wuthering Heights*. Charlotte never wrote better; the criticism and the memoir are masterpieces, and every heavy, doom-laden letter enriches the literature of grief. Even after this distance of time they are almost unbearable to read.

The impression they leave is of courage in the face of suffering, of obstinacy even ('would that my sister added to her other great qualities the humble one of tractability'). This is the Emily Brontë who cauterized herself after she had been bitten by the dog, who did not quail before Branwell's drunken threats of violence, who carried on her ordinary household duties until the day of her death, and implored but one thing—'in life and death a chainless soul with courage to endure'. For Emily Brontë, in her last phase, existence meant suffering, and stoicism was the only way to meet it. Courage is life-giving, but stoicism as thorough-going as this amounts to a denial of life, or rather of life's power to give happiness, and is usually the fruit of some bitter experience. Was there such an experience in Emily's case?

Charlotte said that she was 'torn struggling from a happy life', but was she? Do the facts bear this out? Before Branwell's funeral she caught a cold, she would have no 'poisoning doctor' near her and three months later she died. It looks like suicide.

Shirley, some critic has remarked, could not have written *Wuthering Heights*, and it is worth while to take a look at Charlotte's other portrait of her sister (and there is no doubt at all that *Shirley* was modelled on Emily), begun before Emily's illness and completed after her death. We see a lady of means and leisure, at once practical and idealistic, full of interests outside herself, but given to fits of passionate and melancholy brooding, not quite of the world, perhaps, but accepting it and sharing its joys and sorrows. Charlotte was a most acute observer, and in *Shirley* we can feel the glow of Emily's presence as she appeared in Ellen Nussey's recollections of her, 'a child in spirit for glee and enjoyment'. Shirley is strong and independent and reserved, but we do not feel that she is using these qualities to confront a private sorrow or to keep the world at bay. She draws her strength from Nature and is on the happiest terms with it, and on the whole, with her fellow creatures. 'Too innocent for Hell, too mutinous for Heaven', someone says of her, but that does not mean she was a misfit on earth. Far from it. We remember Catherine's dream in *Wuthering Heights* in

which the angels flung her out of heaven and she awoke on the
moors above Wuthering Heights sobbing for joy; remember,
too, a significant verse in one of Emily's own poems addressed
to Nature:

> *Few hearts to mortals given*
> *On earth more wildly pine;*
> *But none would ask a heaven*
> *More like this earth than thine.*

Shirley was obviously very difficult to manage, a Tartar, like
her dog; but she is a creature of light and air, she does not cast
a shadow. Life is glorious to her.

The impression of strength is confirmed by Ellen Nussey,
whose letter to Clement Shorter tells so much and so little:

> Her extreme reserve seemed impenetrable, yet she was intensely
> lovable; she invited confidence in her moral power. Few people have
> the gift of looking and smiling as she could look and smile. One of
> her rare, expressive looks was something to remember through life,
> there was such a depth of soul and feeling, and yet a shyness of
> revealing herself, a strength of self-containment seen in no other.
> She was in the strictest sense a law unto herself, and a heroine in
> keeping to her law. She and gentle Anne were to be seen twined
> together as united statues of power and humility.

The impression of strength persists, but it is strength in sunlight, almost, one might say, strength through joy. The only
shadows are the bouts of homesickness, so acute as to constitute
an illness, which attacked Emily on the rare occasion when she
left Haworth. Only two of her letters have been preserved; both
to Ellen Nussey, both businesslike in tone, both relating to
Charlotte's absence from home. One contains a rather scornful
reference to Charlotte as being likely to vegetate in Brussels till
the age of Methuselah for mere lack of courage to face the
voyage (the courage-complex again). An unkind comment,
anyhow, and an imperceptive one, if Emily did not know the
reason why Charlotte lingered in Brussels. These, the three
birthday letters she exchanged with Anne and an early diary
fragment in which she makes what is almost a joke about peeling
potatoes, are all, apart from her literary work, that has come
down to us over Emily's signature.

But five French essays, five *devoirs*, that she wrote for M.
Heger in Brussels, still survive. Whether they make good

Charlotte's assertion that 'Ellis will not be seen in his full strength until he is seen as an essayist', I should not like to say. They are tinged with that mid-nineteenth-century French rhetoric which May Sinclair thought had such a disastrous effect on Charlotte's prose (in *Shirley*). But they are not juvenilia. Emily was 24 when she wrote them; her spirit was quite unbending, she did not share Charlotte's reverence for M. Heger and we may assume that the sentiments are her own—the more confidently because, in the case of one essay, the pupils were allowed to choose any subject they liked. Emily chose Harold on the eve of the battle of Hastings, and it shows that in certain moods Emily was in love with defeat and possibly with death. Here we see Emily's picture, in the summer of 1842, three or four years before *Wuthering Heights* was written, of what human stature should attain to. Harold is the incarnation of her hero-worship. He is a glorious, effulgent figure on whom no shadow of mortal frailty rests. To Emily the portrait does not seem to be ironical; the fact that Harold is to be disastrously defeated and die the next day does not affect her estimate of him; it does not seem to matter; what matters is that Harold's nature partakes of the divine. The figure, indeed, is all the more splendid because it is isolated against a background of failure and, like the Boy on the Burning Deck, is thus redeemed from any taint of worldly success.

All the Brontës were hero-worshippers, the figure of the Duke of Wellington haunted their minds almost from infancy. In *Shirley* we are given a list of Shirley's heroes. They included soldiers, lawgivers and philosophers, and all were, or could be regarded as, benefactors and models to mankind.

Heathcliff too is of heroic stature; he too faces defeat and prays for death to liberate him from his chains. But what a difference between him and King Harold! Emily never claims for Heathcliff that he had a spark of the divine; if he is an angel he is a fallen angel, utterly fallen. The idealizing part of Emily's imagination was either dead or dormant when she drew his portrait, three years or so after she had painted Harold's. There is, indeed, an assurance of immortality in *Wuthering Heights*, but no moral grandeur attaches to it. Heathcliff's wickedness is often condemned by Nelly Dean, but never, I think, by Emily; it seems as though, by this time, moral considerations no longer weighed with her. 'I shall be incomparably beyond and above you all', says the dying Catherine, but there is no indication that she was referring to a moral eminence; indeed, her life of almost unbridled selfishness would have made any such claim ridiculous.

Here a date seems important. The year 1835 was a disastrous year for Emily and a year of disgrace for all the Brontës. Emily was recalled from Roe Head School after three months, suffering from a homesickness so acute that Charlotte thought she might die. In the same year, the plan of sending Branwell to London to study art either did, or did not, fall through; but in either case, the Black Bull began to claim more and more of his copious spare time. The sisters were compelled to watch their darling, their genius-to-be, changing before their eyes, to be gradually replaced by 'the hopeless being,' as Emily called him, whose every action was to bring them misery and shame.

Was 1835 a turning-point? Emily's poetic output began in the following year, and lasted for a decade. Even if they are not autobiographical, the poems are extremely personal; it is difficult to believe that in most cases the moods and emotions they express are not Emily's own. Even in the Gondal poems we find the same antithesis that dominates *Wuthering Heights*; cold, northern, windswept Gondal is continually contrasted with Gaaldine's 'Eden's isle beyond the southern sea. Her tropic prairies bright with flowers and rivers washing free'—nearly always to the disadvantage of the latter:

> *What flower in Ula's garden sweet*
> *Is worth one flake of snow?*

Emily asks; and answers her question in another poem:

> *But lovelier than cornfields all waving*
> *In emerald and scarlet and gold*
> *Are the slopes where the north-wind is raving,*
> *And the glens where I wandered of old.*

Is it too fanciful to think that Emily's symbolizing mind, like Branwell's, clothed homely things in the disguise of romantic exaggeration, so that a house becomes a hall, a church a minster or cathedral, that Gondal itself was no further from Haworth parsonage than Wuthering Heights, and that the stormy seas on which its inhabitants embarked could in many cases be identified with the few miles of railway line and heather that separated home-keeping Emily from absent Anne, or Branwell or Charlotte? The dungeon walls on which the Gondalians wrote, the Palaces of Instruction from which they fled, the prison caves in which they languished, what are these but the schools and governess-ships which kept the Brontë children from home and Haworth?

Miss Branwell came from Penzance; she never reconciled herself to the harsh climate of Yorkshire, its blunt, outspoken people and their independent ways. She never stopped telling her nieces and nephew how superior Cornwall was. Is it possible that this started in Emily's mind the habit of grouping the episodes of her imaginative life into categories of North and South—her natural puritanism and patriotism making her believe that the North was superior to the South because it was more uncomfortable?

The Gondal poems, and still more effectively the names and initials which are inscribed above them, provide Emily with countless alibis against identification, which no research has been able to shake. Like Morgiana, she puts a cross on every door. Many have tried to read the signs and build a theory on internal evidence, only to leave themselves looking absurd and justifying Lady McCarthy's sweeping remark that 'no one sensible has ever written about the Brontës' (which goes for me, too).

Most enthusiastic of all, and most demonstrably mistaken, was Miss Virginia Moore, who declared that Emily was in love with a man called Louis Parensell, whose name was faintly pencilled over one of the poems. Miss Moore combed Yorkshire in vain for bearers of the name of Parensell, only to learn that she had misread the words and that Louis Parensell should read 'Love's Farewell'.

Mr. Charles Morgan comes much nearer the mark, I think, when he suggests that Emily's increasing loneliness and misery came from the loss of the anthropomorphic vision which had visited her in childhood and which never returned again; her wretchedness and even her sense of guilt arose from the feeling that she had done something to alienate it. She had lost her companion in the other world, which was so much more real to her than this. But, alas, here the dates are against him; for the famous poem in which she describes most triumphantly the vision and its comforting effect ('He comes with western winds') is one of the last she wrote.

One thing seems certain: the poems are a record of deep and

increasing unhappiness; and as certainly they hark back to a
time before 1836, when Emily was happy.

> *Harp of wild and dreamlike strain*
> *When I touch thy strings,*
> *Why dost thou repeat again*
> *Long forgotten things?*
>
> *Harp, in other earlier days*
> *I could sing to thee*
> *And not one of all my lays*
> *Vexed my memory.*
>
> *But now if I awake a note*
> *That gave me joy before,*
> *Sounds of sorrow from thee float*
> *Changing evermore.*
>
> *Yet, still steeped in memory's dyes,*
> *They come sailing on*
> *Darkening all my summer skies*
> *Shutting out my sun.*

Besides these visions of lost happiness, we find in the poems
abundant traces of other emotions, difficult to reconcile with the
strength, self-sufficiency and stoicism of her usual portrait:
regret, remorse, guilt, despair, kindness, solicitude, tenderness;
yearning for absent friends and the grief of separation; passionate love for someone who is dead or who no longer cares; the
longing to be loved and comforted:

> *If grief for grief can touch thee,*
> *If answering woe for woe,*
> *If any ruth can melt thee,*
> *Come to me now!*
>
> *I cannot be more lonely,*
> *More drear I cannot be!*
> *My worn heart throbs so wildly*
> *'Twill break for thee.*
>
> *And when the world despises—*
> *When heaven repels my prayer,*
> *Will not mine angel comfort?*
> *Mine idol hear?*
>
> *Yes by the tears I've poured thee,*
> *By all my hours of pain,*

> *Oh I shall surely win thee*
> *Beloved, again!*

And there are the so-called 'poems of guilt':

> *There let thy bleeding branch atone*
> *For every torturing tear;*
> *Shall my young sins, my sins alone,*
> *Be everlasting here?*

The Brontë children, we know, appropriated Cowper's most despairing poem, 'The Castaway', and made it their own; Caroline recites it to Shirley, and Shirley wonders how she could repeat it with a steady voice.

Moreover, they were all, at one time or another, subject to great depression of spirits, and the thought of death was so much in their minds that they may be said to have lived with it. Many writers of the Romantic movement were half in love with easeful death, but with the Brontës it was not a flirtation. The deaths of their elder sisters, Maria and Elizabeth, left a wound that did not heal. Emily seems to have had an intuition of her own early death, and in some moods to have welcomed it with ecstasy for its own sake, as a fulfilment, not merely as a deliverance from unhappiness:

> *Fall, leaves, fall; die, flowers, away;*
> *Lengthen night and shorten day.*
> *Every leaf speaks bliss to me*
> *Fluttering from the autumn tree.*
>
> *I shall smile when wreaths of snow*
> *Blossom where the rose should grow;*
> *I shall sing when night's decay*
> *Ushers in a drearier day.*

But there was another, contradictory strain in her that clung desperately to life; she was aware of the contradiction and was trying to resolve it when she wrote:

> *Alas, the countless links are strong,*
> *That bind us to our clay,*
> *The loving spirit lingers long*
> *And would not pass away.*

The wind of genius bloweth where it listeth and can turn wreaths of vapour into symbols of dread. It may have pleased

Emily's fancy to imagine herself pining from hopeless love; that is a favourite daydream of adolescence, and for all the maturity of her outlook, one part of Emily's mind never grew up; at the age of 27 she was still playing at Gondal with Anne. Nor can those who are not subject to moods realize their bewildering effect amounting almost to a change of personality, on those who are.

The year 1845 is another turning-point. Branwell returned home for good, if good is the word. The news of his ignominious dismissal from Thorpe Green came soon after, and Charlotte left Ellen Nussey in no doubt as to what his presence meant for the family: 'So long as he remains at home I scarce dare hope for peace in the house.'

In the three and a half years between Branwell's return and Emily's death, she wrote only five poems. Instead of writing poetry she wrote *Wuthering Heights*, but *Wuthering Heights* must have been finished at least eighteen months before she died; during those last eighteen months her literary output was practically nil, unless, as some think, she was at work on another novel, which has been lost. What was the reason? I can't help thinking it was unhappiness, unhappiness at the spectacle of Branwell's gradual disintegration. But the signs are, as always, confusing.

Many of the poems, both the early ones and the late ones, are laments: laments, it seems to me, for her sister Maria's physical, and for Branwell's spiritual death. I once lent Emily's poems to a friend of mine, but he didn't like them and declared she had used the word 'dreary' eight-seven times. I counted up the number of times she had used the word 'glorious', or some derivation of it, and it came, I think, to eighty-one. She uses the word 'happiness' too, but on the whole her poems do not exhibit a middle register of feelings: they alternate between 'dreary' and 'glorious', and 'dreary', it has to be admitted, predominates.

Emily, in her birthday letter dated 30 July 1845, astonishingly expresses the wish that everyone could be as comfortable and as undesponding as she it. Yet in the following month she concludes one of her latest and saddest poems with the stanza:

> *Better that I, my own fate mourning,*
> *Should pine alone in the prison gloom*
> *Than waken free on the summer morning*
> *And feel they were suffering this awful doom.*

And there is another poem entitled 'Claudia' (a name which never again occurs in Emily's Gondal nomenclature). Besides being a beautiful poem, it illustrates, extremely well, the dream-like transitions that are a feature of Emily's poetry; and it, too, mentions the 'doom'. Whether the doom was imaginary or real, it left its mark on her poetry, not wholly for good. At the beginning she was an experimentalist in the best sense; any idea that caught her fancy she would follow up; her mind was a garden stocked with many different flowers. As time passed she began to lose this versatility of subject and to concentrate on themes which (as I think) bore on her own case. The bird-note of tremulous lyricism is more rarely heard, the throb of rhetoric more often; a vehement, compelling, personal conviction (which is not quite the same thing as the artist's conviction) speaks through them, and the garden is sparsely cultivated with prize blooms.

At first she is a landscape painter, content to record the visual aspects of Nature. But as sorrow entered more deeply into her spirit she began to ask of Nature a deeper message than it could give her visual sense. At first, Nature did not fail her; she owed Nature most, though not all, of her moments of ecstasy:

> *What language can utter the feeling*
> *That arose when, in exile afar,*
> *On the brow of a lonely hill kneeling*
> *I found the wild heath growing there.*

Nature reconciled her to the idea of death, for the poem continues:

> *It was scattered and stunted, and told me*
> *That soon even that would be gone.*
> *It whispered 'The grim walls enfold me;*
> *I have bloomed in my last summer's sun.'*

But a rival to Nature soon forced an entrance to her heart:

> *How sweet it is to mark those clouds*
> *Break brightly in the rising day;*
> *To see the sober veil that shrouds*
> *This summer morning melt away.*

> *O sweet to some, but not to her*
> *Unmarkeds't once at Nature's shrine,*
> *She now kneels down a worshipper*
> *A mad adorer, love, to thine.*

Love is the disease of her spirit, Nature is its cure, but the cure grows less and less able to cope with the disease. Nature would help if it could:

> *Shall Earth no more inspire thee*
> *Thou lonely dreamer now?*
> *Since passion may not fire thee,*
> *Shall nature cease to bow?*
>
> *Thy mind is ever moving*
> *In regions dark to thee—*
> *Recall its useless roving*
> *Come back and dwell with me.*

'I want to be what God made me', Emily is reported to have said. Denied the outlet of love, unable to take its old delight in Nature, Emily's mind turned more and more inwards, trying to find a philosophy that should make her misery more manageable to her. Two lines of thought emerge. One, that tries to see the universe as a moral order, is utterly pessimistic and finds the only remedy in death, where 'conquered good and conquering ill are lost in one repose'. The other, by-passing morals, ignoring, indeed, the world without, finds its consolation in a kind of mystical self-worship:

> *And am I wrong to worship where*
> *Faith cannot doubt nor hope despair*
> *Since my own soul can grant my prayer?*

—and in a longing for immortality as such: 'I have cast my anchor of desire deep in unknown eternity', she says. Thus she makes her longing for death a positive thing, not a cowardly, negative withdrawal from life. In 'Last Lines' she celebrates the final triumph of her spirit over its doubts and fears: 'No coward soul is mine.'

But 'Last Lines' is not the last poem she wrote. She wrote two more, one a variation of the other, and they show that in her efforts to come to terms with the universe she had not forgotten that there were other people in the world besides herself. How did she regard them? One might have supposed that her sufferings would have taught her indifference, or even tolerance, but they did not. Hard on herself, she was equally hard on the rest of mankind. She always shunned society; that might have been due to shyness, but in the light of these poems it seems to have been misanthropy. Perhaps she had always had misanthropic moods.

> *First melted off the hope of youth,*
>   *Then fancy's rainbow fast withdrew,*
> *And then experience told me truth*
>   *In mortal bosoms never grew.*
>
> *'Twas grief enough to think mankind*
>   *All hollow, servile, insincere—*
> *But worse to trust to my own mind*
>   *And find the same corruption there.*

So she wrote, perhaps in her haste, at the age of 19. Charlotte and Branwell, in their chronicles of Angria, had written about wars, and wars in which plenty of lives were lost. But into those dry, brilliant, ironical effusions human emotion enters hardly at all. Nearly all that happens is told with lighthearted mockery, or, when Branwell holds the pen, with the professional precision of a historian, relieved by flourishes of rhetoric. Emily and Anne, on the other hand, took their wars to heart. 'The Fall of Zalona' is a record of intense suffering and misery. Man's inhumanity to man seems to have become an obsession with Emily; she came to regard war as senseless and debasing. In one of the last poems Lord Julian is not reproved, far from it, for having had no heart to fill a patriot's grave and for preferring love to fighting. Both Emily's last two poems are poems about war. One is an atrocity story which strikes a strangely modern note, told by an ideological soldier of fortune:

> *Enthusiast—in a name delighting—*
> *My alien sword I drew to free*
> *One race, beneath two standards fighting,*
> *For loyalty and liberty.*
>
> *When kindred strive—God help the weak!*
> *A brother's ruth 'tis vain to seek;*
> *At first it hurt my chivalry*
> *To join them in their cruelty;*

but soon he was as hardened as they and took the same delight in torture, both with tongue and dagger:

> *Twice in my arms, twice on my knee,*
> *You stabbed my child and laughed at me*

moans the narrator's miserable victim, the master of the house where his momentarily victorious enemies were billeted. Soon the tables are turned, and it is the narrator's child whose life is threatened; incontinently he repents and begs for mercy for the boy, which is granted, but the story does not end happily. The other poem is a variant of this, and was written, if the date has been rightly deciphered, seven months before Emily died:

> *Why ask to know what date—what clime?*
> *There dwelt our own humanity,*
> *Power-worshippers from earliest time,*
> *Foot-kissers of triumphant crime*
> *Crushers of helpless misery,*
> *Crushing down Justice, honouring Wrong:*
> *If that be feeble, this be strong.*
>
> *Shedders of blood, shedders of tears:*
> *Self-cursers avid of distress;*
> *Yet mocking heaven with senseless prayers*
> *For mercy on the merciless.*

Thus Emily threw her sceptre—not at the injurious gods, for she was too proud to believe in any control outside herself, but at our own humanity, whose deeds had made our earth a hell.

Socrates said that a man became a misanthrope by being let down by one person, and it is curious that a contemporary reviewer of *Wuthering Heights* surmised that the writer of it had suffered not disappointment in love, but 'some great mortification of pride', which had so embittered his spirit that he had prepared this stinging story in vengeance on his species, and had flung it, crying 'There, take that!' with cynical pleasure in the very teeth of human kind. I do not feel that *Wuthering Heights* is a deliberate attack on human nature (only the character of Joseph is drawn with hatred), but I do think that she wrote it with a spirit that (to quote her own words) had been so 'altered and hardened' by experience that she could no longer take pleasure in what daily life had to offer or in the give-and-take of ordinary human relationships, and had to look beyond them for spiritual satisfaction. Like the prisoner with whom she so often compares herself, her only joy lay in the hope of escape. 'What irks me most is this shuttered prison, after all. I'm tired of being enclosed here. I'm wearying to escape into that glorious world, and to be always there: not seeing it dimly through tears and yearning for it through the walls of an aching heart, but really with it and in it.' She wanted to realize, as Lord David Cecil has justly said, the immortality of the soul in this world.

But the world is very much with us in *Wuthering Heights*; all the characters, except Heathcliff and Catherine, are *terre-à-terre* human beings. The ingenious devices by which Heathcliff, in his career of vengeance, annexed the property of his enemies are correct according to law. And the world wins in the end, for Heathcliff is worsted and the moral order which the lovers had flouted resumes its sway.

How contradictory the evidence is! And what makes it all the more muddling, Branwell, too, suffered from the anguish of lost happiness: he was haunted by the death of their eldest sister, who had been a mother to them all. So, too, was Emily; in her poems she invokes Maria, glad that she cannot share their earthly woe. That Emily resented the world's criticism of Branwell is obvious. Did that make her hate the world? Did the belief that she, as Branwell's chief supporter, also incurred the world's disdain, stiffen her resentment against it, provoking her to inquire by what right it issued moral judgments, since it was so far from moral itself? Did she think attack was the best means of defence?

> *And when I hear thy foes deride*
> *I must cling closely to thy side.*

How deeply had Emily anchored her hopes in Branwell, before she anchored them in Eternity? In her poems she speaks of him as if he was dead—as indeed he was, the Branwell in whom all their hopes had centred. He was dead and the living Branwell was a monster whom the virtuous soul must shun.

> *Oh dream, where art thou now?*
> *Long years have passed away*
> *Since first from off thine angel brow*
> *I saw the light decay.*

So for a moment the clues seem to point our way, the fragments of the jigsaw to fall into place, and to show a coherent picture: the picture of a sister so devoted to her brother that his fall from grace changed her whole outlook. She would not and could not condemn him. From the hell-fire moralist of at least one of the Brussels essays, she became the amoralist writer of *Wuthering Heights*.

Heathcliff is not a portrait of Branwell, but he might be a portrait of the 'iron man' whom, in his Byronic, satanic moods, Branwell would have liked to think himself. But a moment later doubts occur, we remember a score of facts that do not fit, indications that lead in other directions, and the picture dissolves —to be reconstituted, but as what? For Emily Brontë really lived, she is there, at the heart of the myths and legends that have grown up round her, and we cannot help speculating about her life, any more than we can help speculating about Shakespeare's.

Any picture can be made tendentious, but let us close with a happy one, and to obviate the risk of distorting it to fit some theory, let Emily paint it in her own words. The extract comes from her second birthday letter, written in the summer of 1845, three and half years before her death:

> Anne and I went on our first long journey by ourselves together, leaving home on the 30th of June, Monday, sleeping at York, returning to Keighley Tuesday evening, sleeping there and walking home on Wednesday morning. Though the weather was broken we enjoyed ourselves very much, except during a few hours at Bradford. And during our excursion we were: Ronald Macalgin, Henry Angora, Juliet Angusteena, Rosabella Esmaldan, Ella and Julian Egremont, Catharine Navarre, and Cordelia Fitzaphnold, escaping from the palaces of instruction to join the Royalists who are hard driven at present by the victorious Republicans. The Gondals still flourish bright as ever. I am at present writing a work on the First Wars.

I should like to point out, for the benefit of those who think that the Gondal poems were a kind of literary exercise making a coherent saga based on Emily's imaginary, not her real experience, that very few of the names listed occur in the poems of either Emily or Anne. And another question: was Emily's prose chronicle of Gondal ever completed? I doubt it. 'I have a good many books on hand,' she wrote, 'and as usual I make small progress with any.'

IV

NATHANIEL HAWTHORNE

(1)

NATHANIEL HAWTHORNE was a name as well
known in my youth on this side of the Atlantic as on the
other. There were fewer books then, and his were easy
to get hold of: *Tanglewood Tales* was a regulation Christmas
present for children. I don't remember what first attracted me
to him, unless it was the title of his novel, *The Scarlet Letter*,
which rather surprisingly appeared on my grandfather's book-
shelf. I suppose I was intrigued by the name—I had no idea
what it meant, but imagined it was a communication—the sort
of letter that one person writes to another. But why *scarlet*?
I vaguely asked myself. Was the paper scarlet, or the ink?
No doubt my interest would help to support the publishers'
contention that the title of a book makes a lot of difference to
its sales. I have always thought that a novel gave life to its title
—not the other way round. *Tom Jones, Emma, Jane Eyre,*
Adam Bede—would those titles attract one, but for the book
behind them?

But for whatever reason—and it may have been deeper and
more telepathic than the mere words would suggest—I was
drawn to *The Scarlet Letter*, and when I was at school I read it.
I asked my music-master, Percy Buck, whom I rightly regarded
as an authority on culture, what he thought of Hawthorne. He
said, 'Ah, yes, that golden pen!' or words to that effect. But
I knew he must be right, and soon afterwards wrote an essay on
Hawthorne, based rather slavishly on Sir Leslie Stephens's
Hours in a Library, in which I set forth his ideas about the novel,
slightly diluted by my own.

How easy it seemed then! I had no one to contradict me, and
I laid about me with a confidence that I am far from feeling now.

There is an ambiguity in the events of Hawthorne's life just as there is an ambivalence of thought in his books. There is plenty of evidence about his life, supplied by himself, his wife Sophia, his son Julian, and his friends. But just as his stories are written in a sort of mental twilight where ideas are hard to descry and even objects are not always what they appear to be at first sight, so with his life. There *is* a lot of evidence, but much of it is conflicting and in some cases, just when we need them most, the clues are missing. Hawthorne used irony plentifully throughout his stories often with deliberate intent to avoid being pinned down to a meaning; and he used it too when he was writing about himself. And besides irony and ambiguity, there is exaggeration and even downright mystification.

His earliest American ancestor came from England to Massachusetts in 1630. He was called William Hathorne, and Hathorne remained the family name until shortly after Nathaniel graduated from Bowdoin College, when he changed it to Hawthorne—quite why is not explained. Perhaps he thought Hawthorne more euphonious, perhaps he liked the idea of being two people, so to speak, at the same time. Or could it have been because his Hathorne ancestors had done something he preferred to forget? Towards the end of the seventeenth century occurred the Salem witchcraft trials, in which two Hathornes, father and son, took an only too active part. Not only the supposed witches, but also the Quakers, were objects of Puritan persecution; and one of the victims was believed to have laid a curse on Nathaniel's ancestor.

> The figure of that first ancestor [Hawthorne wrote in his Introduction to *The Scarlet Letter*] still haunts me. He was a soldier, legislator, judge; he was a ruler in the Church; he had all the Puritanic traits, both good and evil. He was likewise a bitter persecutor, as witness the Quakers who have remembered him in their histories, and relate an incident of his hard severity towards a woman of their sect, which will last longer, it is to be feared, than any record of his better deeds, though these were many. . . . His son, too, inherited the persecuting spirit and made himself so conspicuous in the martyrdom of the witches that their blood may fairly be said to have left a stain upon him . . . I know not whether these ancestors of mine bethought themselves to repent and ask pardon of Heaven for their cruelties, or whether they are now groaning under the consequences of them in another state of being. At all events I, the present writer, as their representative, hereby take shame upon myself for their sakes, and pray that any curse

incurred by them—as I have heard, and as the dreary and unpros-
perous condition of the race, for many a long year back, would
argue to exist—may be now and henceforth removed.

Whether Hawthorne believed in the existence of this curse,
it would be hard to say. So many of his remarks are to be taken,
as Sir Thomas Browne (who also believed in witchcraft) said,
'in a soft and flexible sense, and not brought to the rigid test
of reason'. But he wrote as if he believed in it; it coloured his
imagination; more than any other single element in his mental
make-up, it conditioned, if it did not inspire, his work. And one
does not have to be unduly superstitious to trace its workings,
or the fear of its workings, in his own life. He was a haunted
and unhappy man—according to one biographer, he was only
really happy for two years, the first two years of his married
life. And there are two periods in his career—towards the
beginning and at the end—which it would be quite tempting to
explain by supernatural causes.

He was born on 4 July 1804, in Union Street, Salem. His
father, a ship's captain, died four years later, leaving a widow,
aged twenty-seven, and three children—Elizabeth, Nathaniel
and Louisa. Louisa was Hawthorne's favourite sister, but it
was Elizabeth who played the greater part in his literary
development, for it was she whom, later on, he deputed to
choose from the local library the books he wanted to read.
Dante, Cervantes, Edmund Spenser, Bunyan, Thomson (of
The Castle of Indolence) and Dr. Johnson were among his
favourites. He cannot have remembered his father with any
distinctness, but I suppose that is no reason why Captain
Hathorne should not have given him the Freudian traumas that
one biographer has credited him with. American critics are more
prone than we are to draw conclusions from internal evidence
and from psychological findings, but certainly *Alice Doane's
Appeal* is a very odd story, and if it indicates anything apart
from what it says, might well confirm Hawthorne's expressed
admiration for Godwin's novel, *Caleb Williams*.

After his father's death the Hawthornes moved to Nathaniel's
maternal uncle's house in Salem. His mother gave way to grief.
'His love of solitude', says Mr. Newton Arvin, one of the most
perceptive of Hawthorne's many biographers, 'was co-operating
with his introspective habits, and the progress of both was to be
fortified by circumstance. For that matter he could not remember

the day when intense solitude had not been preserved by the most important members of his family.'

Five years had passed since the time of the *accident*, since Captain Hathorne's ship had come back from Guiana without him, and Nathaniel's mother had eaten no meals with the rest of them in all that period. 'What had begun as the expression of violent grief . . . had taken a turn not at all uncommon in New England, and had settled into the dreary rite of a monotonous sorrow: a torpid habit. If the shadow of that ancestral curse was to have assumed substance and depth, it could hardly have borne more heavily than this.' Many years later, in fiction, Hawthorne was to describe 'a forlorn widow whose grief outlasted even its vitality, and was saddest then'.

'A torpid habit!' That was what his own temperament was going to make only too fatally easy for him to acquire: was not the malediction of the poor witch, Rebekah Nurse, doing its work at last in setting him this early model of torpidity?

There are three points in this passage that I should like to comment on. 'The accident' referred to occurred when Hawthorne was nine. He injured his foot playing ball at school, had to go on crutches, and did not recover from his lameness till he was twelve. What result this calamity may have had on his psychological development we can only guess. Secondly his mother's addiction to solitude shows that his own may have been hereditary: it had, at any rate, an example in her, and in the rest of his family, for I believe at one time there were four members of the Manning household who all took their meals in their own bedrooms. How different domestic arrangements then must have been from those of our own day! Lastly there is the curse. But might not this have started operating with the accident?—or even earlier, with the death of Hawthorne's father from yellow fever? A curse that could only produce 'a torpid habit' is not a serious one—we might all of us suffer from it, without the intervention of a witch. And in that connection, giving the influence of witchcraft on Hawthorne's mind its due, for he was obsessed by it—and *The House of the Seven Gables*, and to some extent *The Scarlet Letter*, depend on it—he also wrote the enchanting story *Feathertop*, in which a witch, though not an estimable character, is presented with a certain playful sympathy.

While living at his uncle's house Hawthorne, as well as

attending various schools, went on reading and among the books listed was Rousseau. Mr. Arvin says:

> At the age of ten there is probably not much harm even in Rousseau, if these ideal and moonshiny writers [Spenser, Thomson, and Rousseau] are taken along with the proper infusion of reality in the form of baseball games, snowball fights and marbles.

This regrettable and Philistine utterance is unworthy of Mr. Arvin and one even wonders, from this side of the Atlantic, whether baseball was already a popular game or even established in New England in 1814. But to dismiss Rousseau as an 'ideal and moonshiny' writer whose influence might have been counteracted by a few stiff games of baseball (if it then existed) is a more serious error. I should not like to start a controversy on the question of whether Rousseau was a good influence or a bad, but it is incontestable that he was an *enormous* influence, one of the most powerful single influences mankind has ever had—morally, emotionally, and politically—and on a precocious boy of ten the impact of his ideas may have been overwhelming. From him Hawthorne the democrat may have imbibed his left-wing tendencies, for we do not hear of them as existing among his progenitors, and he may also have imbibed a doctrine that had much more far-reaching effects and may have affected the whole tenor of his thoughts. 'The General Will cannot err', proclaimed Rousseau. He was not the first to enunciate this idea: St. Augustine with his *Securus judicat orbis terrarum* had said much the same thing. But Rousseau gave it a new and terrific impetus, and whatever its source, the idea split Hawthorne's attitude towards human nature into two. One part of him believed that the General Will could not err; in the sphere of morals, as in other spheres, its authority was absolute. At least half the themes of his stories originate in the notion of someone, usually a man, unwilling or unable to identify himself with the General Will, and thereby suffering agonies of guilt and frustration. Hawthorne calls this unwillingness, or inability, to co-operate with the General Will, the sin of Pride: to 'cut oneself off from the magnetic chain of humanity', as he puts it, is the worst thing a man can do.

So much for one side of him—the Rousseau side. But the other side—the Calvinist side—completely parted company with Rousseau, and believed in the innate depravity of the human race. He agreed with the prophet Jeremiah that the heart of man is desperately wicked. How would he have felt about the human heart if he had lived in the days of the concentration camp, the labour camp, the gas chamber, the atom bomb, and so on? Were they not manifestations of the General Will, or of a will sufficiently widespread, and widely subscribed to, to be called general?

What Hawthorne felt, as opposed to what he thought of it, is illustrated in many, if not most of his stories. It is embodied in the group of hostile women who confronted Hester Prynne when she came out of prison, and in the mob who tarred and feathered the (as far as we know) blameless and exemplary Major Molineux. Never, as far as I can remember, except at the end of *The Scarlet Letter* where Hester's fellow towns-women are said to have relaxed their rigour towards the adulteress, does he present the crowd, the multitude, the 'onlie begetters' of the General Will, as anything but ignorant, prejudiced and cruel. Yet it is they whom by implication, and sometimes by precept, he urges us to imitate. In later years (as we shall see) he tried to resolve this contradiction—not very successfully, to my mind. Hawthorne *thought* that human nature was good, but was convinced in his heart that it was evil. At least that is how I interpret his dilemma, and it is a hypothesis which seems to explain the two periods of his life—one early, the other late—which have baffled his biographers.

Thanks to the financial help of his uncle, Richard Manning, he went to at least two schools and then to Bowdoin College, a university in Maine, where he made many friends, and behaved in a fairly normal way, to the relief of his biographers, most of whom are anxious to play down the charge of eccentricity. Today in America, and perhaps in England, we must all be as like each other as we can be. He got into scrapes (not very serious scrapes) and was fined for them. He smoked and drank (he was fond of cigars and champagne), he played cards, he went for walks (walking was always one of his favourite pastimes) and generally behaved in a conventional manner. He did not especially shine at his studies, though he was tolerably good at Latin prose: he was anything but a prize-boy, but he took his degree. Among the friends he made were Horatio Bridge, to whose encouragement he owed so much, and Franklin Pierce—who was to become President of the

United States. He also had, so his biographers tell us, two or three girl-friends, but they do not loom so large as perhaps his biographers would like them to. There is a marked tendency, on the part of some of his biographers, to make him out more normal, or at any rate more conformist, than he was. He graduated in 1825, and then the question arose, what was he to do in life? To his sister Louisa he wrote:

> I have thought much upon the subject, and have finally come to the conclusion that I shall never make a distinguished figure in the world, and all I hope or wish is to plod along with the multitude.

How Rousseau would have applauded this resolve! Already in 1821, when he first went to Bowdoin, he had been considering the question of his future, and he wrote to his mother:

> I have not yet concluded what profession I shall have. The being a Minister is of course out of the Question. I should not think that even you could desire me to choose so dull a way of life. As to Lawyers, there are so many of them already that one half of them (upon a moderate calculation) are in a state of actual starvation. A Physician seems to be Hobson's Choice, but yet I should not like to live by the diseases and infirmities of my fellow creatures. And it would weigh very heavily on my conscience if in the course of my practice I should chance to send any unlucky patient *ad inferum*, which being interpreted is 'to the realms below'. What do you think of my becoming an author, and relying for support upon my pen? . . . Indeed, I think the illegibility of my handwriting is very author-like. How proud you would feel to see my work praised by the reviewers as equal to the proudest productions of the Scribbling Sons of John Bull? But authors are always poor devils, and therefore may Satan take them!

Nevertheless he decided to become an author and then began the long period of apprenticeship in 'the dismal chamber under the eaves', which was to last from 1825 to 1837—'the solitary years'. It was then that he began to develop what he called his 'cursed habit of solitude'.

How solitary was in fact his life in Herbert Street and how far did it represent a deliberate withdrawal from the world? Proust, as we know, chose to live for part of his life in a cork-lined room, but that, so I believe, was because he hated noise, not because he shunned society, for society was, or had been,

the breath of his nostrils. Hawthorne, as far as we know, had
no hatred of noise, and while he was at the university he had
been as sociable as the next man, making friends, joining clubs,
and so on. Yet during these twelve years he was a virtual
recluse, and it hardly seems a sufficient explanation to say that
all this time he was practising the craft of writing. Nor, though
his mind's bent was inward-turning, was he oblivious to the outside world; on the contrary he was in some ways very observant,
both of Nature and of human nature. His writing shows a
painter's eye, he observes with loving exactitude, and never
more than in the *Twice Told Tales*, the fruit, though not the
first-fruit, of his years of seclusion. Were they founded on the
notes and reflections and observations he had made while he
was still attached to the magnetic chain of humanity? Like
Henry James, his first biographer, he was always taking notes
to be used later for fictional purposes, although, again like
James, he very often did not use them. It is, of course, unsafe
to assume that a novelist's work is autobiographical in any
direct sense; but it is plausible to assume that his work is a
transcription, an anagram of his own experience, reflecting its
shape and tone and tempo, and its main preoccupations. And
it is true that most of Hawthorne's best stories, including
The Scarlet Letter, do portray the predicament of someone who
has parted company with his fellows, and who, because of some
act of sin and the guilt that follows, is ostracized, or self-
ostracized, from society and lives in isolation, tormented by his
conscience. We know of no reason why Hawthorne should have
felt guilty. Herman Melville, who seems to have enjoyed his
confidence, for a short time at any rate, more than any other
man, suggests that Hawthorne may have done something to
feel guilty about. But their correspondence has been destroyed,
as were Hawthorne's letters to Horatio Bridge. Mr. Waggoner
has suggested an Oedipus motive and a possible sister-fixation
indicated in the story *Alice Doane's Appeal*, but these are assump-
tions that cannot be proved. All we really know is that Hawthorne shut himself up for twelve years, in what he called this
dismal chamber, and that, for whatever reason, these years
were unhappy.

'I was like a person', he says, 'talking to himself in a dark
room.' But writing many years later to his friend Richard
Henry Stoddart, he says:

It was my fortune, or misfortune, just as you please, to have some slender means of supporting myself, and so, on leaving college in 1825, instead of immediately studying a profession I sat myself down to consider what pursuit in life I was best fit for. My mother had now returned, and taken up her abode in her deceased father's house ... in which I had a room. And year after year I kept on considering what I was fit for, and time and my destiny decided that I was to be the writer that I am. I had always a natural tendency (it appears to have been on the paternal side) towards seclusion, and this I now indulged to the utmost, so that for months together I scarcely held human intercourse outside of my own family; seldom going out except at twilight, or only to take the nearest way to the most convenient solitude, which was oftenest the sea-shore ... Once a year, or thereabouts, I used to make an excursion of a few weeks, in which I enjoyed as much of life as other people do in the whole year's round. Having spent so much of my boyhood and youth away from my native place, I had very few acquaintances in Salem, and during the nine or ten years that I spent there, I doubt whether so much as twenty people in the town were aware of my existence. Meanwhile, strange as it may seem, I had lived a very tolerable life, always cheerful, and enjoyed the very best bodily health. I had read endlessly all sorts of good and good-for-nothing books, and in the dearth of other employment had early begun to scribble sketches and stories, most of which I burned.

This account does not appear to be strictly accurate. It represents Hawthorne as being happier in the 'dismal chamber' than from other accounts he was. It says he lived there for only nine or ten years, whereas most of his biographers say twelve. He attributes his tendency to solitude to his father's family, whereas it was equally pronounced in his mother's. He says he burned most of his sketches and stories, whereas as far as we know he only burned seven, and forty happily survived; he makes no mention of his novel, *Fanshawe*, which he published at his own expense in 1828.

He was so profoundly dissatisfied with *Fanshawe* that he set about destroying every copy he could lay hands on—as George Moore did, with his novel *Spring Days*—with so much success that it was not until after his death that a copy could be found for reissue.

Fanshawe is a romantic novel, influenced by Sir Walter Scott. It moves creakily, the characters are wooden, the plot is improbable and undramatic. Altogether it gives few signs of promise. Fanshawe himself is a fabulous student, doomed to an early death because he is a 'solitary being' who is 'unconnected with the world, unconcerned in its feelings, and uninfluenced by it in any of his pursuits'. Here we see already emerging what was to be the chief figure in Hawthorne's carpet.

I have dwelt perhaps at undue length on this period of Hawthorne's life, because it seems to me to contain the essence of the man and his work, and they are almost indistinguishable —the work is a projection of himself. Also because it is a mystery —if indeed it be a mystery—which has always intrigued me.

At last, as Hawthorne himself put it, 'the world called me forth', and he renewed his relations with society. Perhaps it was the favourable reception of the *Twice Told Tales*—Longfellow's review was particularly enthusiastic—which made him feel that at last he was a figure in the literary world, and not 'the obscurest man of letters in America'. In the same year he met Sophia Peabody, a dentist's daughter. He became secretly engaged to her, and after three years, when Hawthorne was thirty-eight, they were married. The fact that he described their married life as 'the solitude of a united two' shows that his ideas had not altogether changed. But the circumstances of his life had changed. In 1839, no doubt in order to make money as well as to open relations with the world, Hawthorne became a weigher at the Boston Custom-House, a post he held for two years. He then took part in that strange socialistic, idealistic experiment, which the Transcendentalist philosopher, Margaret Fuller, had started at Brook Farm. Twelve years later, it gave him the subject and the material for his novel, *The Blithedale Romance*. He stayed there for only seven months, but it was a rather long interlude in what, to judge from Hawthorne's letters to Sophia, was a passionate courtship. To me, those letters seem to protest too much. The continual use of the second person singular, the thou's and thee's, the reference to his wife as 'my Dove', or, more frequently and facetiously, as 'a certain Dove', are too full of literary device to be convincing emotional outpourings, and I suspect that Sophia was only a temporary escape from his sense of inner solitude. She, however, seems to have worshipped him. Hawthorne, as all his photographs and portraits show, had more than his share of good looks.

'What a beautiful smile he has!' Sophia wrote. 'He has a celestial expression.' And again, 'he looked extremely handsome, with sufficient sweetness in his face to supply the rest of the world, and still leave the ordinary share to himself . . . He looked like the sun shining through a silver mist when he turned to say good-bye.'

After the marriage they took a house, the Old Manse, at Concord. Here, according to one biographer, 'he indulged his unsociability without opposition and even with Sophia's abetment'. 'During those three years,' a contemporary says, 'he was not seen by more than a dozen of the villagers.' But another biographer says that the Hawthornes' life at the Manse was surprisingly hospitable—not at all a solitude à *deux*—and gives a list of the friends they entertained—Emerson, Thoreau, Ellery Channing and many others. How difficult it is to get at the truth.

But not being a Transcendentalist—indeed just the opposite, for Hawthorne believed in Original Sin whereas the Transcendentalists, if I am not mistaken, believed in the innate goodness of man—he was not on intimate terms with the Concord group. Of Emerson, the high-priest of Transcendentalism and already a figure of international renown, he said that though Emerson was 'a poet of deep beauty and austere tenderness, he sought nothing from him as a philosopher'. He thought more of Thoreau, a man as solitary as himself, for though Thoreau, he said, was 'not an agreeable person', 'his books were the work of a true man and full of true thought'.

Hawthorne's chief friends were not drawn from the literary world. The exceptions were Longfellow, with whom his friendship remained unclouded, and Herman Melville. Emerson, Thoreau, Ellery Channing, James Russell Lowell and Oliver Wendell Holmes were friends as far as his innate shyness and reserve would let them be.

Financial stringency, and the owner's wish to return, drove the Hawthornes from their Eden, the Manse. Their next stopping-place (all Hawthorne's abodes were transitory) was in his mother's house in Salem. In Salem, after some political intrigue, at which, strangely enough, he was quite an adept, Hawthorne obtained the post of surveyor at the Salem Custom-House, and none too soon, for Sophia's first baby was just about to be born. He held the job for three years, when he lost it, as he had got it, for political reasons. His work at the Custom-House was not laborious: he had plenty of time for creative work; but the mental inertia to which he was so often a victim, returned to him.

My imagination [he wrote] was a tarnished mirror. It would not reflect, or only with miserable dimness, the figures with which I did my best to people it. The characters of the narrative would not be warmed or rendered malleable by any heat that I could kindle at my intellectual forge ... The same torpor, as regarded the capacity for intellectual effort, weighed upon me in the chamber which I most absurdly called my study.

But they were not barren years, all the same, for within a year of leaving the Custom-House Hawthorne wrote *The Scarlet Letter*.

The Scarlet Letter established his fame; *The House of the Seven Gables* increased his popularity; *The Blithedale Romance* diminished but did not seriously damage it. These three novels, all written in less than three years, when Hawthorne was between forty-six and forty-nine, were the peak, if we except some of the short stories, of his artistic achievement. They brought him money enough to buy himself a house of his own —in Concord, a house he characteristically called The Wayside —but not enough to bring him financial security. That, no doubt, was the reason why he accepted the offer of his old friend, Franklin Pierce, now President of the United States, to be the American Consul in Liverpool.

To Liverpool he went in 1853 and there he remained until 1857. After that he travelled, to Rome and Florence, to France and Switzerland, with his wife and his three children. He was a passionate and conscientious sightseer, with, in England, a special love of cathedrals. Who can forget his descriptions of the Close at Peterborough and the Close at Salisbury? He saw them with the eyes of someone who had always hungered for England—*Our Old Home*, as he was later to entitle a thick volume of reminiscences; but though he loved it, he could not altogether love the English: he regarded them with a critical eye. The characteristic duality of attitude in Hawthorne, which would neither accept nor reject, is never more in evidence than in his copious accounts of his experiences in England. Or for that matter his experiences in other countries. In a sense the past was his native country, the climate most congenial to his mind: his best stories are set in the past, or in some timeless epoch that suggests the past. He knew instinctively how to select from the past the furniture, so to speak, that he needed, whereas the present baffled him with its variousness. His last novel, or I should say, his last completed novel, *The Marble Faun*, which he finished in England in 1860, after his return from the Continent, is like a guidebook to Rome and has indeed often been read as one.

The Hawthornes, five of them now, returned to the United States, in the summer of 1860. At one time it looked as though only four would come back, for Una had been very ill with Roman fever. Much of their time in Italy had been almost unbearably anxious. Now *The Marble Faun* had been well received; the family were back at Hawthorne's beloved Wayside, and all seemed set fair.

But it wasn't. In England Hawthorne had pined for America, or at any rate for Americans; in America he pined if not for the English, at any rate for England. But the truth is, he could not be happy wherever he was: it was not in his nature to be.

During the last four years of his life he started four novels, but could finish none of them. This inability distressed him greatly. In January 1864 he told his publisher, Fields, that his mind had 'lost, for the present, its temper and fine edge', and he could not finish the book that Fields had announced. 'Say to your *Atlantic* readers', he said, 'that Mr. Hawthorne's brain is addled, at last.'

Was it addled? It does not seem to have been so, for although three of the unfinished works were not up to Hawthorne's best, the last he was engaged on, *The Dolliver Romance*, is, as far as it goes, fully up to his old standard. But all the same it is difficult to account for the creative frustration, amounting almost to a mental breakdown, of these tragic final years. Every biographer of Hawthorne has tried to explain the falling off; but may not the true explanation be that temporarily, at any rate, he had written himself out? In the twenty-three years since the first volume of *Twice Told Tales* was published he had written, in all, nearly twenty books; and only in the period of his greatest productivity had he been a prolific or a ready writer. He had to force himself to write. With his innate sense of guilt he blamed himself for the barrenness of his Muse, though it was only comparative: many great novelists, Stendhal and Flaubert, for instance, wrote much less than he did. He blamed himself; but why should anyone else blame him, or seek some other explanation than mental exhaustion for his inability to complete his work? The mere act of writing might be an effort, to anyone with a standard as high as Hawthorne's, but to finish the work off, to pull it together, to present it as a rounded whole, needs a still greater effort, and it is not surprising that Hawthorne, whose inspiration always came from within, was incapable of it.

A breakdown there was, both mental and physical, and the physical breakdown is hard to account for—it is the second baffling period of Hawthorne's life, and his treatment of it, or lack of treatment, is equally baffling.

What was his malady? Apparently he had a premonition of death, but except among very primitive peoples men and women don't die just because they think they will.

Hawthorne seems to have gradually faded out of life. The Civil War depressed and bewildered him; if not actually a 'Copperhead' as the northern dissentients from the war were called, he did not believe that any decision could be reached by force of arms. His pen-portrait of Abraham Lincoln was so unflattering that it had to be left out of the article he wrote, 'Chiefly about War Matters', for the *Atlantic*. His old friend and benefactor, Franklin Pierce, the ex-President, was highly unpopular because of his lukewarm attitude to the war. Nevertheless, out of loyalty and affection, Hawthorne dedicated *Our Old Home* to him, regardless of the disapproval of Harriet Beecher Stowe.

Under the worry of this, and his anxiety for the health of his daughter Una, Hawthorne's condition continued to deteriorate, and it is surprising that his wife, family and friends were not more concerned for him than they appear to have been. His wife did say, however, that he was 'very indisposed and that it was imperative for him to change the air and scene'. Accordingly he took that hopeful journey with his friend and publisher, Ticknor, which ended so tragically with Ticknor's death from pneumonia in Philadelphia. On his return Mrs. Hawthorne was frightened by his appearance and by his extreme weakness, but she still thought that a 'serene joy' would restore his health. Hawthorne did not want to consult a doctor, but unknown to him his wife arranged for him to see Oliver Wendell Holmes, who gave him a very unfavourable report. 'The Shark's tooth has got him', he is reported to have said. What did this mean, cancer? To the layman it sounds like that, but the word has never been mentioned in connection with Hawthorne's illness. Another journey in search of health was prescribed, this time in the company of Franklin Pierce. But the two friends had only been away a week when Pierce, going into Hawthorne's room early in the morning, found him dead.

A strange end—to die in a hotel away from his family and his home. What prompted Hawthorne to do it, unless it was a last bid for solitude? In *The Blithedale Romance* there is a passage which seems prophetic. Coverdale, who to some extent represents Hawthorne in the novel, is lying in bed so ill that he does not expect to live. But he is comforted by the presence and kind ministrations of the stalwart Hollingsworth. Coverdale says:

> Happy the man that has such a friend beside him when he comes to die! and unless a friend like Hollingsworth be at hand—as most probably there will not—he had better make up his mind to die alone. How many men, I wonder, does one meet with in a lifetime, whom he would choose for his death-bed companions!

Hawthorne did not choose his wife or his children for this sad office, he chose his old friend Franklin Pierce, who had the bedroom next to his, with an open doorway through which he could watch his friend; and though he did not actually see Hawthorne die (he died peacefully in his sleep) his presence must have brought him comfort akin to the comfort that Hollingsworth brought to Coverdale.

(2)

I once stayed for a few days with Mrs. Wharton, that rather formidable lady and considerable novelist, in her beautiful house at St. Brice just outside Paris. She was, like her great friend Henry James, an expatriate American, and her standards in every department of life and living were of the highest and most uncompromising: it was said (by Mr. Raymond Mortimer, I think) that she despised the rich for not being writers, and writers for not being rich. I had no claim to be thought either, and have never been able to understand why she invited me to stay, especially as she was ill at the time. Soon after my visit she died: I hope it was *post* and not *propter hoc*. She spent most of the day lying on a chaise-longue. There were plenty of chairs in the house but they were almost all too precious to sit on.

I didn't talk to her much about books, or anything else, as far as I remember, but I did once speak to her of Nathaniel Hawthorne, expressing my admiration for his work, and awaiting a Sibylline reply. I got the reply, but it was not what I expected.

'I don't like his books', she said. 'He started all that nonsense about style.'

I was aghast at this verdict, and I still am. For surely no novelist writing in English has ever written better prose than Hawthorne?—at least, that has always been an article of faith with me. Thackeray is perhaps his equal, but Thackeray, as a craftsman of words, did not fly as high as he did. Thackeray's style was a perfect instrument for saying what he had to say: but it is self-effacing, you cannot enjoy it for itself, as you can Hawthorne's.

Someone has said that Hawthorne's literary style was antiquated, even in his own day. Perhaps it was; I am no judge of that. But if it was, so also, I am told, was the style of John Sebastian Bach in his day. I dare say it would not be difficult to find examples of other artists who have chosen, or been impelled, to express themselves in modes used by their predecessors: Beddoes, for instance. It would be still easier to find examples of artists working in a style of their own invention. But I cannot see there is any virtue in that, any more than there is a virtue in contemporaneousness—a quality which some critics rate highly. There certainly is—or may be—a virtue in originality, but originality can be garbed in the oldest clothes as well as in the latest fashion.

As regards fiction, it would be difficult to distinguish what Hawthorne says from his way of saying it—*le style est l'homme*. As it was with Milton—but in Milton's case the style is so pronounced that, as far as his writing goes, the saying might be reversed—*l'homme est le style*. Hawthorne was certainly original, as original in his own, much less spectacular way, as Edgar Allan Poe was in his. The two writers have a good deal in common. They were among the earliest practitioners of the short story; they both freely used the supernatural; they both saw reality in an aspect very different from that of our daily experience. Realism, except as an end to an utterly non-realistic effect, was quite outside their range or intention as writers. And the aesthetic side of their art (if the pleonasm may be forgiven), the craft of writing, in fact, meant much more to them than it meant to their colleagues on the other side of the Atlantic —Jane Austen, Flaubert and Thackeray excepted.

But there was a great difference between the two, and it soon became apparent to Poe, if not to Hawthorne. Hawthorne used craftsmanship as a means to an end—to make his work as beautiful as might be to the eye and ear and mind. With him it was an instrument, with Poe it was an aim—Poe thought that certain combinations of words would, by the interrelation of their sound, produce an effect that was independent, or partially independent, of their literal meaning.

At least this was Poe's recipe—or, in a famous passage describing the genesis of his poem *The Raven*, he said it was— for writing poetry. And its influence is evident in his stories too. He uses words for their sound effects, to awaken reverberations in the reader's mind that mere meaning could not. 'For the love of God, Montresor!' exclaims the victim, about to be walled up, in *A Cask of Amontillado*, and the cry goes on echoing in one's consciousness with a life of its own, beyond its verbal meaning and the dismal circumstances of the story.

But there was another and deeper difference between Poe and Hawthorne, as Poe was soon to discover. Poe was one of the first critics to hail the *Twice Told Tales*. 'Mr. Hawthorne's distinctive trait', he said, 'is invention, creation, imagination, originality—a trait which, in the literature of fiction, is positively worth all the rest . . . Mr. Hawthorne is original at *all* points.' But later, in 1847, reviewing the *Mosses from an Old Manse*, he revised his opinion. Hawthorne was no longer, to Poe, 'The example, *par excellence*, of the privately-admired and publicly-unappreciated men of genius.' Poe now found him 'peculiar and *not* original, and infinitely too fond of allegory . . . Let him mend his pen, get a bottle of visible ink, come out from the Old Manse', etc.

Allegory was the rock on which, so to speak, Poe and Hawthorne split. In spite of their otherworldliness, their fantasy, their insight into abnormal states of mind, Poe's tales are quite different from Hawthorne's. They are not allegories; they are not symbolic; they are not concerned with morality nor have they a moral. They take us into another world, as Hawthorne's do, and often into a world of horror, as Hawthorne's sometimes do; but they are, as he described them, 'tales of mystery and imagination'. If they have under- and overtones of meaning, those meanings are not concerned with ethics. One reads them for the story, and for its impact on the imagination.

Poe was more original and more inventive than Hawthorne. He was the most outstanding innovator in the field of fiction there has ever been. He invented the detective story, the treasure-hunt story, the horror-story *per se* (the horror-comics of today descend from him), he might almost be said to have invented the short story. He was, like Frederick II, *innovator mirabilis*; he was perhaps the first writer to approach art in a scientific spirit, and the first to exploit the possibilities of the subconscious, though he did not know it by that name. Hawthorne exploited it too, but always with the intention of throwing light on the human predicament in its entirety—with special reference to its moral predicament—which had little interest for Poe.

If we except *Fanshawe*, that premature product of his pen, Hawthorne was a short-story writer before he was a novelist, and although *The Scarlet Letter* is the peak of his achievement (and even *The Scarlet Letter* is really a *nouvelle*) the short story is his natural medium, as it was Hans Andersen's, who, though he lived longer, was almost his contemporary. His imagination had much in common with Hans Andersen's. It was rather more moralistic, but the author of *The Snow Queen* could have written *The Snow Image*, though I doubt if Hawthorne could have written *The Snow Queen*. Hawthorne wanted to get away from the temporary, and still more from the contemporary, into an indefinite era where his characters could be seen in isolation without having to conform to any more mundane rules than those of the human heart.

Critics have been right in insisting that his stories need the element of *distance*, distance in time. Many great novelists have needed it. It has been said, with some truth, that nearly every great novelist has written about a period at least forty years earlier than the time when he was putting pen to paper. That is roughly true of *War and Peace*, of *Vanity Fair*, of *Wuthering Heights*, and of *Don Quixote*. Their authors looked back to a time when the past was as clear as a mirror, undisturbed by the distracting phenomena of the present.

But Hawthorne needed a longer distance in time than that. He needed it, not so much to clarify his vision, but as to interpose a blur, a slight fog between him and his subjects, through which his readers could only vaguely descry what was happening and therefore be the less able to say 'This is, or is not, like life as we know it.' Of his four chief novels, only *The Scarlet Letter* has its action in the past—the past of 1690, or thereabouts, when witches and Quakers in New England were still liable to execution for their practices or their opinions. But it is not an historical novel in the sense that it tries to *evoke* the past. It uses the past as a medium for the presentation of moral issues which Hawthorne felt could not be so forcibly presented in the materialistic daylight of 1850.

For by 1850 materialism had taken its hold of America as firmly as it had of England. The paradox is that all the important writers of Hawthorne's day—himself, Emerson, Thoreau, Melville and Poe—were strongly anti-materialistic and anti-rationalistic, much more so than their English contemporaries, who were romantic no doubt, but who accepted the Universe (to quote Carlyle's young friend), at any rate in its social manifestations, far more readily than they did on the other side of the Atlantic. Realism did not flourish in fiction until its tenets had taken root in the man in the street.

Hawthorne was not immune from realism in his attitude towards money: he had a Yankee shrewdness in that respect. And in a furtive, half-ashamed way, it comes into his novels. Little Pearl, Hester Prynne's daughter, is left well off; the surviving Pyncheons inherit a fortune through Judge Pyncheon's death; not the least part of Zenobia's tragedy is that she was financially ruined, or thought she was, when she committed suicide.

But it is all faery gold, not gold that has been worked for, gold that is an object of existence, as it is in Balzac. And it is of little importance, as a criterion of human endeavour, in Hawthorne's *Twice Told Tales* and his *Mosses from an Old Manse*, stories which, if not the summit of his achievement, are the most characteristic of his genius. Poe thought that the *Mosses* showed a falling-off, and Hawthorne, too, thought he could go no further in that direction, but most critics would agree that they contain some of his best work—*Young Goodman Brown, The Birthmark, Rappacini's Daughter, The Celestial*

Railroad, Feathertop, Egotism, or The Bosom Serpent, The Intelligence Office, Roger Malvin's Burial, The Old Apple Dealer, The Artist of the Beautiful. They, with the stories from the *Twice Told Tales* and *The Snow Image*, are among the first, and in my opinion the best, short stories ever written.

What lies behind them? What (to use an ugly phrase) is their motivating inspiration?

To answer that I should have to discuss a subject I am utterly unqualified to comment on—the Sin of Pride. First because it is not a sin I suffer from myself (at least, I think not, unless my acceptance of the flattering invitation to speak in Cambridge is a sign that I do), and secondly because it is a theological sin, and I am no theologian, except in so far as I know that Pride is the worst of sins, and the father of them all. It is the sin by which (if ambition is a form of pride) fell the Angels. The Church—all the Churches—have been against it —partly, I feel (as a staunch individualist), because the exercise of private judgment is an offence against whatever religious body one may happen to belong to. It is an assertion of the self against the superior authority of the many.

I don't think that many people nowadays suffer from the sin of pride—one almost wishes they did, for at any rate, if it took the form of proper pride, it would prevent them from doing a great many of the things they do. The prevailing sin of our day, I should say, is dishonesty: I could fill books with instances of dishonesty that have come my way: the contractual basis of society is threatened by it. And I can hardly think of one instance of the sin of pride.

But it was the sin of pride that seems to have obsessed Hawthorne, pride in various forms. The pride of birth which wrapped Lady Eleanor literally in the infected mantle which gave her smallpox. 'The curse of Heaven has stricken me', she cries, 'because I would not call man my brother or woman sister. I wrapped myself in pride as in a mantle, and scorned the sympathies of Nature, and therefore has Nature made this wretched body the medium of a dreadful sympathy.' Ethan Brand, who spent his life looking for the Unpardonable Sin, found it at last. 'It is a sin that grew within my own breast,' he said, 'standing erect with a pride that distinguishes all enthu-siasts of his stamp, a sin that grew nowhere else. A sin that triumphed over the sense of brotherhood with man or reverence

for God! and sacrificed everything to its own mighty claims!
The only sin that deserves the recompence of immortal agony!
I incur the guilt. Unshrinkingly I accept the retribution!'
Hawthorne explains how Ethan Brand had developed his
intellect at the expense of his heart.

> Where was the heart? That indeed had withered, had contracted,
> had perished! It had ceased to partake of the universal throb. He had
> lost his hold of the magnetic chain of humanity. He was no longer
> a brother—man, opening the chambers, or the dungeons, of our
> common nature by the key of holy sympathy, which gave him a right
> to share in all its secrets: he was a cold observer, looking on man-
> kind as the subject of his experiment and at length converting man
> and woman to be his puppets and pulling the wires that moved
> them to such degrees of crime as were demanded for his study.
> Thus Ethan Brand became a fiend.

It is almost impossible not to suspect in this passage, and in
many others like them, a self-criticism of the lonely writer in
his dismal chamber, unable to mix with his fellows, although
at the same time wanting to, and speculating about them in
the detached manner of a Flaubert—or a fiend. As we shall see,
Miles Coverdale in *The Blithedale Romance*, who is usually
thought to be a projection of Hawthorne himself, was that sort
of man. But is not every novelist, however much he may
participate, as Dickens and Balzac did, in the hurly-burly of life,
condemned to be an observer of the human scene, as much as a
painter is, or used to be, an observer of the pictorial scene?
And might it not be said that the contemporary painter's dislike
of representation (especially of the human face and figure, for
we have very few portraitists nowadays) is a development of
the same tendency of withdrawal from the 'magnetic chain of
humanity' that Hawthorne lamented in himself?

As for the sin of using human beings for one's own purposes, and not as an end in themselves (which Kant believed
to be the cornerstone of ethics) we have only to glance at the
events of the past fifty years to realize how often, and how
disastrously, men have used other men for their own purposes.

Hawthorne was a prophet, if not of things, at any rate of
states of mind to come. Dreams meant a great deal to him, and
the dubious hinterland between sleeping and waking; he was
the predecessor of such writers as Kafka and Camus, and that
is one reason why his work has aroused so much interest lately

in the United States, where psycho-analysis has taken a firmer
hold even than it has here. The sense of guilt which runs
through many of his stories saddens them. He had, as someone
has said, a sentimental Victorian sense of the function of women
(especially pretty young women, like Phoebe in *The House of
the Seven Gables*) to save men from themselves. He had a soft
place in his heart for women. But they are not (with certain
exceptions, Hester Prynne, Zenobia) the most convincing or
the most clearly realized of his characters. Despite scriptural
authority to the contrary he may have thought that Eve was
not really involved in the sin of Adam.

No novelist had a more wakeful sense of humour than Hawthorne, but his playfulness, his conceits, are meant to raise a smile
not a laugh. When there is a laugh in his stories it is nearly
always a bitter, anti-social laugh—a laugh at somebody's
expense, like the bitter laugh at the expense of Major Molineux,
in which Robin, his kinsman, joins in spite of himself.

My Kinsman, Major Molineux is one of the earliest and the
best of Hawthorne's short stories, though not one of the most
characteristic, perhaps because it does not wear its moral on
its sleeve. It has a dream-like quality, the quality of nightmare
with a nightmare's sense of anxiety and frustration and impend-
ing calamity. Young Robin sets out to seek his fortune in a
distant and to him quite unknown city. I believe it to have been
Boston. He has been told to ask for his kinsman, Major Molineux, the great man of the place, whom he has never met, but
who will be sure to help him. He arrives towards the close of
day, and immediately sets about asking for his kinsman: but the
answers he gets from the townsfolk are always hedging,
ambiguous, or slightly sinister. The hours pass and his quest is
not rewarded. At last he finds himself among a group of
spectators, including an 'old citizen', thronging the streets,
watching a procession. It is a torchlight procession and in the
midst of it is Major Molineux, tarred and feathered, who is
being drummed out of the town—we are not told why.

And lastly there sailed over the heads of the multitude a great broad
laugh... In front of the Gothic window stood the old citizen, wrapped
in a wide gown, his gray periwig exchanged for a nightcap... and
his silk stockings hanging about his legs. He supported himself on his
polished cane in a fit of convulsive merriment, which manifested
itself on his solemn old features like a funny inscription on a tomb-

stone. The contagion was spreading among the multitude when all at once it seized upon Robin, and he sent forth a shout of laughter that echoed through the street: every man shook his sides, every man emptied his lungs, but Robin's shout was the loudest there. The cloud-spirits peeped from their silvery islands, as the congregated mirth went roaring up the sky! The Man in the Moon heard the far bellow. 'Oho,' quoth he, 'the Old Earth is frolicsome tonight!'

The leader gave the sign, the procession resumed its march. On they went, like fiends that throng in mockery around some dead potentate, mighty no more, but majestic still in his agony. On they went, in counterfeited pomp, in senseless uproar, in frenzied merriment, trampling all on an old man's heart. On swept the tumult, and left a silent street behind.

Robin comes to his senses, not quite knowing if it has been a dream. He tells his companion he is tired of town life, but his companion suggests that he should give it a further trial. 'As you are a shrewd youth,' he says, 'you may rise in the world without the help of your kinsman, Major Molineux.'

This is the most ambiguous of Hawthorne's stories. What are we to make of it? It is not a tract against pride, for there is not a word to suggest that Major Molineux was not an exemplary old gentleman, quite innocent of that, and other sins. Robin joins in the hue and cry against him—and what is that hue and cry but an expression of the General Will of the cruel and ignorant populace, inflamed by blood-lust, the very people that Hawthorne is always urging us to associate ourselves with? It is hard to resist the conviction that for all his protestations of love for his fellows he was at heart a misanthrope.

The sin of singularity, which is Hawthorne's main theme, is illustrated in many of his stories and is not always directly connected with the Sin of Pride. *The Ambitious Guest* who wants to leave a name behind him (surely a praiseworthy ambition) is overwhelmed by an avalanche, as is the group of kindly people who give him shelter. *The Artist of the Beautiful* who spends his life in the endeavour to construct by art a butterfly so beautiful that it will be indistinguishable from Nature's own product, sees his life's work ruined by the careless grasp of a child's hand, and gets very little sympathy for it, from Hawthorne or anyone else, though his friend the blacksmith, with his physical strength and his hammer and anvil, is portrayed as an invaluable member of society—simply, it seems, because he was not an artist of the beautiful—though many blacksmiths have been, and perhaps still are. Then there is *The Birthmark* —a very touching story which, like *The Artist of the Beautiful*, is a warning against the quest for perfection. A man marries a beautiful girl who has no moral defects and only one physical defect—a birthmark, the fleshly imprint of four fingers on her cheek. He is not satisfied with her other qualities, outstanding as they are; he can only see her in terms of the Birthmark. She consents to have it removed by surgery: the operation is successful but the patient dies.

All these stories and many more—*The Great Stone Face* is one—seem to be intended to discourage the individual's—anybody's—quest for perfection—and as such are especially directed against the artist, whose quest perfection has to be. Does Hawthorne mean that the artist—and there has been none more scrupulous and painstaking than he—is to be condemned because of his unlikeness to the Common Man (beloved of Rousseau)? Is it a feeling of guilt, which he expresses so eloquently in his Introduction to *The Scarlet Letter*, that his seafaring Puritan forebears would have found no relish of salvation in a life devoted to scribbling? Or is it some deeper and more tragic idea, that the artist's calling, with its accompanying quest for perfection, however imperfectly realized, inevitably separates the artist from his fellows, who have no such preoccupations and are content to go down undistinguished from the cradle to the grave?

Such a conviction might be the secret of Hawthorne's unhappiness, which he tried to conceal from himself by all kinds of devices—marital pleasure, family life, mixing with the common man in custom-houses and consulates, speaking at Lord Mayor's banquets (he hated public speaking but inured himself to it), intensive sightseeing in England and on the Continent (he was in the van of American sightseers, hardly a cathedral passed him by), and finally by sheer hard work, for in spite of long periods of non-productivity, and a natural inertia, he left behind him at least twenty-five volumes.

I suppose he felt he must justify himself in the eyes of God and man—as regards the former a vain hope, for in Thy sight shall no man living be justified.

To say this is to narrow down and limit the appeal of Hawthorne's stories—the two volumes of *Twice Told Tales*, the two

volumes of *Mosses*, and *The Snow Image*. If in the main they
come back to one theme, the sin or folly of aiming at something
which one's fellows do not aim at, they contain so much else—
lovely descriptions of natural scenery, many characters, old and
young, lovingly observed, without reference to the good or the
bad—thoughts and reflections of beauty and depth and humour,
which come straight from Hawthorne's artistic sensibility, and
have nothing to do with his convictions (whatever they were)
about human nature, fallen or unfallen. However little he may
have enjoyed his own life, he enjoyed the life of the world outside in manifold forms, and celebrated it and enhanced it. He
embellished it with the beauties of his mind and his literary
style which (despite Mrs. Wharton) was a wonderful instrument.

Hawthorne, like Henry James, had an inferiority complex
about the possibilities that the American scene afforded a
novelist compared with those that were native to England and
the continent of Europe. The disabilities the two writers complained of were different, but in my opinion equally mistaken.
Take Hawthorne's first. In his Introduction to *The Marble
Faun* he wrote:

> No author, without a trial, can conceive the difficulty of writing
> a romance about a country where there is no shadow, no antiquity,
> no mystery, no picturesque and gloomy wrong, nor anything but a
> commonplace prosperity, in broad and simple daylight, as is happily
> the case with my dear native land.

Henry James Junior (as he was still called when he published
his study of Hawthorne in 1879, fifteen years after the latter's
death) also discussed, apropos of Hawthorne's *American Notebooks*, the difficulties and handicaps under which an American
novelist of that time laboured. As I said, they were very different
from the disabilities that Hawthorne complained of.

> As I turn the pages of his journals [James wrote], I seem to see the
> image of the crude and simple society in which he lived. I use these
> epithets of course, not invidiously but descriptively; in one's desire
> to enter as closely as possible into Hawthorne's situation, one must
> endeavour to reproduce his circumstances. We are struck by the
> large number of elements that were absent from them, and the
> coldness, the thinness, the blankness, to repeat my epithet, present
> themselves so vividly that our foremost feeling is that of compassion
> for a romancer looking for subjects in such a field. It takes so many

things, as Hawthorne must have felt later in life when he made the acquaintance of the denser, richer, warmer European spectacle—it takes such an accumulation of history and custom, such a complexity of manners and types, to form a fund of suggestion for a novelist . . . The negative side of the spectacle on which Hawthorne looked out, in his contemplative saunterings and reveries might, indeed, with a little ingenuity, be made almost ludicrous; one might enumerate the items of high civilisation, as it exists in other countries, which are almost absent from the texture of American life, until it should become a wonder to know what was left. No State, in the European sense of the word, and indeed barely a specific national name. No sovereign, no court, no personal loyalty, no aristocracy, no church, no clergy, no army, no diplomatic service, no country gentlemen, no palaces, no castles, nor manors, nor old country-houses, nor parsonages, nor thatched cottages, nor ivied ruins, nor cathedrals, nor abbeys, nor little Norman churches; no great universities nor public schools—no Oxford, nor Eton, nor Harrow; no literature, no novels, no museums, no pictures, no political society, no sporting class—no Epsom, nor Ascot!

Did Henry James write this passage with his tongue in his cheek? A little, perhaps, but not entirely, for he goes on to say what were the American novelist's compensations, besides 'that American humor, of which of late years we have heard so much', and they were not very impressive, at least as far as Hawthorne was concerned.

'Hawthorne's entries are to a great degree accounts of walks in the country, drives in stage-coaches, people he met in taverns.' (One doesn't think of Henry James as frequenting *taverns*, but they have given many a novelist valuable material—George Eliot and Thomas Hardy, for instance.) James goes on to say, 'The minuteness of the things that attract his attention and that he thinks worthy of being commemorated is frequently extreme, and from this fact we get the impression of a general vacancy in the field of vision.' Then he quotes:

Sunday evening, going by the jail, the setting sun kindled up the windows most cheerfully, as if there were a bright, comfortable light within its darksome stone wall.

Again,

I went yesterday with Monsieur S. to pick raspberries. He fell through an old log bridge—looking back, only his head and shoulders appeared through the rotten logs and among the bushes.

Again,

> A shower coming on, the rapid running of a little bare-footed boy, coming up unheard, and dashing swiftly past us, and showing us the soles of his naked feet as he ran down the path and up the opposite side.

I suppose that the *nominativus pendens* in this and the preceding quotation may be forgiven an author who was jotting down notes; but they are rather surprising in a prose-writer as scrupulous as Hawthorne. James goes on:

> In another place he devotes a page to the description of a dog whom he saw running round after its tail: in still another he remarks, in a paragraph by itself, 'The aromatic odour of peat-smoke in the sunny autumnal air is very pleasant.' The reader says to himself that when a man turned thirty gives a place in his mind—and his inkstand—to such trifles as these, it is because nothing else of superior importance demands admission. Everything in the notes indicates a simple, democratic, thinly composed society; there is no evidence of the writer finding himself in any variety and intimacy of relations with anyone or with anything. We find a good deal of warrant for believing that if we add that statement of Mr. Lathrop's about his meals being left at the door of his room, to rural rambles of which an impression of the temporary phases of the local apple-crop were the usual, and an encounter with an organ-grinder or an eccentric dog the rarer, outcome, we construct a rough image of our author's daily life during the several years that preceded his marriage.

Perhaps we do, but I think that James misses the point, here, just as he misses it, perhaps on purpose, in his list of the phenomena, useful to a novelist, that were lacking from the American scene of Hawthorne's day. What would the author of *The Scarlet Letter* have made of Eton and Harrow, or Epsom and Ascot? Not that any of those places, I am sure, are lacking in picturesque and gloomy wrongs—perhaps they are richer in such subjects than was the New England of Hawthorne's day. But could he have made them illustrative of his special moral preoccupations? Could he have portrayed a member of Pop or of the Philathletic Club withdrawing himself from the society of his school-fellows because of some picturesque and gloomy wrong that he had committed or fancied he had committed? It isn't impossible, any more than it is impossible that a reckless habitué of Epsom or Ascot should go home and commit suicide.

But somehow one doesn't see Hawthorne in that *galère*. As for 'abbeys, cathedrals and little Norman churches', Hawthorne had his fill of them when he came to England, and has left lovely accounts of them in his *English Notebooks*—but they wouldn't have nourished his novelist's gift—they would have choked it with a surfeit, just as the ancient monuments of Rome nearly did. Just as England itself did, when, after his return to America, he tried to make it the scene of two novels, *The Ancestral Footstep* and *Dr. Grimshawe's Secret*—neither of which was he able to finish.

No, Hawthorne's sense of romance was transforming rather than interpretative: the more commonplace the object, the better he could invest it with his own special imaginative quality.

Of course Hawthorne knew more about his own country than we, in another country, and in another day and age, can hope to do. As I said, the tide of materialism was already rising in New England, as it was in England. Yet how comes it that the American writers of that time—Emerson and Thoreau, Poe and Hawthorne and Melville, and a little later, Walt Whitman and Henry James himself—were among the least materially-minded of any group of authors? Henry James, to be sure, in his later life, may have fallen for the worldly lures of Eton and Harrow, Ascot and Epsom, or for the wealth and fashion that they represented—for I can't imagine him ever describing those institutions and functions realistically. One remembers how impressionistically but untechnically he described a game of golf; and the thought of Milly Theale or Maggie Verver attending the celebrations of the 4th of June at Eton makes one's mind boggle. And as for Hester Prynne being there, dressed so unfashionably in her Scarlet Letter, it is inconceivable.

No, in spite of what Henry James and Hawthorne himself thought and said, New England gave Hawthorne just what his imagination needed. *A Rill from the Town Pump* (to quote the title of one of his stories) was a more rewarding subject for him than the fountains of Versailles or Trafalgar Square, or even the fountains of Rome. Henry James makes fun of the small beer that Hawthorne chronicles in his notebooks—'the general vacancy of the field of vision', 'the setting sun on the windows of the jail', 'the plight of Monsieur S., only his head and shoulders appearing through the rotten logs and among the bushes', 'the dog running after its own tail', and 'the pleasant aromatic odour of peat-smoke'—all those *choses vues*, though trivial to a sophisticated mind, are extremely important in Hawthorne's case, because they reward the efforts—in some cases the *desperate* efforts—he made to get out of the prison of his mind and establish a contact with the humdrum life of the ordinary man (sacred symbol). They were valuable to him precisely because they were objective, and not subjective; they proved to him, and to his readers, that the world had an independent existence apart from his consciousness of it—which is a thing that James, with all his talent for digesting his impressions, could not do. James wouldn't have realized the importance of a mere external event, such as a dog chasing its own tail.

But to return to the world of fashion, and of clothes, throughout the ages a vital subject, in which women always, and men now—especially young men—are passionately interested. Hawthorne was interested in clothes too, but as symbols, not as fashion plates. We shall see to what poetic use he puts the Scarlet Letter that Hester Prynne was compelled to wear. And he makes equally effective use of an article of clothing in one of his earliest and best stories, *The Minister's Black Veil*. It tells how the saintly Father Hooper, the minister revered and adored by all his flock, suddenly took to wearing a black veil, behind which his features were invisible, unless his breath lifted a corner of the veil and allowed a glimpse of them. Why, and for what sin he had committed, he adopted this strange disguise, we are never told; but he wore it for years, until his dying day. On that day the minister attending his death-bed begged Father Hooper to take it off, indeed he tried to take it off himself. But Father Hooper, with a sudden access of strength, resisted this intolerable intrusion on his privacy. 'Dark old man,' exclaimed the affrighted minister, 'with what horrible crime upon your soul are you passing to the judgment?' But Father Hooper was not even abashed. 'Why do you tremble at me alone?' cried he, turning his veiled face round the circle of pale spectators. 'Tremble also at each other! I look around me and lo! on every visage a black veil!'

The tremendous effect of this climax cannot be conveyed by a brief extract; but brief as it is it shows that Hawthorne was more in his element with clothes, even if they only consisted in a double row of crape that symbolized some picturesque and gloomy wrong, native to New England, than he would have been as a fashion-reporter, or even as an observer of fashions, at Ascot or Epsom in Old England. He tried, he tried hard, and the effort may have helped to bring about his early death, to isolate from the great mass of English legends and ghost stories one that would suit his purpose, and he thought he had found it. But the bloody footprint in the English castle which appears in more than one of his last novels, did not lead to anything, whereas *The Minister's Black Veil*, if one surrenders to its magic, leads to a great deal.

(3)

Hawthorne wrote *The Scarlet Letter* soon after his enforced retirement from the Salem Custom-House. It was a short novel, judged by the standards of those days, perhaps not more than 70,000 words. It was his intention to publish other stories with it, to eke out its length; but in the end he, or his publishers, wisely decided not to, and hit on the compromise of a long introductory essay, which he called *The Custom-House*. Hawthorne was pleased with it, and peversely used to say that the book owed its success to its preface—for he did not believe that *The Scarlet Letter* would be any more popular than his short stories had been. The preface is an account of his experiences at the Salem Custom-House, of his colleagues there and of the three and a half hours a day—not a very exacting stint—that he devoted to the service of Uncle Sam. He lost his job as a result of a change in the administration: General Taylor was elected President and Hawthorne had to go. It is not surprising that he looked back on the Custom-House with mixed feelings.

It is a strange experience [he wrote], to a man of pride and sensibility, to know that his interests are within the control of individuals who neither love nor understand him, and by whom, since one or the other must needs happen, he would rather be injured than obliged. Strange too, for one who has kept his calmness throughout the contest, to observe the bloodthirstiness that is developed in the hour of triumph, and to be conscious that he is himself among its objects! There are few uglier traits of human nature than this tendency—which I now witnessed in men no worse than their neighbours—to grow cruel merely because they possessed the power of inflicting harm. If the guillotine, as applied to office-holders, were a literal fact instead of one of the most apt of metaphors, it is my belief that the active members of the victorious party were sufficiently excited to have chopped off all our heads and have thanked Heaven for the opportunity!

How, one wonders, did Hawthorne reconcile this bitter comment with his oft-repeated cry that a man must 'not cut himself off from the magnetic chain of humanity'? If there were so little virtue in mankind, what profit, least of all what moral profit, was there for a man of 'pride and sensibility' to rub shoulders with it? Hawthorne, as we have seen, continually inveighs against the sin of pride which he identifies with a tendency to shun the society of the common man, as he himself had for twelve years 'under the eaves' of his mother's house at Salem. Hawthorne's anti-pride complex seems like self-criticism. It is not generally construed as such, but we need an hypothesis to account for the feeling of guilt which is, emotionally, the dominant figure in his carpet, so to speak. It was through pride —the pride of thinking himself better than, or at any rate different from, his neighbours—that Ethan Brand became a fiend. But does anyone suffer, or has anyone ever suffered, from that form of pride? Recluses there have always been, and always will be; but surely their bent for solitude has its origin in other causes than pride—in some fundamental incompatibility with their fellows, perhaps, due to whatever cause. For some reason they feel themselves to be outcasts, and in an instinct of self-justification they hit out at society—as Byron did, as Emily Brontë did, as Hawthorne did. Ostensibly Hawthorne idealizes society: over and over again he writes of it as the norm of feeling and behaviour to which everyone should conform, and which he ignores or defies at his peril. But when he *presents* society, when he shows it in operation, above all when it is voicing its moral judgments, he presents it with horror and contempt—and never more than at the opening of *The Scarlet Letter*, when Hester Prynne comes out of prison, and there is only one voice among the congregated women spectators which speaks for her.

Despite his protestations to the contrary, it seems as though, in his deepest feelings, Hawthorne was a misanthrope. He professed to believe in the standards of ordinary human nature as a criterion of goodness to which we must all subscribe, but he didn't really. Really, he believed, as his fellow-puritans did, in the depravity of the heart of man, and never more profoundly than when they got together and delivered judgment on someone whom they thought to be a sinner—or merely unfortunate, or merely different from themselves.

In the course of his enchanting introduction to *The Scarlet Letter*—so much more 'genial' than the story that was to follow —Hawthorne tells how he came across, in the Custom-House, a bundle of papers and the scarlet letter itself—the letter A— which had been embroidered and prettified by Hester Prynne's own hands. This discovery, he said, gave him the idea for the story which has fascinated and saddened readers from that day to this.

Hawthorne was, of course, perfectly entitled to fictionalize the origins of his tale, just as other novelists before and since have fictionalized theirs. But as a matter of fact the idea of *The Scarlet Letter* had been in Hawthorne's mind long before he worked at the Salem Custom-House. *The Scarlet Letter* was published in 1850. In 1837 appeared the first volume of *Twice Told Tales*, the fruit of his solitary labours 'under the eaves'. A second collection of *Twice Told Tales* was published, I think, in 1851, and among them was one called *Endicott and the Red Cross*, about a Puritan stalwart in New England who resisted the tyranny of Charles I and Archbishop Laud. When the story opens, various malefactors, for the most part guilty of moral and doctrinal deviation from the Puritan code, are undergoing punishments suitable to their offences. Among them

> was a young woman, with no mean share of beauty, whose doom it was to wear the letter A on the breast of her gown in the eyes of all the world and her own children. And even her own children knew what that initial signified. Sporting with her infamy the lost and desperate creature had embroidered the fatal token in scarlet cloth with gold thread and the nicest art of needlework, so that the letter A might have been thought to mean Admirable, or anything rather than Adulteress.

Hawthorne goes on to say:

> Let not the reader argue, from any of these evidences of iniquity, that the times of the Puritans were more vicious than our own, when, as we pass along the very street of this sketch, we discern no badge of infamy on man or woman. It was the policy of our ancestors to search out even the most secret sins and expose them to shame, without fear or favour, in the broadest light of the noon-

day sun. Were such the custom now, perchance we might find materials for a no less piquant sketch than the above.

Well, this story, *Endicott and the Red Cross*, though only published in the second volume of *Twice Told Tales*, was actually written before the first volume appeared in 1837, but for some reason was not included in them. It shows that the idea of *The Scarlet Letter* had been in Hawthorne's mind for many years before he made the supposed discovery of the object itself in the Custom-House at Salem. It also shows that, in those earlier years, he did not take the idea of adultery so seriously, or, playful and ironical though he was, he could not have suggested that the A might stand for 'Admirable'. Such a cynical interpretation of the fatal emblem would have torpedoed the whole conception of *The Scarlet Letter*, which depends for its terrific force on the author being able to persuade his readers that adultery is one of the worst of sins. Admirable, indeed! The thought crosses one's mind, Did he have his tongue in his cheek when he wrote that?

'Resist the Devil and he will flee from you' is a counsel of Holy Writ. Hawthorne appears to have thought that the way to salvation was through mingling with people whose hearts were just as depraved as, or more so than, his own—if, as I think we can fairly claim, it was his own heart that he was worried about. Why, just because you happen to have measles yourself, are you any the better for rubbing shoulders with people who also have measles? The minister who pronounced Hawthorne's funeral oration called him 'the friend of sinners'. Someone more illustrious than he was also called the friend of sinners, and no doubt it could be maintained that Christ thought it was a duty to associate with such people. But may that not have been His reaction against the Scribes and the Pharisees, who were so critical of Him, whereas those who had fewer moral pretensions than the Pharisees welcomed Him?

There is no evidence that Hawthorne regarded himself as a 'do-gooder' and wanted to align himself with society in order to reform it. Such an idea would have been abhorrent to him, for it would have fostered the sin of pride. No, it was he who was to be the gainer from this dubious experience of exploring what he called 'the foul cavern of the human heart'. A very recent writer on Hawthorne, and a perceptive one, Miss Millicent Bell, quotes from a letter Hawthorne's great friend Bridge wrote to

him in 1837, when the first volume of *Twice Told Tales* was in
the press.

'I have been trying to think what you are so miserable for',
wrote Bridge. 'Although you have not much property you have
good health and powers of writing which have made and can still
make you independent.' Miss Bell comments:

> Hawthorne was miserable, despite the healthy cast of his own nature,
> in the realisation that his profession isolated him. He was prepared
> to be a critic of solitude not only because he loathed its effects upon
> the solitary individual but because he longed for the world of
> steady purpose and happy labour, the rounded lives of the fisher-
> men and farmers he met on his walks.

With all respect to Miss Bell, who knows the subject much
better than I do, I can't believe this, any more than I can believe
that an artist's life condemns him or her to solitude. It is true
that the artist's calling, of whatever kind, does drive him into
himself during the time that he is exercising his art—but perhaps for that very reason, most artists, at least those of my
acquaintance, are among the most sociable of human beings,
once their work is over. In London, Paris, and doubtless in New
England they join themselves into groups, often with a name
that reflects their united aim, and haunt cafés, restaurants and
clubs where they can meet people like-minded with themselves.
It has been said, perhaps with truth, that 'social life is death
to the artist', but that implies, I think, the kind of social life
that fashionable hostesses provide, or used to provide, for the
literary and other lions in whom they happened to be interested
—occasions which, however glittering in themselves, did little
to foster art, and were, in fact, a distraction from it. But Hawthorne, whose chief literary friends were Longfellow, Emerson
(with whom he was never on easy terms), Thoreau, Margaret
Fuller, the Alcotts, and Herman Melville, did not enjoy fashionable social life—*le monde*—until he came to Europe where, it
has to be admitted, in spite of the fact that his hours of employment at the Liverpool Custom-House were nominal, he did not
get as much work done as he would have liked to, or as he
thought he ought to. So many of Hawthorne's occupations
turned to guilt in his mind and none more tormentingly than
lack of occupation.

The Scarlet Letter, as we all know, is a study in guilt and the separation from one's fellows that guilt, or a guilty secret, leads to. Perhaps I should say a study in sin, rather than a study in guilt, for in 1850 they still believed in sin, which was one reason for the popularity of *The Scarlet Letter*. Sin is a theological concept which may be why, in the early years of this century, when Christianity began to lose its hold, interest in Hawthorne waned. But guilt is psychological, and as soon as it established itself in the public mind as the guilt-complex, interest in Hawthorne revived. Otherwise, why have so many books been written about him during the last decade?

There are four chief characters in *The Scarlet Letter*—Hester Prynne, the adulterous wife, Roger Chillingworth, her husband, Arthur Dimmesdale, her lover, and little Pearl, their daughter, the child of sin. It has almost no social context, because the characters are almost always seen in isolation; and when seen together, as they occasionally are, their isolation is the more pronounced, since each member of the quartet, except for Pearl, is involved in sin. Hester is trying, with only moderate success, to compound for her sin by a life of good works and industry (she is an expert needlewoman); the public shame she incurs by having to wear the scarlet letter works as a sort of expiation leaving her conscience troubled, but with some sense of good, inside her and outside, to uphold it; Arthur Dimmesdale, the minister worshipped by his flock, would like to confess his sin, but dare not, and suffers even more intolerably from his sense of guilt; Roger Chillingworth, the wronged husband, is in the toils of sin, because his one aim is to burrow into Dimmesdale's consciousness and inflame his sense of guilt to the point of despair and madness. He has no feeling of guilt himself, but living with one aim, and that a wicked one, he is cut off from communion with his fellows. Alone of the four, little Pearl is sin-free and guilt-free. She is a naughty child, it must be confessed, always asking her elders awkward questions, and indulging her bad temper, but she is a sprite, an elf, who has escaped the consequences of the Fall.

There are few novels, then, with as little social context as *The Scarlet Letter*, and yet there are few novels in which social context counts for so much. The disapproval of her Bostonian neighbours accounts for Hester Prynne's ostracism; the dread of it, should his sin be revealed, accounts for Arthur Dimmesdale's misery. Pearl is shunned by her fellow children. Only

Roger Chillingworth, the really guilty one, is immune from the fact, or fear, of society's disapproval. His failure to enslave the soul of Arthur Dimmesdale kills him, but that is his own personal failure, with which social sanctions have nothing to do. Hawthorne believed in immortality, but he holds out no hope for Chillingworth in the next world.

It is a fact to be noted that Hawthorne's dread of sin is not because it separates the soul from God (which I believe is the orthodox view) but because it separates a man from communion with his fellows. But why should it if, as his story *Young Goodman Brown*, so forcibly points out, we are all sinners?

As is the case with so many first novels, *The Scarlet Letter* is Hawthorne's best. In it he follows his own bent, which was to present his characters from the inside. He tells us, with some care, what they looked like: but he never tries to establish much external reality for them: they are enclosed by their situation, and the special reality which their situation, *vis-à-vis* each other, imposes. The book has a poem's unity of feeling: it is perhaps the only novel which is a perfect work of art, because none of its happenings are out of key with the rest.

It has defects, of course, and unresolved discords. Hawthorne skates over the fact that Hester Prynne married Roger Chillingworth without loving him. Why did she, when her youth and beauty might have procured for her a more worthy suitor than this dried-up old man? The wrong she did to Chillingworth is played down—after all, no one compelled her to marry him—and is lost sight of in his vindictiveness and her love for Arthur Dimmesdale with its tragic outcome. Hawthorne's sympathies are more completely with her than perhaps they should have been.

If we look for the secret of the novel's hold on popular favour (it still sells, I am told, 2,000 copies a year in America), we can find it in the fact that it completely realizes its author's aim—which so few novels ever have. Not many people, nowadays, think adultery a serious matter, yet Hawthorne persuades us to take it as seriously as if it were apartheid or slum-clearance or capital punishment or some other question that can still arouse our moral passions. And even if its style is antiquated, *The Scarlet Letter* is, of course, most beautifully written, a thing which people still appreciate, whatever Mrs. Wharton may have said.

And though the theme of adultery as a cardinal sin may be so

old-fashioned as to be almost unreal, Hawthorne's analysis of
the emotions is strangely up to date. Many writers, before him,
had realized that hatred is akin to love: but none of them,
I fancy, had described what has lately come to be called 'the
love-hatred relationship' as clearly as Hawthorne does. Commenting on Roger Chillingworth's attitude to Hester (and to
Arthur) he remarks:

> It is a curious subject of observation and inquiry, whether hatred
> and love may not be the same thing at bottom. Each, in its utmost
> development, supposes a high degree of intimacy and heart-know-
> ledge; each renders one individual dependent for the food of his
> affections and spiritual life upon another: each leaves the passionate
> lover, or the no less passionate hater, forlorn and desolate by the
> withdrawal of his subject. Philosophically considered, therefore,
> the two passions seem to be essentially the same, except that one
> happens to be seen in a celestial radiance, and the other in a dusky
> and lurid glow. In the spiritual world the old physician and the
> minister—mutual victims as they have been—may, unawares, have
> found their earthly stock of hatred and antipathy transmuted into
> golden love.

There are many instances of Hawthorne's insight into abnormal psychological states of mind. In the chapter entitled
The Minister in a Maze he portrays Arthur Dimmesdale return-
ing from his meeting in the woods with Hester, in which she has
persuaded him to leave Boston, go abroad, throw away the
Scarlet Letter and live joyously with him in sin. The kind-
hearted and tolerant reader of today cannot help hoping they
will do so: they have suffered so much, they have received from
the scourge of conscience (not to mention the material scourge
which, quite how I cannot imagine, Arthur Dimmesdale applied
to his own shoulders) double for all their sins. But Dimmesdale
cannot envisage his future with the burden of sin removed, and
the conflict which has been raging in him, between desire and
guilt, reaches a new pitch of intensity, comparable to that of
Phèdre or Macbeth. But instead of trying to convey his desperation by images connected directly with it—'tomorrow and
tomorrow and tomorrow'—Hawthorne adopts another way of
showing Reason toppling from its throne. It is reminiscent of
the dirty songs and snatches that Ophelia sings when her
wretchedness at last gets the better of her. Mr. Dimmesdale
behaves quite out of character.

At every step he was incited to do some strange, wild, wicked thing or t'other, with a sense that it would be at once involuntary and intentional, in spite of himself, yet growing out of a profounder self than that which opposed the impulse

—the subconscious self, I suppose, but what novelist before Hawthorne had so categorically recognized its existence?

The minister encounters three respected and devout members of his flock. To the old deacon he is tempted to utter certain blasphemous suggestions respecting the communion-supper; to the elderly woman who has lost most of her relations and friends he wants to say something that would blast her faith in immortality, and into the tender bosom of a beautiful young girl he would drop a germ of evil 'that would be sure to blossom darkly soon, and bear black fruit betimes'.

The fact that he does none of these things is imputed to the confusion in his mind which paralyses his tongue.

And in another respect Hawthorne seems to have been far in advance of his time. He recognized the interdependence of mind and body in the matter of physical illness. If he did not actually use the term psycho-somatic he knew what it meant, as did Roger Chillingworth, who was using psycho-somatic methods to break down Arthur Dimmesdale's health.

The Scarlet Letter is an almost unrelievedly gloomy story— gloomier even than *Madame Bovary*. In *Madame Bovary*, as Henry James suggested, the characters are not, as representative human beings, worth the trouble that Flaubert spent on them, and his pessimistic conclusions have therefore the less force. But in *The Scarlet Letter* it is not so; Hester and Arthur are valuable human beings in themselves, and would have been so to the community, if the community would have allowed Hester to be, and if Arthur's conscience would have allowed him to be. The human heart contains in itself the seeds of its own destruction—that is Hawthorne's conclusion.

And be the sad and stern truth spoken [he says], that the breach which guilt has once made into the human soul is never, in this mortal state, repaired. It may be watched and guarded so that the enemy shall not force his way again into the citadel, and might even, in his subsequent assaults, select some other avenue in preference to that where he had formerly succeeded. But there is still the ruined wall, and near it the stealthy tread of the foe that would win over again his unforgotten triumph.

Later on, as we shall see, Hawthorne revised his view of Sin
as a purely destructive agent, in fact he went back on it, and
already in *The Scarlet Letter* there are signs of his coming
change of attitude. But in this book the moral balance between
the individual's sin (however excusable) and the right of conscience and the community (however ill-informed) to judge it,
is evenly maintained, and the effect of the story, both moral and
aesthetic, depends on this. We must believe that Hester and
Arthur were sinners and that conscience and the community
(which so often join forces) had the right to condemn them.

★

But a recent critic, with an outlook of his own, thought
otherwise. In his *Studies in Classic American Literature* (1924)
D. H. Lawrence discusses *The Scarlet Letter* on the whole very
sympathetically. But he reads into it, as might be expected, his
own message, not Hawthorne's. Writing in an anti-American
and misogynist mood, he, almost makes Hester Prynne the
villain of the piece, thereby agreeing with her Puritan neighbours, though on very different grounds.

The Scarlet Letter gives the show away.

You have your pure-pure young parson Dimmesdale.

You have the beautiful Puritan Hester at his feet.

And the first thing she does is to seduce him.

And the first thing he does is to be seduced.

And the first thing they do is to hug their sin in secret, and try to
understand.

Which is the myth of New England . . .

Dimmesdale was seduced gloatingly. Oh, luscious sin!

He was such a pure young man that he had to make a fool of purity.
The American psyche.

Of course, the best part of the game lay in keeping up pure
appearances.

The greatest triumph a woman can have, especially an American
woman, is the triumph of seducing a man, especially if he is pure.

And he gets the greatest thrill of all in falling—'Seduce me, Mrs.
Hercules.'

And the pair of them share the subtlest delight in keeping up pure
appearances, when everybody knows all the while. But the power of
pure appearances is something to exult in. All America gives in to
it. *Look* pure!

To seduce a man, to have everybody know.

To keep up appearances of purity. Pure!
This is the great triumph of woman.

The minister's great longing is to escape from Hester—who is
really a witch.
A devil she is, and a devil she will be. And most men will suc-
cumb to her devilishness.
The minister's great longing is to escape from her, as he proves
when, dying on the scaffold, he expresses the fear lest, because of
their sin, he may meet her in the next world.

I suppose there is something to be said for this interpretation
of the story, but I wonder what Hawthorne would have made
of it.

★

The Scarlet Letter had an immediate success. It was a best-
seller. Quite what that phrase (if it existed in 1850) would have
denoted in the number of copies sold, I can't say; or how much
money Hawthorne made from it. What was the size of the
reading public in the United States of that day? What proportion
of it bought books, and what proportion borrowed them from
libraries? By today's standards I should guess that *The Scarlet
Letter* was a *succès d'estime*. It founded his literary reputation,
but it did not bring him a fortune, or anything like it. He was
still in need of money now that he had lost his job at the Salem
Custom-House, and had only his pen to rely on to make a living.
This consideration undoubtedly had its effect on his second
novel. *The Scarlet Letter* had been acclaimed in England as
well as in America. It had fulfilled one of Hawthorne's ambitions: it proved that an American writer could achieve fame
equal to that of any of the scribbling sons of John Bull. So far as
fiction was concerned it had put America on the map. But it had
a drawback which no one was quicker to acknowledge than
Hawthorne himself. It was too gloomy. One remembers the
scene in which Hawthorne read the closing passages to his wife,
how his voice rose and fell with emotion and how she went to
bed with a headache. Laugh and the world laughs with you,
weep and you weep alone, as another and lesser American writer
was to say long after Hawthorne's death. Would the public
stand for another novel of the unrelieved gloom of *The Scarlet
Letter*? Its author was not the only person to wonder if it would.
In his work the least materially-minded of great novelists,

Hawthorne was not the least materially-minded of men; even if his circumstances as a married man with a family would have allowed him to be, constitutionally he wasn't. He was enough of a man of affairs to hold down, for a time, three jobs—at the Boston Custom-House, the Salem Custom-House, and the Consulate at Liverpool—all of which involved a great deal of business and understanding of money-matters. And apart from this, Hawthorne had his hard-baked side, derived no doubt from his Puritan ancestors but also ingrained in himself. He was not a money-grubber, but money was seldom absent from his thoughts.

But this was not the only reason why he decided that his next novel should be more cheerful than *The Scarlet Letter*. There was a deeper reason and one that reflected the fundamental dichotomy in his nature—or if not in his nature, in the nature of his thought. By nature he was, as we know, a solitary. There has been a tendency among recent writers to play down his instinct for solitude. On both sides of the Atlantic some form of collectivism has been gaining ground at the expense of the individual. Line up with one's fellows, join the queue—that is the cry. And with one side of him, Hawthorne would have backed it up. He was, as we know, obsessed by the sense of sin, whether a general conviction of the depravity of the human heart, or, as Herman Melville once suggested, some sin of his own, or both, doesn't greatly matter—much as one would like to know what his own sin was, supposing he had committed one. What does matter is the paradox, which none of his critics seems to have noticed, in his moral outlook. He believed, with most orthodox Christians, that the greatest sin is the sin of pride—not, apparently, because it cuts one off from God, but because it cuts one off from one's fellows. Over and over again his stories illustrate the danger of pride: it was owing to pride that Ethan Brand became a fiend. It is dangerous to argue from internal evidence, but there is much that points to the fact that in denouncing pride Hawthorne was criticizing himself—the solitary living under the eaves, who would not go out to mix with his fellows and often waited until nightfall before he would go out at all.

But at the same time he illogically held the view that the only way to salvation was to mingle with one's fellows, and the more commonplace they were, the better. If, one asks oneself,

the human heart is so depraved, why go out into the highways
to associate with it? A man is known by the company he keeps;
surely it would be better to remain wrapped up in oneself,
cultivating any good qualities one happens to possess, than join
(for instance) a mob of hooligans such as tarred and feathered
poor Major Molineux, who, as far as we know, was innocent
of any crime?

Later we shall see how Hawthorne tried to resolve this paradox, but when he wrote *The House of the Seven Gables* he was
determined to show he was not the misanthrope of *The Scarlet
Letter*. He would take a more genial view of mankind than he
did of the Puritans who had persecuted Hester Prynne more than
a century and a half before. Indeed, *genial* is a word that occurs
quite often in the book.

It does not fit in very easily, however, until the final chapters
when Hawthorne stretches probability to its utmost to bring
about a happy ending. Those chapters are full of misplaced
ingenuity. It is rather shocking that an artist as scrupulous as
Hawthorne could have descended to all these tricks and subter-
fuges, tying up all sorts of loose ends that didn't need tying up,
using machinery that was already out of date in the time of *The
Castle of Otranto*.

This doesn't prevent *The House of the Seven Gables* from being
a very enjoyable novel. It is in fact Hawthorne's most enjoyable
novel, for it contains much of his happiest (in both senses of the
word) ideas. Indeed, it only errs in so far as it strays in the
direction of geniality. What Hawthorne really thought of
geniality (as distinct from what he thought he ought to think
of it) is presented most brilliantly in the portrait of the iniquitous Governor Pyncheon, the villain of the piece, whose smile
was so genial, so sultry, that it tempted flies to come and buzz
in it. Governor Pyncheon was Salem's pin-up boy; he was a
success figure, admired by everybody except by his cousin
Hepzibah, whose near-sighted scowl made her an object of
universal suspicion and dislike. Poor Hepzibah, who had a life-
interest in the House of the Seven Gables, but who had been
robbed of her inheritance by this same cousin—just as her
brother, Clifford, had been robbed of his liberty by a trumped-
up charge of murder, engineered by his genial cousin, the future
Governor of Massachusetts.

Nothing in Hawthorne is more imaginative, more amusing,

and more touching than his evocation of the House of the Seven Gables itself—it lives for us more vividly, perhaps, than any other house in fiction—except for *Wuthering Heights*. The gables, the Pyncheon Elm overhanging them, Alice's Posies growing on them, the abandoned garden, Old Maule's Well, the fountain whose waters had turned brackish, and above all, perhaps, the chickens, so ancient and dilapidated, are unforgettable conceptions.

Nor can I subscribe to the views of some critics who find the characters unsatisfactory because, from a realistic standpoint, they are insufficiently individualized. Hawthorne created very few characters whom we recognize as persons, existing in their own right. Hester Prynne is one; Zenobia in *The Blithedale Romance* is another. As his notes show, he wanted to be interested in human beings for themselves, as Jane Austen was, as Dickens was, as all the great English Victorian novelists were. But try as he would, he was more interested in what they *represented*, above all in their moral aspect, and as they illustrate the operations of the Moral Law.

Politically, Hawthorne was decidedly Left Wing. As his story *Lady Eleanor's Mantle* shows, he associated the established order—the Establishment, as some people now call it—with the Sin of Pride. *The House of the Seven Gables* is a tract against pride—especially pride as exemplified in what Tennyson called long descent. Hepzibah, that emblem of out-worn gentility, is absurd; the Pyncheon chickens, so exhausted racially that they can hardly produce an egg, are absurd. Clifford Pyncheon, her brother, released after thirty years of imprisonment for a crime he had never committed, is not absurd—he is too pathetic to be absurd—but in so far as he represents a decaying social order, which had lost whatever *raison d'être* it ever had, he is doubly an object of pity—not only for his own ruined life, but for the outworn social order that he represents. Judge Pyncheon, who hopes to do the brother and sister out of their meagre inheritance, is a pillar of that social order, a success figure, anything but a figure of fun. Of all his creations, not excluding Roger Chillingworth, Judge Pyncheon is the one that Hawthorne hates the most—he has not a good word or a sympathetic thought for him, and one feels that it must have been an effort for Hawthorne not to have made the Judge murder his uncle, as well as plant the supposed murder on

Clifford. Can it be that Hawthorne equated wickedness with worldly success, and can it be that his own lack of worldly success, until he wrote *The Scarlet Letter*, predisposed him to this view?

It is said that Hawthorne modelled Judge Pyncheon on the man who, for political reasons, got him sacked from the Custom-House. It was an act of revenge, and as such, one would have thought, rather out of Hawthorne's character.

But if in life Judge Pyncheon was an emblem of success, in death, with all his machinations come to nought, he is absurd. Fifty or more years ago I read the chapter entitled *Governor Pyncheon*—and thought it one of the most outstanding examples of sustained rhetorical prose in English literature, and when I re-read it, not long ago, I could still remember many of the sentences in which Hawthorne, with incomparable eloquence, and irony, contrasts the present condition of the Judge, bereft of life, with the Judge of a few hours before, with all his plans for worldly advancement, all his powers for mischief, still active in him.

Rise up, Judge Pyncheon! The morning sunshine glimmers through the foliage, and, beautiful and holy as it is, shuns not to kindle up your face. Rise up, thou subtle, worldly, selfish, iron-hearted hypocrite, and make thy choice whether still to be subtle, worldly, selfish, iron-hearted and hyprocritical, or to tear these sins out of thy nature, though they bring the life-blood with them. The Avenger is upon thee! Rise up, before it is too late!

What! Thou art not stirred by this last appeal? No, not a jot! And there we see a fly—one of your common house-flies, such as are always buzzing on the windowpane—which has smelt out Governor Pyncheon, and alights, now on his forehead, now on his chin, and now, Heaven help us, is creeping over the bridge of his nose towards the would-be chief magistrate's wide-open eyes! Canst thou not brush the fly away? Art thou too sluggish? Thou man, that hadst so many busy projects, yesterday! Art thou too weak, that wast so powerful? Not brush away a fly? Nay, then, we give thee up!

And Hawthorne does give him up, in more ways than one. It is not true, as has sometimes been said, that Hawthorne felt some compassion for all his characters. He had none for Judge Pyncheon, none for the Puritans who persecuted the Quakers in *The Gentle Boy*, none for *The Man of Adamant*, who, in my opinion, deserved it. Self-righteous he may have been, a religious paranoiac who thought that he was right, and all the world was wrong; but he was, I suspect, a projection of Hawthorne himself and the cave to which he betook himself to be out of humanity's way was a refuge resembling the 'eaves' under which Hawthorne spent his semi-solitary years. Hawthorne makes much of the sin of pride which cuts a man off from 'the magnetic chain of humanity', but if humanity is like his view of it in *The Gentle Boy* and *My Kinsman, Major Molineux*, anyone might not only be excused but applauded for running away from it, and so avoiding 'the contagion of the world's slow stain'.

But to return to *The House of the Seven Gables*. It is the only one of Hawthorne's novels in which there is a moral scapegoat. The other characters are not blameless, with the exception of Phoebe, who in Hawthorne's eyes can do no wrong; but there is no moral balance in this book as there is in the others. All the culpability falls on Judge Pyncheon: it is he who, morally and physically, is the victim of Old Maule's curse. Its effect appears to expire with him: when he is dead, all the others live happily ever after, enjoying the added advantage of his wealth.

Apropos of Phoebe, I should like to point out how seldom Hawthorne lets his conviction of the depravity of the human heart extend to women. In giving them this immunity he seems to disregard the story of the Fall and the doctrine of Original Sin—for it was Eve who offered Adam the apple. There are a few instances of bad women in his stories: Lady Eleanor, in *Lady Eleanor's Mantle*, incurs a very harsh retribution for indulging in the Sin of Pride: but she is an aristocrat, and pride of birth is something that Hawthorne as a democrat could not easily forgive. And there is a painted harlot in *Major Molineux* whose intentions are not too good. But in the main Hawthorne lets women off very lightly—especially, one suspects, after he had fallen in love with Sophia Peabody. Perhaps this was due to chivalry; perhaps also to a realistic conviction, which no one could dispute, that women are by nature less criminal, if not less sinful, than men.

In his preface to *The House of the Seven Gables* Hawthorne gives his famous definition of a Romance.

When a writer calls his work a Romance [he says], it need hardly be observed that he wishes to claim a certain latitude, both as to its fashion and material, which he could not have felt himself entitled to assume, had he professed to be writing a Novel. The latter form of composition is presumed to aim at a very minute fidelity, not merely to the possible but to the probable and ordinary course of man's experience. The former—while as a work of art it must rigidly subject itself to *laws*, and while it sins unpardonably so far as it may swerve aside from the truth of the human heart— has fairly a right to present that truth under circumstances, to a great extent, of the author's own choosing or creation. If he think fit, also, he may so manage his atmospherical medium as to bring out or mellow the lights, and deepen and enrich the shadows, of his picture. He will be wise, no doubt, to make a very moderate use of the privileges here stated and, especially, to mingle the Marvellous rather as a slight, delicate and evanescent flavour than as any portion of the actual substance of the dish offered to the public. He can hardly, however, be said to commit a literary crime even if he disregard this caution . . .

The point of view in which this tale comes under the Romantic definition lies in the attempt to connect a bygone time with the very present which is flitting away from us. It is a legend prolonging itself from an epoch now gray in the distance, down into our own broad daylight, and bringing along with it some of its legendary mist, which the reader, according to his pleasure, may either disregard or allow it to float imperceptibly about the characters and events for the sake of a picturesque effect. The narrative, it may be, is woven of so humble a texture as to require this advantage and at the same time to render it the more difficult of attainment . . .

'The more difficult of attainment.' Hawthorne is not the only author to have chosen the hard way to write a novel. Emily Brontë did the same; but *Wuthering Heights* gains greatly in depth and variety of viewpoint from its complex method of narration; and the same is true in a different way of *The House of the Seven Gables*, where past and present meet and overlap and enrich each other.

(4)

I have quoted the reasons given by Nathaniel Hawthorne and Henry James as to why, in the middle of the nineteenth century, it was difficult, if not impossible, for an American to write a novel based on ordinary American life. In their notions of what an American novel of that period *could* be based on, they were,

I imagine, thinking of different types of fiction. Hawthorne was thinking of the Romance, for which, in the introduction to *The House of the Seven Gables*, he claimed special immunities and privileges. The Romance, he said, in effect, did not need to imitate the surface of daily life: it had its own laws of its author's own devising: it only sinned if 'it swerved aside from the truths of the human heart'.

The Blithedale Romance was the third of the novels which Hawthorne wrote in such quick succession after his dismissal from the Salem Custom-House. It is also the one novel in which he, I won't say tried to imitate, but in which he is not altogether disregardful of the surface of ordinary life. It was founded, he tells us in the preface, on his experiences at Brook Farm, that socialistic, idealistic, Utopian community of Transcendentalists. He joined it in April 1841, and stayed there, on and off, until October. He had some idea, apparently, of marrying Sophia Peabody, to whom he was already engaged, and taking her to live at Brook Farm with him—a truly Utopian idea, but with Hawthorne theory always counted for more than practice. His mother and sisters urged him to come home, and finally he did —disillusioned but not disgusted with this new failure to make satisfactory contact with the Common Man—that mythical personage whom Hawthorne admired and despised so much.

Blithedale was sufficiently like Brook Farm for Hawthorne to write a preface at once admitting and denying that it was. It is the first instance I know of in which a novelist declares that his characters are entirely fictitious. It has often been done since, and perhaps for the same reason, that the author knows quite well that they are not.

But perhaps I may be forgiven for quoting what Hawthorne himself says about the reality, and the unreality, of the Blithedale setting, for it is an excellent instance of his characteristic gift of saying two opposite things at the same time. Truth to him was always two-faced, if not double-faced. His ideas meant more to him than the characters in which he embodied them, and this may partially account for the inconclusiveness that hangs about this work—the effect of his double—or treble—vision. He could not commit himself—as his illustrious contemporaries, Emerson and Thoreau and even Melville, always could. 'Publish yourself of a personality', said Emerson, or words to that effect. Meaning, I suppose, make up your mind what you

like, and what you are like, and let everyone know that this is
the sort of person you are. 'Cast the bantling on the rocks', and
it will make good in the face of every hardship of circumstance
and public disapproval. This was Emerson's creed, the creed of
the uncompromising individualist. But it was not Hawthorne's.
Hawthorne said he could get nothing out of Emerson's philosophy, although he liked the man. Not only did Hawthorne see
through a glass darkly, but he saw himself in a glass darkly.
The cloud of unknowing was denser, in his case, than it has been
for any other novelist of equal stature.

Let us hear what he says himself.

In the *Blithedale* of this volume many readers will probably
suspect a faint and not very faithful shadowing of Brook Farm, in
Roxbury, which now a little more than ten years ago, was occupied
and cultivated by a company of socialists. The author does not wish
to deny that he had this community in his mind, and that (having
had the good fortune, for a time to be personally connected with it)
he has occasionally availed himself of his actual reminiscences, in
the hope of giving a more life-like tint to the fancy-sketch in the
following pages. He begs it to be understood, however, that he
has considered the institution itself as not less fairly the subject of
fictitious handling than the imaginary personages whom he has
introduced there. His whole treatment of the affair is altogether
incidental to the main purpose of the romance; nor does he put
forward the slightest pretensions to illustrate a theory, or elicit a
conclusion, favourable or otherwise, in respect to socialism.

In short, his present concern with the socialist community is
merely to establish a theatre, a little removed from the highway
of ordinary travel, where the creatures of his brain may play their
phantasmagorical antics, without exposing themselves to too close
a comparison with the actual events of real lives. In the old countries,
with which fiction has long been conversant, a certain conventional
privilege seems to have been awarded to the romancer; his work
has not been put exactly side by side with Nature and he is allowed
a license with regard to everyday probability, in view of the improved
effects which he is bound to produce thereby. Among ourselves, on
the contrary, there is as yet no such Faery Land, so like the real
world, that in a suitable remoteness one cannot well tell the
difference, but with an atmosphere of strange enchantment, beheld
through which the inhabitants have a propriety of their own. This
atmosphere is what the American romance needs. In its absence,
the beings of imagination are compelled to show themselves in the
same category as actually living mortals; a necessity that generally

renders the paint and paste-board of their composition too painfully discernible. With the idea of obviating this difficulty (the sense of which has always pressed very heavily upon him) the author has ventured to make free with his old and affectionately remembered home at *BROOK FARM,* as being certainly the most romantic episode of his life—essentially a daydream and yet a fact—and thus offering an available foothold between fiction and reality. Furthermore, the scene was in good keeping with the personages whom he desired to introduce.

These characters, he feels it right to say, are entirely fictitious. It would indeed (considering how few amiable qualities he distributes among his imaginary progeny) be a most grievous wrong to his former excellent associates, were the author to allow it to be supposed that he had been sketching any of their likenesses. Had he attempted it, they would at least have recognised the touches of a friendly pencil. But he has done nothing of the kind. The self-concentrated Philanthropist; the high-spirited Woman, bruising herself against the narrow limitations of her Sex; the weakly Maiden, whose tremulous nerves endow her with Sibylline attributes; the Minor Poet, beginning life with strenuous aspirations which die out with his youthful fervour—all these might have been looked for at *Brook Farm,* but by some accident, never made their appearance there.

But is this strictly true? Nathaniel Hawthorne appeared at Brook Farm, and in the guise of Miles Coverdale the minor poet, he certainly appeared at Blithedale. Most of his biographers are agreed that Coverdale was a projection of Hawthorne—he had the qualities which Hawthorne lamented in himself—he was the cold-hearted observer, watching, even spying upon, his fellows in the Blithedale experiment. At Brook Farm there were eight of them; in *The Blithedale Romance* Coverdale concentrates his attention on four—himself, Priscilla (whose portrait suggests Sophia Peabody), the queenly Zenobia who had certain likenesses to Margaret Fuller—his wife's great friend and the *grande dame* of the Transcendentalist movement. The fourth was Hollingsworth, ex-blacksmith and philanthropist, whose belief it was that criminals could be reformed by kindness. He has no prototype in real life, as far as we know— unless he embodies Emerson's idealism and individualism, which Hawthorne so much distrusted. And there is a shadowy fifth, who though not an inmate of Blithedale, appears and exercises a malign influence on its fortunes—the mysterious

Westerveldt, with his good looks, his black beard, and his gold teeth.

Miles Coverdale, the narrator of the story, arrives at Blithedale, as Hawthorne arrived at Brook Farm, in an April snowstorm, and immediately catches cold. The cold develops into a serious chill, pneumonia perhaps, from which he does not expect to recover. Hollingsworth, the blacksmith-philanthropist, ministers to him. (In this connection I might mention, to show how far Hawthornian studies have gone in the United States, that the names of his characters have undergone much scrutiny: we have Chillingworth and Hollingsworth, Coverdale and Dimmesdale: what do these worths and dales imply?) Hollingsworth appears to be an angel of light, and as we know, Coverdale said how lucky would a man be to have such a friend at his bedside when he was dying. Seizing upon this, D. H. Lawrence, in his analysis of the plot of *The Blithedale Romance*, observes:

> I, Nathaniel, at once catch cold and have to be put to bed. Am nursed with inordinate tenderness by the blacksmith, whose great hands are gentler than a woman's, etc. The two men love one another with a love surpassing the love of women, so long as the healing and salvation business lasts. When Nathaniel gets well and wants to have a soul of his own he turns with hate to this black-bearded, booming Salvationist. Hephaestos of the Underworld. Hates him for tyrannous monomaniac.

Lawrence goes on.

> Plot II. Zenobia, that clever, lustrous woman, is fascinated by the criminal-saving blacksmith, and would have him at any price. Meanwhile she has the subtlest current of understanding with the frail but deep Nathaniel. And she takes the White Lily, half pityingly half contemptuously, under a rich and glossy dark wing.
> Plot III. The blacksmith is after Zenobia, to get her money for his criminal asylum: of which, of course, he will be the first inmate.
> Plot IV. Nathaniel also feels his mouth watering for the dark-luscious Zenobia.
> Plot V. The White Lily, Priscilla, vaporously festering, turns out to be the famous Veiled Lady of public spiritualist shows: she whom the undesirable Husband, called the Professor (Westerveldt) has used as a medium. Also she is Zenobia's half-sister.
> Débâcle.
> Nobody wants Zenobia in the end. She goes off without her flower. The blacksmith marries Priscilla. Nathaniel dribbling confesses that he, too, has loved Prissy all the while. Boo-hoo!

It may well be that Lawrence's synopsis of the plot of *The Blithedale Romance* tells us more about himself than it does about Hawthorne, or his book. I have quoted it partly for that reason, and partly because it shows the inherent difficulty of commenting on Hawthorne's work. So many constructions can be put on his stories that every reader will probably find a different one. This is not true of most of the great novelists. Most of them, to a more or lesser degree, consciously or unconsciously, try to interpret life and impose a meaning on it. With Sir Walter Scott and Jane Austen the tale's the thing: they present life as it is, or was, and the events they describe have their face-value, behind which they do not expect us to look. Tolstoy, Dickens, Stendhal, all had axes of different sorts to grind, but any reader can tell what they were: they stand out a mile, but even with those writers the story comes first. It gives us the facts on which we form our judgment and if we don't want to look beneath the surface we can read the story for its own sake. George Eliot was full of moral and extra-fictional preoccupations, but even *Middlemarch* could be read for the story, for the interest in what happens and is going to happen, regardless of the fact that it also reflects a view of life.

But it is not so with Cervantes or with Dostoevsky. With them you have to look for an under-meaning, or an over-meaning, and so it is with Hawthorne. D. H. Lawrence described *The Scarlet Letter* as the triumph of Sin, just as he said that Dostoevsky's characters were 'sinning their way to Jesus'. It is a half-truth, but only a half-truth, and his analysis of *The Blithedale Romance*, so it seems to me, leaves out more than half that Hawthorne meant to say, precisely because Lawrence re-created the book in the image of his own thought, and left out the spiritual and moral meanings which meant so much (we must suppose) to Hawthorne. It doesn't greatly matter that he vulgarized it, in word and thought, for a vulgar version of a high-falutin' pretentious story may be salutary: it pricks a bubble that ought to be pricked. But the same tactics, if applied to certain aspects of Lawrence's own work, might make it sound half-baked and even ridiculous.

The Blithedale Romance has always been the least popular of Hawthorne's novels except with one or two critics (there are always those) who think it the best. There is a chill at the heart of it: the cold that Coverdale caught in the April snowstorm is never really expelled by the summer heat and Coverdale's arduous labours in the manure-heap and on the milking-stool. This is partly his own fault: he was always lamenting his coldness of heart, his tendency to spy on other people instead of feeling with and for them—just as Hawthorne was. When Coverdale takes a holiday from Blithedale in an inn in a nearby town, he spends much of his time drawing aside his bedroom curtains and watching Zenobia and Priscilla and Westerveldt who, by a very strange coincidence, were also taking a rest from Blithedale in a house on the other side of the street. Eventually, shamefaced, he calls on them and gets the rough side of Zenobia's tongue.

By this time the collective purpose of the little colony had broken up, under the stress of irreconcilable personal feelings: so, Hawthorne suggests, it will always be with any idealistic enterprise. Zenobia is the chief sinner and also the chief sufferer: it is a *sine qua non* with Hawthorne that sin brings suffering. There is hardly one happy sinner in his works, except such fiends in human shape as Westerveldt and Chillingworth. These men are emblems of evil, familiars, leeches, who live on the misery they can cause their victims and are happy doing it. What was Zenobia's previous relationship with Westerveldt, the mesmerist; how he got her into his clutches, and how they were both able to victimize Priscilla, the blameless Veiled Lady of their experiments, we are never told. Zenobia paid for it, whatever it was, by the loss of Hollingsworth's love. She took her own life, and the discovery of her drowned body is the most dramatic and remarkable set piece in all Hawthorne's work.

Zenobia's tragedy becomes the main theme of the story, but there are others nearly as important. What does Coverdale amount to, with his exquisite sensibility and his personal ineffectiveness? What are we to make of Priscilla, the Veiled Lady, Zenobia's minion, with whom Coverdale so surprisingly declares he was in love? And what of Hollingsworth, the blacksmith-philanthropist?

I think that Hawthorne started by being more interested in Hollingsworth than in any of his other characters, for Hollingsworth was to illustrate the folly of philanthropy, and his plan for the reformation of criminals through an appeal to their higher instincts.

'Much as I liked Hollingsworth,' Coverdale said, 'it cost me many a groan to tolerate him on this point. He ought to have commenced his investigation of the subject by perpetrating some huge sin in his proper person, and examining the condition of his higher instincts afterwards.'

This seemingly flippant remark is really crucial to Hawthorne's thought. He does appear to have believed, as Sherwood Anderson did after him, that there was something purging to the soul in committing a crime. Hollingsworth doesn't commit one; but his monomania on the subject turns him into a raging egotist and helps to bring about Zenobia's death. He didn't care for her so much as for the money he hoped to get out of her to further his plan.

But this issue is never fully developed; it peters out, as do other issues in the story, in the tragedy, I will not say the melodrama, of its end. As a novel *The Blithedale Romance* is not a complete success; it tries to include too many issues, and between them falls to the ground. As for Old Moodie and his two daughters and the chain of coincidences they represent, no one in this or any age could swallow them. But what lovely writing there is in the book, what poetry.

★

In *The Marble Faun*, the last novel which Hawthorne left as he meant to leave it (if we except the conclusion tacked on at the end as a sop to those readers who wanted explanations of various mysterious happenings), there are more coincidences and there is still more poetry. As for the coincidences, we must remember that until the time of Flaubert or thereabouts, when Realism began to take possession of the novel, the novel-reading public didn't mind coincidences, in fact it rather welcomed them. It preferred events which were startling and surprising to those which were lifelike and inevitable. It wanted to be taken out of itself, not driven into itself. Improbability didn't matter, because a spice of improbability lent flavour to the dish. Samuel Richardson knew as much about the workings of the human heart (at any rate of the female human heart) as any novelist ever has: Dr. Johnson's famous tribute to him was well deserved. But as far as the action of the story goes, *Pamela* and *Clarissa* are full of the wildest improbabilities. Nor did Fielding or Smollett adhere to probability; they didn't regard it as a virtue, their aim was to surprise and entertain the reader with a series of plausible if unlikely happenings.

And poetry! Re-reading *The Marble Faun* may make us feel that Hawthorne was poet first, moral philosopher second, and novelist third. Not that the book lacks drama; in some ways it is the most dramatic of Hawthorne's romances. It centres round a murder, and the murder is magnificently described. Donatello, the young Italian count who bears such a striking resemblance to the Faun of Praxiteles in the Capitoline Museum in Rome, throws Miriam's persecutor off the Tarpeian Rock. That is the crucial episode of the story. Until the murder happens, Donatello has been gay, happy, carefree, a child of Nature, Adam before the Fall. After the murder he is stricken by the pangs of awakening conscience and becomes a different kind of being, a being like the rest of us, a sinner, Adam after the Fall. This is the subject of the book, Donatello's transformation. In England it was published under the title of *Transformation*—its third alternative title, *The Romance of Monte Beni* (Monte Beni was the name of Donatello's castle in Tuscany), is misleading and also irrelevant.

Round Donatello are grouped the three main personages of the story: Miriam, a woman of exalted but dubious parentage whose surname (presumably Italian) we are never told; Hilda, a young New England girl, pure as a dove, and surrounded by doves in the tower where she keeps alight the lamp which has burnt before the statue of the Virgin for four hundred years; and Kenyon, also from New England.

All three are artists. Miriam, a native of Rome, is a portrait-painter, Hilda is a copyist and Kenyon is a sculptor: these two have come to Rome to study and practise art. It is through their eyes that Hawthorne looks at Rome and at the Tuscan country-side when the scene shifts to Monte Beni.

Sometimes Hawthorne does not bother to give his impressions of Rome through their eyes—he just describes it. Rome went to his head, and the obsession found relief in some of the loveliest word-paintings ever penned. Who can forget his account of St. Peter's, or of the Carnival, or of the Campagna, or of the Pantheon? They are infused with a poetry and a sensibility which never flag.

They are not only word pictures: Hawthorne's feeling for Rome expresses the ambivalence of all his thought. He loves and hates it, he feels (as many have) the accumulated wickedness of its past, just as much as he is fascinated by the decaying grandeur of its present—the heritage of its past: and those two views symbolize his divided feeling for human nature—its grandeur and its squalor. It is the same with his attitude to the Roman Catholic Church, so wonderfully expressed in the scene in which Hilda confesses to the priest (in St. Peter's) that she has been an eyewitness of Donatello's murder of the Capuchin monk. This experience has destroyed her peace of mind—she thinks it is driving her mad. The act of confession restores her to herself; she is touchingly grateful; but when the priest tells her that she, being a heretic, has no right to take advantage of the Confessional, and ought to embrace the Roman Catholic faith herself, she rounds on him with some spirit.

Hawthorne's attitude to the Church of Rome is ambivalent like so many of his attitudes, like Hilda's own attitude. She went—and it was a dangerous errand—to observe, as Hawthorne says,

> how closely and comfortingly the Popish faith applied itself to all human occasions. It was impossible to doubt that multitudes of people found their spiritual advantage in it, and would find none at all in our own formless mode of worship; which, besides, so far as the sympathy of prayerful souls is concerned, can be enjoyed only at stated and too unfrequent periods. But here, whenever the hunger for divine nutriment came upon the soul, it could on the instant be appeased. At one or another altar the incense was forever ascending; the mass always being performed and carrying upward with it the devotion of such as had not words for their own prayer. And yet if the worshipper had his individual petition to offer, his own heart-secret to whisper below his breath, there were divine auditors ever ready to receive it from his lips; and what encouraged still more, these auditors had not always been divine, but kept, within their heavenly memories, the tender humility of a human experience. Now a saint in heaven, but once a man on earth.

And it is the same with St. Peter's itself. Hilda's first impression of it—like so many other people's—was disappointing. The preconception of St. Peter's was, as Hawthorne says,

> a structure of no definite outline, misty in its architecture, dim and gray and huge, stretching into interminable perspective, and over-arched by a dome like the cloudy firmament. Beneath that vast breadth and height, as she had fancied them, the personal man might

feel his littleness and the soul triumph in its immensity. So in her earlier visits when the compassed splendour of the actual interior glowed before her eyes, she had profanely called it a great prettiness: a gay piece of cabinet work on a Titanic scale: a jewel casket, marvellously magnified.

This latter image best pleased her fancy; a casket, all inlaid on the inside with precious stones of various hue, so that there should not be a hair's breadth of the small interior unadorned with its resplendent gem. Then, conceive this minute wonder of a mosaic box, increased to the magnitude of a cathedral, without losing the intense lustre of its littleness, but all the petty glory striving to be sublime. The magic transformation from the minute to the vast has not been so cunningly effected but that the rich adornment still counteracts the impression of loftiness. The spectator is more sensible of its limits than of its extent.

But there came a day when Hilda saw St. Peter's differently, when it asserted its spiritual significance, and gave her, if not the original conception she had formed of it, something more awe-inspiring.

The pavement! It stretched out illimitably, a plain of many-coloured marble, where thousands of worshippers might kneel together, and shadowless angels tread among them, without brushing their heavenly garments against those earthly ones. The roof! The dome! Rich, gorgeous, filled with sunshine, cheerfully sublime; and fadeless after centuries, those lofty depths seemed to translate the heavens to mortal comprehension, and help the spirit upwards to a yet higher and wider sphere. Must not the faith, that built this matchless edifice, and warmed, and illuminated and overflowed from it, include whatever can satisfy human aspiration at its loftiest, or minister to human necessity at the sorest? If religion had its material home, was it not here?

These and similar passages, taken out of their context, may seem inflated, and guidebooky, but they have their justification in that they suggest the turmoil in Hilda's mind which came from witnessing the murder, and impelling her towards the only act she can think of that will restore her sense of innocence—confession, and it does so; confessing, she recovers her innate Puritanism. After a mysterious disappearance of four days, which the story as originally written did not explain, she returns to her tower. The doves which, all except one, had taken flight with her, also return, and the Virgin's lamp is relit.

Of the four main characters in *The Marble Faun* Hilda is the most effectively realized, and the most useful for Hawthorne's purposes—for it is through her eyes that he records his Roman impressions, when he does not, rather shamelessly, record them through his own. As I said before, the town pump was more of an inspiration to him than the Fountain of Trevi. Rome was too great a challenge, and, with Rome he bit off a bigger bit than he could chew. But it is in Hilda's changes of mood towards the things that Hawthorne held most valuable—because in them he saw the spirit of man in its highest development—that is to say, in works of art—that he most vividly illustrates the effect of sin and crime on a spirit unwilling to recognize or accept them. After her experience on the Tarpeian Rock she could not take her old pleasure in the pictures she used to copy—she could hardly look at them without distaste.

Miriam and Donatello are overwhelmed by Donatello's crime; they appear mysteriously in garbs of penitence, we do not know what their ultimate fate will be, and Hawthorne himself is very cagey about it. To forestall, or perhaps to meet criticisms on this score, he observes, airily but also truly,

> The actual experience of even the most ordinary life is full of events that never explain themselves either as regards their origin or their tendency.

The problem of how omniscient a novelist should be, or pretend to be, is one that will never be solved. Hawthorne, perhaps too often, took refuge in ignorance.

Kenyon, the American sculptor whose Cleopatra is going to be a masterpiece, is a shadowy figure, less distinct than his countrywoman, Hilda, if more distinct than Miriam and Donatello. There is a justification for this: artists who live for their art have less personality than other people have to spill around. But even if he hasn't much personality of his own he has an eye for other people's. In his long *villeggiatura* with Donatello he observes the change that has come over Donatello's character after the murder (all Hawthorne's characters are clearer when he analyses them than when he presents them). The interlude at Monte Beni, which gives Hawthorne his chance to describe the Tuscan landscape, has a further purpose: it shows us Kenyon observing the change which transforms the Faun into a human being. He knows that Donatello is suffering from guilt, though not until much later does he learn why.

And here I will interrupt myself for a moment to point out that in three of Hawthorne's novels one of the chief characters is haunted by a familiar—a demon in human form who sucks out his life-juices. In *The Scarlet Letter* it is Dimmesdale who is haunted by Chillingworth; in *The Blithedale Romance* Zenobia is mysteriously in thrall to Westerveldt—why, we are not told; and the same situation repeats itself in *The Marble Faun*, where Miriam is victimized by the Capuchin monk whom Donatello, to rid her of the incubus, or succubus, hurls from the Tarpeian Rock.

Did Hawthorne, one asks oneself, ever come across an example of this situation in real life? Could he have been a victim of it himself? I don't think I have ever known an instance of an *âme damnée*, a vampire battening on the spiritual and physical life of his host. Yet that is what Iago was to Othello; and if our psychological perceptions were keener than they are, we might find a similar phenomenon in the lives of our friends; or even in one's own life—disquieting thought.

But Kenyon meant to be a good angel, not a bad one, to Donatello when he took him for that long ramble over the Tuscan countryside which ended at the market-place in Perugia where, under the majestic statue of Pope Julius III, he hands Donatello over to Miriam, who, with Kenyon's connivance, has suddenly and conveniently appeared. The Pope seems to be giving them his blessing. Will all go well? Kenyon hopes so.

Miriam was a partner in Donatello's guilt, Hilda was not, and she cannot forgive Miriam, her erstwhile dear friend, who had stood much in the same relation to her as Priscilla had to Zenobia. But Hilda is a stronger character than Priscilla was, and cannot reconcile herself to their crime. When, by chance, they find Miriam kneeling in the Pantheon (of which Hawthorne gives us so vivid a description) Kenyon tries a last appeal to her heart. It is a striking passage, and perhaps sums up what Hawthorne himself thought about crime and its consequences on the individual.

Donatello, he says,

'perpetrated a great crime, and his remorse, gnawing into his soul, has awakened it, developing a thousand high capabilities, moral and intellectual, which we never should have dreamed of asking for, within the scanty compass of the Donatello we knew.'

'I know not whether this is so,' said Hilda, 'but what then?'

'Here comes my perplexity,' continued Kenyon. 'Sin has educated Donatello, and elevated him. Is sin, then, which we deem such a dreadful blackness in the universe, is it like sorrow, merely an element of human education through which we struggle to a higher and purer state than we could have otherwise attained? Did Adam fall that we might ultimately rise to a far loftier paradise than his?'

'Oh hush,' cried Hilda, shrinking from him with an expression of horror which wounded the poor speculative sculptor to the soul. 'This is terrible, and I could weep for you, if you indeed believe it. Do you not perceive what a mockery your creed makes, not only of all religious sentiments, but of moral law? and how it annuls and obliterates whatever precepts of heaven are written deepest within us? You have shocked me beyond words!'

So they let Miriam go without speaking to her, and throw in their lot with each other, a happiness which is denied to Miriam and to Donatello, who apparently expiates his sin in a dungeon. Miriam said to Hilda, as one friend to another, 'You need a sin to soften you.' But Hilda was incapable of sin and remained, comparatively at least, unsoftened.

Hawthorne once wrote to his wife, 'I first look at matters in their darkest aspect, and having satisfied myself with that, I begin gradually to be consoled, to take into account the advantages of the case, and thus trudge on, with the light brightening around me.' But, as one critic has remarked, the light never grows very bright. Another critic, Mr. Mark Van Doren, comments:

Hawthorne himself seems unable to decide whether it is altogether well that Sin has produced a world wherein [here he quotes from Hawthorne] 'the entire system of men's affairs . . . is built up purposely to exclude the careless and happy soul'. We are all, he says, 'parts of a complicated scheme of progress, which can only result in our arrival at a colder and drearier region than we were born in'.

In spite of its many beauties, *The Marble Faun* is, I think, the weakest of Hawthorne's novels, or, I should say, of his romances, for the human interest, which after all is the main point of a novel, has the Italian setting to compete with, as well as the moral ideas which are more important to Hawthorne than the characters who embody and exemplify them.

A continuous reading of Hawthorne's novels and short stories is a saddening experience, for although his view of the human lot is no more pessimistic than, say, Hardy's or Flaubert's, and though he may have persuaded himself that Sin like sorrow is educative, his insistence on it is in the long run depressing. And this is because he isolates it from the other activities and aspects and elements in human life, and only sees his characters *sub specie moralitatis*, if there is such a phrase. He rubs our noses in it. Perhaps no one would deny, especially today, that Sin is the most important single element in human life: the existence of the atom bomb, and all that it implies, proves that Hawthorne was no dreamer or irresponsible pessimist, as Emerson was an irresponsible optimist when he declared on his fifty-eighth birthday, 'I could never give much reality to evil and pain.' Hawthorne, who seems to have thought that only evil and pain were real, may have been nearer the mark.

American biographers and critics have ransacked Hawthorne's life and works so thoroughly that there seems no general aspect, or individual point, which they have not ferreted out. Yet I think there is one that has not had much attention drawn to it, and that is, his pacifism. He disliked the American Civil War so much that he could hardly take sides in it. It is not fanciful to suppose that his distaste for what was going on in the world around him helped to account for the unproductivity of his last years. As I said before, the last book he was engaged on, *The Dolliver Romance*, shows him at his best and disproves that his imagination was waning with the waning of his physical powers. One of the four romances that he came nearest to completing (Robert Browning helped to fill in the gaps and give it some kind of shape) was called *Septimus Felton, or the Elixir of Life*—the sub-title in itself may have shown Hawthorne's preoccupation with death. The story as a whole is spoilt by the complexities and ingenuities of its plot—the exact prescription of the elixir, and its connection with the Bloody Footstep in the English castle which fruitlessly haunted Hawthorne's imagination.

The story is set in the year 1776, at the time of the American War of Independence, and the unheroic hero, Septimus Felton, is a Hawthorne-like character with Indian blood in his veins and a murderer among his ancestors. We may assume, I think, that his attitude towards the War of Independence reflects Hawthorne's own attitude to the Civil War.

Septimus [we are told] felt himself strangely ajar with the human race, and would have given much either to be fully in accord with it, or to be separated from it forever.

'I am dissevered from it,' Septimus says. 'It is my doom to be only a spectator of life, to look on as one apart from it. Is it not well, therefore, that sharing none of its pleasures, and happiness, I should be free of its fatalities, its brevity? How cold I am now, while this whirlpool of public feeling is eddying round me! It is as though I had not been born of woman.'

Septimus's imagination keeps reverting to this idea of undying-ness; but meanwhile the war-fever takes hold of him, though the cause for which it is being fought does not. He goes out with a gun in his hand and meets an English officer, who challenges him; and in a rather confused scene, which is more like a private duel than an incident in war, he kills the officer.

This episode is, to my mind, one of the best things Hawthorne ever wrote: the relationship between the victor and the victim—the former's remorse, the latter's forgivingness are most beautifully and movingly described, and with far more sense of a direct relationship between two people, unimpeded by abstract considerations, than is usual with Hawthorne.

Dying, the English officer bequeathed to Septimus a docu-ment which, genealogically, gave him a claim on a great estate in England, the castle with the Bloody Footstep, and this theme is interwoven, though it never quite coalesces with, his longing to find the elixir of life which is the main subject of the book. His Aunt Kezia, and his Indian ancestor, both had recipes for the elixir, but one ingredient was wanting, the herb *sanguinea sanguinissima*. At last Septimus discovers it, growing on the Englishman's grave, and he prepares the potion, with most unexpected results.

The theme slipped out of Hawthorne's hands; his tired mind could not reconcile the thought behind it with the circumstances in which he sought to clothe it, and the story is only a fragment, a skeleton, of the book it should have been. Yet it contains a great deal of the essential Hawthorne—the contrast between life as it is lived by hopeful and healthy human beings (typified by Robert Hagburn and Rose, Septimus's ex-girl-friend) and those who, like Septimus, would try to find an explanation of life apart from, and almost unconnected with, the mere, gross act of living. It is the essential Hawthornian problem, and it is perhaps a blessing for mankind that so few of us are troubled with it. The only interpretation of life is one that comes out of the act of living—that is, I suppose, Hawthorne's existentialist conclusion, though he could not adapt it to his own life.

Reflecting on what the elixir would bring him, and the advantages of immortality in this world (which is a figure, perhaps, for immortality in the next), Septimus had misgivings.

> Sometimes the prospect a little chilled him. Could he give them all up—the sweet sister; the friend of his childhood; the grave instructor of his youth; the homely, life-known faces? Yes: there were such rich possibilities in the future: for he would seek out the noblest minds, the deepest hearts in every age, and be the friend of human time. Only it might be sweet to have one unchangeable companion; for unless he strung the pearls and diamonds of his life upon one unbroken affection, he sometimes thought that his life would have nothing to give it unity and identity: and so the longest life would be but an aggregate of insulated fragments, which would have no relation to one another. And so it would not be one life, but many unconnected ones. Unless he could look into the same eyes, through the mornings of future time, opening and blessing him with the fresh gleam of love and joy; unless the same sweet voice could melt his thoughts together, unless some sympathy of a life side by side with his could knit them into one; looking back upon the same things, looking forward to the same: the long thin thread of an individual life, stretching onward and onward, would cease to be visible, cease to be felt, cease, by and by, to have any real bigness in proportion to its length, and so be virtually non-existent, except in the mere inconsiderable Now.

It isn't likely that any man, whether he be Septimus Felton or Hawthorne himself, having these ideas, is likely to find much happiness in the 'mere inconsiderable Now', which is, after all, the only moment of time in which we *can* find happiness.

The mind tells the feelings many things which the feelings cannot accept, and vice versa: the heart has its reasons which reason knows not of. Hawthorne was a supreme example of such an ill-regulated personality. His mind could not accept what his heart told him; his heart could not accept what his mind told him.

Like most novelists, Hawthorne had two personalities, one for writing, one for living. Perhaps I should say three: he had a third personality, for loving. If we try to grade them in degrees of happiness, the loving one (let us hope, though there seems to be a doubt about it) came first. The personality for living came second. In his copious notebooks, when he was purely an observer of the scene around him, in America, England, France or Italy, he was tolerably happy, because what he saw, with such meticulous and conscientious observation, took him out of himself. As a sightseer he could be more or less a camera: an instrument that does not feel. And, I suspect, he got a certain sense of virtue, dear to the Puritan heart, from observing mankind and its works—the General Will in its various manifestations, which he felt he ought to admire, and did admire, but which he could not assimilate or love.

But when he was alone, with a pen in his hand, he became the third and the essential Hawthorne, who could see little good in anything that had no relish of salvation in it, and how little that was!

(5)

I meant to say something of Hawthorne's influence on American fiction; but this task, when I came to think about it, seemed to be beyond me. Critics better informed than I have found fundamental points of difference between the novel in England and the novel in America. The American novel is more symbolical, more consciously national (though also more parochial) than the English novel. It is not concerned, as so many of our novels are, with one stratum of society, upper class, middle class, or lower class; or, if it is, it regards such class distinctions *sub specie aeternitatis*, giving little significance to man-made, or rather socially-invented values. There was at one time in some American novels a democracy of drink, which drew millionaires and miners together. They were Americans and they shared this common experience. They also shared other experiences more readily than did the characters in an English novel. But now we have caught them up and maybe surpassed them.

One possible way in which, as I see it, Hawthorne may have influenced the modern American novel is in the *classlessness* of the characters he depicts. When class crops up, as it does, for instance, in *The House of the Seven Gables* or in *Lady Eleanor's Mantle*, it is already on its way out, and only there because it illustrates the sin of pride. But in nearly all Hawthorne's stories complete social equality reigns: the main ranking difference, a moral one, is between those who are proud and stand apart, and those who 'muck in' and accept the common lot.

Social distinctions, as we know, do exist in the United States today; they existed in the time of Henry James and Mrs. Wharton, and they existed, I expect, in Hawthorne's day. But only faintly and with blurred edges. We do not find them in the work of Herman Melville or Edgar Allan Poe. Nor do we find them outstandingly in the work of Faulkner or Hemingway. In their books a man's a man for a' that, though of course, distinctions of wealth do count, as they count, much more strongly, in the novels of Scott Fitzgerald, now so much in vogue. What point (apart from its beautiful writing) would *The Great Gatsby* have, if it were not for the money element? Even if it is a satire on the tycoon-type and on the old rich and the new rich in America, Fitzgerald could not have satirized them had they not already existed. The hero of *An American Tragedy*, one of the great novels of the century, meets his unhappy end through ambitions that are at least as much social as sexual.

At one time theirs was an aristocracy of wealth, whereas ours was of birth. And the Americans have, as we know, an American way of life, which operates however diverse the elements that compose it: whereas we have no English way of life, in the national sense. Yet surely we are more like them than we used to be: the Americanization of England has gone on apace, whereas there has been no corresponding Anglicizing of America. As for snobbery, the terms status-seekers and status symbols were American in origin. But they have been adopted here and the ideas that go with them: a man's social position is judged at least as much by the kind of car he keeps as by (for instance) whether he has been to a public school. I couldn't help feeling gratified when somebody told me that my Rover car was a modest status symbol. Interest in cars is here, as in America, a great social solvent, a powerful agent for democracy, for nearly every man likes to talk about them, without fear or favour, and a good many women too.

In Hawthorne's time there were no cars and in his works, at any rate, no status symbols indicating material wealth, though there were plenty of moral status symbols, as we know—pre-eminently in *The Scarlet Letter*.

Earlier on I quoted the list Henry James made of the elements of civilization that were absent from the social set-up in Hawthorne's day, and which made the task of the American novelist difficult. I won't recapitulate them all. Some were institutional— no Church, no State, no army, no navy, no Eton, no Harrow, no Epsom, no Ascot—while some were material—no abbeys, no cathedrals, no castles, etc. Hawthorne's own list was much shorter, so I will venture to repeat it.

No author without a trial can conceive of the difficulty of writing a romance about a country where there is no shadow, no antiquity, no mystery, no picturesque and gloomy wrong, nor anything but a commonplace prosperity, in broad and simple daylight, as is happily the case with my dear native land. It will be very long, I trust, before romance-writers may find congenial and easily handled themes, either in the annals of our stalwart republic or in any characteristic or probable events of our individual lives. Romance and poetry, ivy, lichens and wall-flowers, need *ruin* to make them grow.

'Ruin to make them grow'! Here Hawthorne implies something which he doesn't imply elsewhere, that a Romance must of its nature be gloomy, regardless of the fact that the word denotes, to most people, the exact opposite—it suggests a love-story that is going to turn out happily. But let that pass. He and Henry James were talking of different things—Hawthorne of the Romance, Henry James of the novel. The deficiencies—the lack of social calories—that would have starved Henry James's muse, had little effect on Hawthorne's, even if he had been able to assimilate them.

But if we survey the American literary scene, before, during, and after Hawthorne's time, *do* we find such paucity of the subjects that Hawthorne required for his romances, or Henry James for his novels?

James Fenimore Cooper was born in New Jersey in 1789. Altogether he wrote about thirty novels—or romances—if romance is an apter name for an adventure-story. *The Last of the Mohicans* came out in 1826, *The Pathfinder* in 1840, *The Deerslayer* in 1841: they had a tremendous success on both sides of the Atlantic. Hawthorne said, 'I do abhor an Indian story', but he could not have denied that Fenimore Cooper had the materials for writing a Romance.

Nor could he have denied it to Washington Irving, whose *Rip Van Winkle*, published in 1820 or thereabouts, was more in his own line of country. According to one of Hawthorne's biographers, Hawthorne never 'learned more from Irving than the secret of his thinnest sentiment', which no doubt is true, but Irving was an author not only much admired in America, but also in England and by Sir Walter Scott. Irving and Cooper came from New York, which may have seemed a different country in those days from New England. All the same, their achievements do rather disprove Hawthorne's suggestion that he was working in an untilled field. Romance had already established itself in popular esteem in the United States, even if it was not the same brand of Romance that Hawthorne favoured.

When Henry James complained of the poverty of the American social scene, he spoke as a novelist, not as a romancer: he thought that the elements that nourish a novelist's gifts were not there. In my childhood I read, or had read to me, four books, all of which I can still remember, in all of which I lived with the characters, their families, their environment, the society they mixed with. Their personal lives, their home life, their friends, the adventures that befell them, at home and abroad, were as real to me as my own life, or more. They were, all three, highly 'socialized' novels, their social context was amazingly rich, and if it did not include the items that Henry James said were essential to a novelist's material, I certainly did not miss them. The atmosphere of domesticity was what I most relished, the interrelation of all the characters, the feeling that they loved each other and were dependent on each other, and were growing up into a world (for most of them were children, rather older than myself) in which these warm, interesting, intimate, above all *safe* relationships, would be continued indefinitely. They were middle-class children, like myself, whose interests were bounded by family activities. I did not mind their not having heard of Epsom and Ascot, for neither had I. I have sometimes thought that whatever imagination I have—the warmest part of it, anyhow—comes from these stories, and is American in origin.

The Wide, Wide World, by Susan Warner (or Elizabeth Wetherell), and *Uncle Tom's Cabin,* by Harriet Beecher Stowe, both appeared in 1851, in the same year as *The House of the Seven Gables.* They are middle-brow novels, no doubt, but they overflow with geniality and an assurance of the sufficiency of ordinary daily life to supply one's moral and spiritual needs.

And so does *Little Women*, by Louisa M. Alcott, which came out in 1868, and its sequel, *Good Wives*. Those four books delighted juvenile, and older, readers on both sides of the Atlantic for more than half a century. Nor were they namby-pamby novels in which everyone is always happy. Ellen Montgomery, the lachrymose heroine of *The Wide, Wide World*, suffered terribly from homesickness and was always rushing upstairs and throwing herself on her bed in a passion of grief. There is the tragedy in *Little Women* when Beth dies; and as for *Uncle Tom's Cabin*, besides the deaths of little Eva and her father, there are enough picturesque and gloomy wrongs connected with the slave trade to have satisfied even Hawthorne.

Mrs. Hawthorne nursed Louisa Alcott through an illness, but there is no evidence that Hawthorne read *Uncle Tom's Cabin*, nor would he necessarily have agreed with its sentiments towards the negroes if he had.

But my point is that the United States of that time was a country fit for heroes and heroines to live in, especially the heroes and heroines of novels, provided they did not ask too much of life, and as far as they could, steered clear of Evil.

Henry James, as we know, was much influenced by Hawthorne, for whom he had a profound admiration, and he, like Hawthorne, was immensely conscious of evil. But he did not regard it in the same way that Hawthorne did. With James it was an almost inevitable concomitant of life. Some of the characters in his novels are driven by their natures and circumstances and ambitions (never, I think, by pride) into courses that seem purely evil—Osmund and Madame Merle, for instance, in *The Portrait of a Lady*, Kate Croy, in *The Wings of the Dove*, Charlotte Stant, perhaps, in *The Golden Bowl*. Whenever they appear they bring a nasty moral smell with them. They are evil because, almost always, their object is to betray innocence, or if it is not their object, it is the means they adopt to gain their ends. Their ends are usually, but not always, money. For money, Osmund and Madame Merle victimize the rich, unsuspecting Isabel Archer; for money, Kate Croy and Merton Densher, her accomplice, make use of Milly Theale; for money, Charlotte Stant tries to keep in the good graces of Maggie Verver, whose husband the Prince has been and still is Charlotte's lover. But though Henry James was so sensitive to evil that even in the case of his minor characters he keeps a sort of chart of their moral temperatures, evil is only one aspect of his multiple awareness. He uses it mainly for aesthetic purposes, to enrich the texture of his books, to induce suspense, to make us take sides with this character against that, to engage our feelings ever more deeply with the plot he is unfolding. He seldom makes it the dominant characteristic of any of his personages, he socialized it, and only once does he show it, as it were, in isolation. The nearest he gets to doing this is in *The Turn of the Screw*, where the children corrupted by Peter Quint and Miss Jessel are emblems of evil first, and human beings afterwards. Evil is the subject of the book and the chief character: we can almost see it stalking about in the shadowy glimpses we get of the butler and his accomplice, and in the beautiful and seemingly innocent faces of the children of whom it has taken possession.

But with Hawthorne Evil was always a thing in itself, and his characters—those that are susceptible to it—are meant to illustrate its workings. Sometimes he calls it the Black Man, a forest-ranging personage who is, to all intents and purposes, the Devil. It is he who accosts Young Goodman Brown, he who haunts the woods where Hester Prynne and her daughter wander in *The Scarlet Letter*. Sometimes he is made more corporeal: he appears in the substantial frame and rubicund countenance of Judge Pyncheon; he gleams at us through Professor Westerveldt's gold teeth; we meet him in the cata-combs at Rome and watch him being hurled off the Tarpeian Rock. He is enough of a human being to be killed by a fall from a precipice, but no more: otherwise he is just an embodiment of evil, like Ethan Brand, after his successful search for the Unforgivable Sin.

This view of Evil as something both inside us and outside us, the human condition, in fact, is implicit in most of Hawthorne's stories. It is the theme of *The Fall of Man*, told with many variations, and leading (in *The Marble Faun*) to the unorthodox conclusion that sin is as inevitable as sorrow, and must be accepted as part of the training of the soul on its way to a higher development: it has a regenerative power.

This preoccupation with sin makes Hawthorne an apocalyptic novelist, just as Herman Melville was in *Moby Dick*, and as Edgar Allan Poe was in many of his tales. Herman Melville saw sin as embodied in the White Whale, with whom Captain Ahab has a fight which might well have figured in the Book of Revelation, the prototype of all stories in which the main, the only issue, is the struggle between the good and the bad. Edgar Allan Poe assumed that Evil is paramount in the world: he didn't bother to account for it, he didn't even say he disliked it: he took it for granted, it was the climate of his mind, and the source of a great deal of his inspiration.

Happily for us, all three authors were able to see the world and human beings in other aspects than the aspect of sin. Hawthorne was an inveterate sightseer; Herman Melville followed the sea in ships, and was quite capable of observing humanity without regard to its virtue or lack of virtue; and Edgar Allan Poe was an untiring literary experimentalist to whom art meant a great deal (as indeed it did to Hawthorne) and to whom illness and premature death (and premature burial) meant more. All three of them were able to use their imaginations on subjects with which Sin had nothing to do. Otherwise we could not get from them the pleasure that we do get. Sin is not an inexhaustible subject, and it can become a monotonous one. We all know the story told of Calvin Coolidge, who went to church and was afterwards asked what the sermon was about. 'It was about sin,' he replied. 'And what did the clergyman say about sin?' 'He was against it.'

We may applaud the brevity of that reply: but so was Dante against sin, and so was Milton (unless, as someone said, he was of Satan's party). Sin was their subject, and on it they wrote two of the great poems of the world. Hawthorne read *The Divine Comedy* and *Paradise Lost*, and no doubt found much in them to suit his temperament. He read Shakespeare too, and as a child was fond of quoting the line:

Stand back, my lords, and let the coffin pass!

But was Hawthorne against sin? The answer, as so often when one tries to pin Hawthorne down, is 'Yes and No'. He was violently against the sin of pride, because it cuts us off from the 'magnetic chain of humanity'—not because, as orthodox Christians hold, it separates the soul from God. Hawthorne had a Calvinistic upbringing, but he was not a Christian; I doubt if he believed in Christ or even in God. His religion (for he must have been religious, or he could not have been so concerned with sin) was a form of humanism akin to Rousseau's.

To oppose the General Will indicated pride, and pride was anathema.

But towards other sins he was not only indulgent, he even advocated them for their redemptive and regenerative value— as did his compatriot, Sherwood Anderson. Until a man had committed a sin, he was an incomplete human being. Adam was a complete human being after the Fall. Before the Fall he was just a Child of Nature—he did not even know that he was naked. Donatello was a Child of Nature, before he murdered the Capuchin monk. Hester Prynne was presumably a Child of Nature (if a married woman can be) until she committed adultery with Arthur Dimmesdale, and gave birth to little Pearl. Pearl, the offspring of Sin (one never knows whether to write it with a capital S or not), is the one happy character in the book.

Hawthorne does not tell us whether she will still be happy if, and when, she has sinned herself, but it is clear that the idea of human nature after the Fall appeals to him more than the idea of human nature before it. We all partake of the sin of Adam, and must bear, or enjoy, the consequences.

Hawthorne's preoccupation with Sin was at once his limitation and his strength; he did not always make the best use of it (if one can make the best use of Sin), but Sin was the attachment to the groundwork of his mind that kept his kite flying. Nor did he believe with Dante, and Milton, and Browning, and the Catholic Church that Good was sure to prevail over Evil. When, after a prolonged tour of the sights of Rome, Miriam, Kenyon and Donatello (Hilda, the fourth member of the quartet, had rather pointedly absented herself, she could no longer associate with the guilt-stained Miriam)—when they come to the Church of the Capuchins, and look at Guido Reni's picture of the Archangel Michael trampling on Satan, the dragon, Miriam, who had been concerned with crime, whereas Hilda had only witnessed it, observes:

That Archangel now—how fair he looks with his unruffled wings, with his unhacked sword, and clad in his bright armour, and that exquisitely fitting sky-blue tunic, cut in the latest Paradisiacal mode! What a dainty air of the first celestial society! With what a half-scornful delicacy he sets his prettily sandalled foot on the head of his prostrate foe! But is it thus that virtue looks, the moment after its death-struggle with evil? No, no; I could have told Guido better.

A full third of the archangel's feathers should have been torn from his wings: the rest all ruffled, till they looked like Satan's own! His sword should be streaming with blood, and perhaps broken half-way to the hilt; his armour crushed, his robes bent, his breast gory; a bleeding gash on his brow, cutting right across the stern scowl of battle! He should press his foot hard down on the old serpent, as if his very soul depended upon it, feeling him squirm mightily, and doubting whether the fight were half over yet, and how the victory might turn! And with all this fierceness, this grimness, this unutterable horror, there should be something high, tender, and holy in Michael's eyes, and around his mouth. But the battle never was such child's play as Guido's dapper Archangel seems to have found it.

Kenyon tells Miriam that she ought to paint the picture of man's struggle against Sin according to her own idea.

'The picture would have its share of truth, I assure you,' Miriam answered; 'but I am sadly afraid the victory would fall on the wrong side. Just fancy a smoke-blackened, fiery-eyed demon, bestriding that nice young angel, clutching his white throat with one of his hinder claws; and giving a triumphant whisk of his scaly tail, with a poisonous dart at the end of it! That is what they risk, poor souls, who do battle with Michael's enemy.'

One has to remember that this speech is put into the mouth of Miriam, who is acquainted with Evil at first hand and twice over—through the agency of the Capuchin monk, with his mysterious hold over her, and through Donatello, who freed her from the monk by murdering him. It was Kenyon, who had no first-hand experience of Evil, who believed it might be educative and a necessary factor in the soul's progress.

In *The Turn of the Screw* the battle is between Good and Evil, between the governess's struggle to save the souls of her charges from destruction, and the Devil who means to keep them. The issue remains in doubt, and in the end the battle is only half-won. The governess rescues the boy, but loses the girl —and if we identify the governess with St. Michael, the Archangel, we can certainly think of her as losing a full third of her feathers. *The Turn of the Screw* is one of the few stories by Henry James in which he recognizes the full force of Evil, as Hawthorne did—nor does he see it as part of a regenerative process, as Hawthorne tried to.

Hawthorne has been said to have had 'the tragic view of life', but what exactly does that mean? It doesn't mean the triumph of Evil over Good—it isn't as simple as that. The tragic hero has potentialities for goodness, or greatness, exceeding those of ordinary men. But in him there is a fatal flaw, either innate, as in Shakespeare, or wished on him by the gods, as in Aeschylus or Thomas Hardy, which makes his gifts of none effect and indeed turns them to poison. This is the case with some of Hawthorne's characters, but not with all. Arthur Dimmesdale succumbs to the doom laid upon him; so does the Man of Adamant, so does Ethan Brand, so does the Ambitious Guest, so, I suppose, does Father Hooper in *The Minister's Black Veil.* But could these characters have escaped their fate? Are they endowed with free-will?

It is hard to answer that question. The cause of tragedy, in most of Hawthorne's stories, is pride, taking the form of egotism. *Egotism, or The Bosom-Serpent* is one of his most characteristic tales. Roderick Elliston believes that he harbours a serpent in his bosom; it has infected his whole being with snakelike qualities. When he speaks, he hisses; when he walks he weaves to and fro as a serpent might. As a result of this lamentable complex, his wife has left him, indeed everybody shuns him, and not unnaturally, for when he meets acquaintances or even strangers in the street he exclaims, to their dismay, 'Ah, I see that you also have a bosom serpent!' This habit, of course, makes him as unpopular with them as they are with him. The old Hawthornian situation of social ostracism repeats itself. But in this story Roderick Elliston is saved, not by his own efforts but by the timely, if unlikely, return of his wife, Rosina.

'Oh yes,' said Rosina with a heavenly smile. 'The serpent was but a dark fantasy, and what it typified was as shadowy as itself. The past, dismal as it seems, shall fling no gloom upon the future. To give it its due importance we must think of it but as an anecdote in our Eternity.'

'An anecdote in our Eternity'! With these words Hawthorne might be thought to affirm his belief in the immortality of the soul. The story also suggests that egotism can only be cured by the intervention of another human being, preferably a woman, best of all by a wife. Egotism is not, I suppose, a peculiarly masculine trait, but most people would agree with Hawthorne that it is more often found in men than in women. Eve was tempted, but Adam fell.

Hawthorne was a religiously-minded man, and *The Scarlet Letter* is one of the greatest of religious novels. But he was not an orthodox Christian, for he nowhere suggests, with any conviction, that Sin can be atoned for by Grace, as an outside agency, or by Repentance, as the sinner's own contribution. The Wages of Sin is death. In Hawthorne's view Sin has to be paid for, not by Christ's suffering on the Cross for the redemption of the world, but by the punishment of social outlawry, or by a gnawing spiritual anguish—a Bosom Serpent. In Arthur Dimmesdale's case only open Confession (which as we know is good for the soul) annuls the sense of guilt. A great effort, a great sacrifice of pride, the turning of oneself inside out, mortification, humiliation—in the eyes of men, not of God—can release the sinner from his sin.

Perhaps confession on the psychiatrist's couch is a kindred but humaner method of attaining the same end.

Like the other New Englanders of his generation Hawthorne was a Puritan and a perfectionist, but unlike them he was not an optimist; he thought that individual personality was a burden, not an inspiration, something to be endured, not to be lived with and enjoyed. Nearly every novelist has a writing-self, that small part of his mental, emotional and imaginative make-up which can fertilize his gift. Often this writing-self is different from and almost opposed to his daily self, and his social self. Thomas Hardy, whose view of the human lot was, in another way, as gloomy as Hawthorne's, was in his private life, I believe, a cheerful and happy man. The Hawthorne who wrote the American, English and Italian notebooks, in which he was observing life as it was, not creating it in his own image, was a happier person than Hawthorne the novelist; and perhaps Hawthorne the married, family man was happier too, if we go by his letters, and Hawthorne the friend was happier too, to judge by his relations with Horatio Bridge and Longfellow and Franklin Pierce.

Yet I feel that his personality was more of a piece than that of most fiction-writers. He says somewhere that he preferred his own society to that of almost anyone else; and most people who knew him remarked that in company he was shy, awkward and reserved. Henry James Senior wrote to Emerson:

Hawthorne isn't a handsome man [this is a curious comment, for almost every other contemporary says he was extremely good-looking, and his photographs and portraits bear it out], nor an engaging one personally. He has the look all the time, to one who doesn't know him, of a rogue who suddenly finds himself in a company of detectives. But in spite of his rusticity, I felt a sympathy with him amounting to anguish and couldn't take my eyes off him all the dinner. The idea I got was, and it was very powerfully impressed on me, that we are all monstrously corrupt, hopelessly bereft of human consciousness, and that it is the intention of the Divine Providence to overrun us and obliterate us in a new Gothic and Vandalic invasion . . . The old world is breaking up on all hands—the glimpse of the everlasting granite I caught in Hawthorne shows that there is stock enough for fifty better.

One reason why Herman Melville dedicated *Moby Dick* to Hawthorne 'in token of my admiration for his genius' was that Hawthorne refused to accept the cheerful humanistic view of Emerson and his fellow-Transcendentalists. 'There is the grand truth about Nathaniel Hawthorne', Melville wrote. 'He says NO in thunder, but the Devil himself cannot make him say Yes. For all men who say *Yes*, lie.' Mr. Mark van Doren comments, 'When Hawthorne read these last sentences, smiling as he regularly smiled at their author's exuberance, he may have remembered Emerson in Concord and wondered whether Melville did not include the local saint among the '*Yes*-gentry'.

Few people, reviewing the history of the last hundred years, would deny that the 'yes-gentry' were wrong, and that Hawthorne was the better prophet. Hawthorne said 'NO in thunder', and in this connection it is interesting to quote the opinion of Edgar Allan Poe, who had admired Hawthorne to begin with, and then changed his mind. 'The author who is merely *at all* times *quiet*', Poe said, 'is of course, upon *most* occasions merely silly and stupid.' Compared with Poe, and compared with many novelists of today, Hawthorne is a 'quiet' writer; but there was a thunder of conviction in him that Poe missed.

Hawthorne is one of the most serious-minded of all novelists, for not only did he take the human predicament for his province (often without giving much personal attention to the individuals who exemplified it), he also saw it mainly under one aspect, the aspect of Sin and Salvation. No theme which depended on those issues was too large for him to tackle. In one of his most exhilarating stories, *Earth's Holocaust*, he depicts an enormous bonfire into which a mob, inspired by revolutionary fervour, throws everything that belongs to the past—art, literature (including Hawthorne's own works), science, every vestige of pre-conflagration civilization including, finally, the Bible. Except for the Bible, which assumed a dazzling whiteness as the finger-marks of human imperfection were purified away, everyone and everything were consumed, leaving only the narrator, the last hangman, the last thief, the last murderer, and the last toper, who handed round a brandy-bottle to keep their spirits up. But presently a 'dark-complexioned personage' (we are in no doubt as to who *he* is) joined the little group.

'There is one thing that these wiseacres have forgotten to throw into the fire,' [this personage says], 'without which all the rest of the conflagration is just nothing at all: yes, though they had burnt the earth itself to a cinder.'

'And what may that be?' eagerly demanded the last murderer.

'What but the human heart itself?' said the dark-visaged stranger, with a portentous grin. 'And unless they hit upon some method of purifying that foul cavern, forth from it will reissue all the shapes of wrong and misery—the same old shapes or worse ones—which they have taken such a vast deal of trouble to consume to ashes. I have stood by this livelong night and laughed in my sleeve at the whole business. Oh, take my word for it, it will be the old world yet!'

To those who are worried by the idea of the hydrogen bomb, this may almost seem a consoling message.

In England there has been no novelist comparable to Hawthorne or to Melville—apocalyptic novelists who felt that the very fabric of the earth is as unstable as it is presented in the Book of Revelation. Hawthorne complained that we, the English, are a beer-drinking, beef-eating, down-to-earth people, and our nineteenth-century novelists did not, on the whole, envisage such drastic changes in the structure of society, much less in the structure of the earth, as were foreseen by St. John the Divine. But there is one English novelist who has certain affinities with Hawthorne, both in mental outlook and in personal characteristics, and that is Emily Brontë.

The likenesses may be accidental and superficial, and in any case they are more noticeable in the characters of the two authors than in their work. It is a long way on the map from Haworth Parsonage to Salem, Massachusetts, but spiritually it is not so far, for puritanism reigned in both places, the Evangelical-Wesleyan Puritanism of Mr. Brontë and his sister, the Calvinist Puritanism of the Hawthornes. In both households there was a zeal for learning. All the Brontë children had it, and if Nathaniel's sisters did not share his passion for reading, at any rate Elizabeth supplied him with the books. They were both middle-class families, though the Hawthornes had come down in the world and the Brontës, thanks to their father's education at Cambridge, had come up. Both families were hard-pressed for money; Mr. Brontë's living was only £200 a year, and I doubt if the Hawthornes had much more. The Brontës, like the Hawthornes, saw little of their neighbours and even under their own roof-tree were inclined to solitude. Mr. Brontë always dined alone, and in the Hawthorne house, as we have seen, at one time four members of the family each ate in separate rooms. And for five years after her husband's death Mrs. Hawthorne took all her meals alone.

Each household, then, was a separate entity, holding little communication with the outside world and, within the house, only an imperfect communication with each other.

The four Brontë children were of course intensely attached to each other, though later they paired off, Charlotte with Branwell, Emily with Anne. Hawthorne was on affectionate terms with both of his sisters. Elizabeth seems to have run errands for him but it was Louisa he loved best.

But family relationships apart, as far as local society went, Emily always shunned it as Hawthorne came to shun it, in a more marked way than she did. She did not spend twelve years in semi-isolation but she would not go out to see people. 'Why should I,' she said in effect, 'when Charlotte will bring it all back to me?' Charlotte loved social life, although when she was famous, and lionized, she was too tired to enjoy it. Hawthorne, when he came to England, was famous, and literary circles, such as Monckton Milnes, welcomed him, but he could not take it. Emily did not live to be lionized, but if she had, she would, I feel sure, still have stuck to her solitary walks on the moors (if indeed they were solitary) just as Hawthorne wore for himself a private foot-path, above and beyond the house he returned to when he came back from Europe, where he could walk alone and undisturbed. He called the house 'The Wayside' to suggest, I suppose, the transitory nature of life, in which we are but caravaners, however many people (as was no doubt the case with him, the famous writer) may drift in to have a look or a drink.

Like Hawthorne Emily Brontë was obsessed by guilt, why, we do not know, any more than we know why he was. Like him, she was much preoccupied by death, and like him she looked over the edge of it into immortality. Like him, when she knew herself to be dangerously ill, she would not seek medical advice: 'I will have no poisoning doctor near me', she said. She did not leave home to die, as he did; but again, like him, she stayed on her feet almost until the hour when death overtook her.

With both of them, a sense of the impermanence of this world, and an interest which, in Emily's case, amounted to a longing for the next, are discernible in their works—in Emily's poems and her one novel; and here and there, in everything that Hawthorne wrote. They had said good-bye to life long before they left it. Emily's death, as described by Charlotte, seems like suicide, and Hawthorne's—he went for a trip with his friend Pierce instead of staying in bed, which would surely have been more sensible—seems rather like it.

If we compare *Wuthering Heights* with *The Scarlet Letter*, we find marked similarities and marked differences. *The Scarlet Letter* was published in 1850; *Wuthering Heights* in 1847; there is no evidence that Hawthorne had read it. Both authors had probably read *The Tales of Hoffmann*; both believed, or half-believed, in the supernatural, at any rate as vehicles for romantic feeling. No one knows how much German literature Emily had read between the intervals of bread-baking and potato-peeling.

The Scarlet Letter and *Wuthering Heights* could be called novels about revenge. Roger Chillingworth revenges himself on Arthur Dimmesdale, his wife's lover; Heathcliff revenges himself on the Earnshaws who had maltreated him as a boy, on the Lintons who had separated him from Cathy—on the world, in fact. Chillingworth's revenge, though it was directed against one person (for he does not, oddly enough, appear to have wished ill to Hester Prynne) was so obsessive that it, too, might be called a revenge against the world. Chillingworth and Heathcliff both succeed in their objectives: Dimmesdale dies from Chillingworth's unrelenting psycho-somatic persecution, and Heathcliff, in one sense more materially-minded, gets hold of the Earnshaw property and the Linton property. But both are disappointed in the end: Chillingworth because Dimmesdale's soul escapes him, and Heathcliff because his longing to be re-united to Catherine makes his success as a land-grabber of small value to him.

Now for the differences between the two books, and the difference between Hawthorne's outlook and Emily Brontë's. *The Scarlet Letter* is a study in sin, and the sense of reconciliation with which every tragedy *used* to end, comes about from the fact that Dimmesdale confesses his sin, in public, and is, we are to suppose, reunited to God, via public opinion, without the sanction of which, in Hawthorne's view, there could be no salvation. *Vox populi vox dei.*

Emily Brontë cared nothing for the sanctions of society— there is no sign that she recognized them. *The Scarlet Letter* and *Wuthering Heights* are alike in the fact that the characters are presented in isolation—in *The Scarlet Letter* against a background of sin, in *Wuthering Heights*, against what? The moors? Nature? Each novel has various supernumerary charac-ters; *The Scarlet Letter* has Governor Bellingham, a well-meaning man, Mistress Hibbens, his sister, a witch—and, of course, the Black Man, whom we need not further describe. *Wuthering Heights* is more fully furnished: there are Nelly Dean, who acts as narrator, Joseph, who acts as chorus, Zillah, the rather mean-minded servant at Wuthering Heights, Mr. Kenneth, the overworked doctor, and Mr. Green, the venal solicitor, suborned by Heathcliff. In neither book do these personages add up to a community, a society, a social background in which, wherever we live, most of us find ourselves. But the social background of *The Scarlet Letter*, though seldom described, makes itself continuously felt. In fact, the scarlet letter itself, as a symbol of sin, gets its force from the multitude of disapproving faces round it. Whereas in *Wuthering Heights* the community as a body that can condemn or condone, or drop in for a chat, or can exert any influence whatsoever on the lives of the Earn-shaws, the Lintons and the Heathcliffs (for we must include Linton Heathcliff, one of the best-drawn characters in the book) —that community doesn't exist. The chief characters are far too much occupied with their own affairs to be even aware of social pleasures or pressures.

Emily Brontë, like Godolphin Horne in Belloc's poem, held the human race in scorn; it was said that of all her acquaintance only Willie Weightman, the ill-fated curate at Haworth, was exempt from Emily's 'liberal scorn'. To her, the strength of private feelings was their own justification: despite all his wickedness Heathcliff is happy in the thought that death will reunite him to Catherine, and he can hardly wait for it. He is, of course, a sinner of the deepest dye; Nelly Dean wonders if he is a ghoul or a vampire; but Emily does not take him to task for his wickedness (though Charlotte did). She seems to regard him as a natural phenomenon, a cliff, perhaps, with heath growing on it.

But willingly as she accepted him as a force of Nature, and the first Catherine as his counterpart, she realized that the social order had its claims, and Wuthering Heights and Thrushcross Grange come together in the persons of Hareton Earnshaw and Catherine Linton—Catherine Heathcliff, as she became for a miserable moment—dull, ordinary people perhaps, but how could society exist without them? To Emily, who seems to have had no social life outside her family, and her experience as a teacher at Miss Patchett's school at Law Hill (and we know how much she hated it), society as such had no reality, and no more meaning than the racing world would have to someone who was not interested in racing. She was an uncompromising individualist: 'No coward soul is mine, no trembler in the world's storm-troubled sphere.' The only allegiance she owed was to God, whom she located in her own breast, and to one or two people for whom her heart bled and burned—we shall never know who they were.

To Hawthorne such an attitude would have denoted extreme spiritual pride; and had he read *Wuthering Heights* he might have attributed the woes of Heathcliff and Catherine Earnshaw to the fact that they never took their neighbours into account; they were 'isolated from the magnetic chain of humanity', and doomed for that reason. Nor would he have been altogether wrong.

On the other hand, Emily Brontë had a much keener sense of personality than Hawthorne had. Nearly all the characters in *Wuthering Heights* are carefully, if not lovingly, observed; and Joseph's every word is faithfully recorded, in its proper dialect, to tether the story to the ground. Joseph is as anti-social as any of the other characters in *Wuthering Heights*, but he is a person first, and an emblem of misanthropy and censoriousness second, whereas most of Hawthorne's characters, though they are never merely types, are symbols of something outside themselves and (to Hawthorne) more important than themselves, because it reflected the ideals and claims of the community, which Emily would never have recognized—except as she would have recognized the fact that if one goes out in the rain it is wise to take an umbrella.

Perhaps the parallel between these writers is not very rewarding except in so far as it illustrates the means whereby two lonely, misanthropic novelists, unwilling or unable for one reason or another to receive sustenance from the community, were still able to produce great works of art. In composing these works they found compensation, and consolation, for whatever it was in their natures that made for solitude, unhappiness, frustration, guilt. Though their circumstances differed, and their aims differed, they were kindred souls who 'desired a better country—that is, a heavenly one'.

(6)

Being a more mongrel race even than Defoe's 'True-born Englishman', the Americans, except in the higher income brackets, are less conscious of social inequalities based on accent, dialect, and so on, than we are. The spoken word, smacking of class and origin, prejudices them less, for or against, than it would us. To each other, perhaps, 'their speech bewrayeth them', but it does not constitute a status symbol. 'An American is an American is an American', as Gertrude Stein might have said.

The speech used by Hawthorne's characters is stylized and semi-poetic. It was his own invention, and probably never used by anyone in any age, not even by the Puritans of the seventeenth century, the period to which (possibly because of the feeling of guilt, the witch's curse laid on his ancestor) his mind compulsively turned. How often in dialogue, trivial or important, do the remarks of the characters end with an exclamation mark—as if they were in a continual state of surprise.

Hawthorne uses exclamation marks more recklessly than any other novelist. Doubtless he read the Bible, for his morality, much as he distrusted it, is founded on the Old Testament, or on a reaction from the Old Testament. In the Old Testament there are very few exclamation marks. Perhaps in those days people were not surprised by anything that happened: they had learned to accept it. Only the Book of Job voices, or rather Job himself voices, an incessant query, emphasized by notes of interrogation, about the human lot; and sometimes these queries overflow into passion, with appropriate exclamation marks, when he feels that his sufferings are greater than he can bear:

> Oh that my words were now written! Oh that they were printed in a book! That they were graven with an iron pen and lead in the rocks for ever!

Most of Hawthorne's characters suffer, or cause others to suffer; and in such cases the exclamation mark represents a *cri de cœur*. But he does not always use it as a symbol of distress or protest; more often to suggest an uncertainty in the speaker's mind, the ambiguity of thought and feeling which always haunted Hawthorne. He did not want to commit himself to a *statement* (any more than Henry James did) which requires a full-stop. He wanted to awake a reverberation of doubt, the doubt from which we all at one time or another suffer, echoing endlessly, not only in accents of surprise or pain, but of wonder, sadness, humour—a recognition of the fact that facts have blurred edges, and that their face-value does not always correspond to their full meaning, which only futurity will reveal.

I dwell on the exclamation mark (if one can dwell on something so transitory) because it has a twofold bearing, or use, in Hawthorne's work. Besides indicating ambivalent states of mind, it is a kind of *literary leveller*, and like the style of which it is an ornament and an accompaniment, it helps us to see the characters *sub specie aeternitatis*, the way that Hawthorne saw them.

I do not know at what period, or in what country, speech was first used by poets and dramatists, and (much later) by novelists, to differentiate (*a*) the social class and (*b*) the personality of the speaker. By Shakespeare's time both methods of differentiation were already established, although the distinction between personality and personality was less marked than that between class and class. Hamlet does not say the kind of thing that King Lear would have said, because he has different things to say, but they speak each other's language, the language of princes; whereas the Fool in *Lear* and the Gravedigger in *Hamlet* are content with proletarian speech.

In Hawthorne's stories, many of which are set in a no-man's-land of time, the speech used by all the characters, whether of high or low degree, is as uniform as it would be in the Old Testament or in Greek tragedy. If there was a difference of social status between (for instance) Elisha and the Shunnamite woman, or between Jezebel and Jehu, it does not appear in their conversation. Whereas even in *The Blithedale Romance*, the novel in which Hawthorne got nearest to his own time—since it was founded on his recent experience at Brook Farm—all the characters talk in the same way. Does his neglect of the nuances of the spoken word as an index of class and character proceed from a conviction that all men and women are fundamentally alike, all victims of the 'human predicament', in whatever language they may express themselves? *What* is said, not *how* it is said, really counts. The diction of Hawthorne's dialogue is a timeless, classless, means of communication, available to all in any walk of life, at any epoch.

He was far more sensitive to moral issues than to personal relationships or to social grades. In so far as he took cognizance of them it was to illustrate the moral ideas on which his stories are based. After all, morality doesn't exist *in vacuo*. It is a concept derived from the behaviour of human beings, as assessed and adjudged by their fellow human beings, according to varying canons and at various periods in history. Some Frenchman said, 'Morality is a delicate sense of a variable custom.' Hester Prynne had a character of her own, a character of much dignity and integrity. But she is primarily the emblem of someone who has been judged harshly by the world, but who (as always in Hawthorne) must submit to the world's moral verdict. Do we align ourselves with it, or with her? This is the alternative that Hawthorne is always putting before us, the clash of moral values from which his inspiration springs, as it was the inspiration of Sophocles when he wrote *Antigone*, the perfect example of the individual's conflict between duty to conscience and duty to the State (or Society).

Hawthorne's characters are not sharply differentiated because they are all caught up in a moral dilemma. Nearly anyone who is in a tight place will react to the *situation* (Antigone was an exception), not in obedience to the dictates of his own character. Still less will he use special words to fit it. Vague cries and shouts, 'Oh!' 'Ah!' 'Help!' etc., will serve his turn—the almost inarticulate language of people unused to violence, but suddenly confronted by it. For there is violence, or an extremity of feeling that may lead to violence, in most of Hawthorne's stories.

*

What was Hawthorne like, as a man, to meet? From his portraits and photographs, which give a much more consistent view of his appearance than his friends, or he himself, give of his character, we know what he looked like: the mass of dark hair, the noble brow, the deep-set eyes, at once brooding and searching, the long drooping moustache which he generally but not always wore—these physical traits are immediately recognizable, and we do not have to say, 'No, there was another Hawthorne, quite unlike this one!'

But when we try to imagine his bearing and behaviour in society we are at once confronted by the usual contradictions. Henry James senior, who would not even allow that he was handsome, said he was like a rogue who suddenly finds himself in a company of detectives. On the other hand his son Julian thought that Hawthorne did enjoy social life, but that owing to his intuitive sympathy with everyone he spoke to, and his desire to meet them half-way, he gave no consistent impression of his personality, with the result that all his interlocutors formed a different idea of him, just as in aftertimes his biographers and readers have.

And his table-talk? Of that we have as far as I know no record except Herman Melville's remark that he said 'NO in thunder', which cannot have been an aid to conversation, although I suppose that Melville was not referring to his spoken word, but to his general attitude to the accepted opinions of his day, especially to the more optimistic ones.

He cannot have talked in the way the characters in his stories talk, or in the parlance of some of the letters he wrote to his wife, which with its 'thees' and 'thous' is almost baby-talk, akin to 'the little language' that Swift used in his *Journal to Stella*. It does not altogether ring true; it is a form of 'talking down', an effort to escape from the harsh realities of adult life that many people have recourse to when talking to their dogs. Sophia seems to have adored him so uncritically that it must have been a temptation to treat her as a pet and caress her with verbal fondlings. It may have been a sort of compensation for the Puritan strictness of his upbringing which discouraged demonstrativeness, although it did not discourage demonstrativeness in his sister Louisa. She wrote him letters when he was at Brook Farm, begging him to come home or even to reply, which have the warmth and spontaneity of love-letters. Why did he not bother to answer? Was it from lack of feeling, or mere carelessness? Was it because, in the ordinary relationships of life, his attitude to himself was too ironical for him easily to accept affection? Friendship, yes: but his friendships were nearly all with men, Horatio Bridge, Franklin Pierce, Herman Melville, Longfellow. There is no evidence that he had any serious friendship, still less any love-affair, with any woman except Sophia. Or could his epistolary silence during the months at Brook Farm (he wrote very little to Sophia, to whom he was engaged), be attributed not to negligence or indifference, but the long hours of manual work (from six o'clock in the morning to seven o'clock at night, according to one account)?

It seems certain that Hawthorne had no natural zest for life, no *joie de vivre*. What he achieved he achieved from a sense of duty, not from inclination. His innate puritanism looked askance on inclination, or so it seems. Although, as we shall see, there was another version of his character, the activity that suited him best, and gave his dual nature its most complete outlet, was sightseeing. As a sightseer he satisfied his ever-alert conscience, for who could say, what American of any epoch could say—and Hawthorne was a pioneer of sightseeing—that it did not enrich the personality, add to the store of learning, and so minister to the greater glory of God (whatever Hawthorne's conception of God was, if he had one)? Also he enjoyed it, not only for its own sake, and its moral function, but for the opportunity it gave him to exercise the powers of his golden pen.

As a sightseer, his son Julian was his constant companion, though only a lad. Julian, because he had access to Hawthorne's papers and to the letters between him and his wife (Hawthorne's letters to Herman Melville were I believe destroyed)—Julian, of course, was in a position to know a great deal about his father, and his biography, *Hawthorne and his Wife*, besides being a very well-written is also a very objective account of their relationship. Indeed, his tone when writing about his parents is sometimes as neutral as if he had been writing about anybody's parents. But since Hawthorne was 38 when he married Sophia, Julian can have known nothing directly about his father's formative years. His father's contemporaries may well have known more; and in any case close relations often know less about each other than outsiders know about them. Despite his objective approach, Julian was attached by piety and loyalty to his father's memory, yet even he admits that there were different and opposing interpretations of Hawthorne's character.

His writings show him as a man of placid temperament, unwilling to commit himself, putting a barrier of humour and irony between him and direct experience. But his son tells us that he was prone to fits of violent rage, which might account for his savage portrait of Judge Pyncheon, said to be founded on a prominent citizen of Salem, who had got him dismissed from his post at the Custom-House, and account, too, for the violence, or threat of violence, which is an element in many of his stories.

Pilgrim's Progress was one of his favourite books, and Mr. Facing-Both-Ways reminds us of him. There were two schools of thought about him, so Julian tells us, to account for his 'extraordinary undemonstrativeness'. Besides being an athlete, Julian, whose obituary notice recorded the facts that he lived to be over 80, and had a chest measurement of 46 inches, was a considerable novelist and *Sebastian Strome* might still be remembered, if the reputation of his father had not eclipsed it.

Trying to reconstruct his father's image, Julian says:

> The most common escape has lain in the direction of constructing an imaginary Hawthorne from what was assumed to be the internal evidence of his writings—a sort of morbid, timid, milk-and-water Frankenstein, who was drawn on by a grisly fascination to discuss fearful conceptions and was in a chronic state of being frightened almost into hysterics by the chimeras of his own fancy. His aversion from bores and ignorant or uncongenial intrusion was magnified into a superhuman and monstrous shyness; in the earlier part of his literary career, opinion was divided as to whether he were a young lady of a sentimental and moralizing turn of mind, or a venerable and bloodless sage, with dim eyes, thin white hair, and an excess of spirituality. ....

Meanwhile another school of Hawthorne analysts has sprung up. . . . These are persons some of whom were acquainted with Hawthorne during his bachelor days and for a time afterwards, and who maintain that he not only possessed broad and even low human sympathies and tendencies, but that he was by no means proof against temptation, and that it was only by the kind precaution and charitable silence of his friends that his dissolute excesses have remained so long concealed. Singularly enough, it is as a tippler that the author of *The Scarlet Letter* most frequently makes his appearance in the narratives of these expositors; he was the victim of an insatiable appetite for gin, brandy and rum, and if a bottle of wine were put on the table, he could hardly maintain a decent self-restraint.

Very naturally, Julian Hawthorne rebuts both of these charges against his father, but surely the truth must lie somewhere between them, between Hawthorne the saint and Hawthorne the sot? The two aspects of him seem to be irreconcilable, unless one regards them as both being forms of withdrawal—one from direct contact with the human race, which his moral sensibility was too delicate to mix with, and the other as a cruder form of escape, in gin and brandy and rum.

He wanted to escape from himself as well as from society, it seems, for he tells Sophia that if it had not been for her, he would have returned to his solitude, his bachelor solitude. She was in complete sympathy with him, she helped him along the way, and yet when he must have known that death was near, he preferred to face it away from home, in the company of Franklin Pierce, his old friend who had not again been nominated for the Presidency.

Julian also reports the legend that Hawthorne's death was due not so much to illness as to a drunken spree with his old friend.

How perplexed grows belief! One thing is certain, that towards the end of his life Hawthorne could not 'finalize' anything he wrote: the 'picturesque and gloomy wrongs' which, despite his statement to the contrary, he had found in abundance in New England, inspired his muse in a way in which the picturesque and gloomy wrongs of Old England, and in Europe generally, did not; even *The Marble Faun*, for all the beauty of its writing, is so choked with picturesqueness that the gloomy wrongs, though certainly existent, do not make their full effect: the setting is too elaborate for the theme. Europe proved a surfeit to his beauty-loving spirit; he could not finalize, in art, the experience it gave him. Why, we shall never know, unless there was some psycho-somatic influence, started by the witch's curse, perhaps, that warred against his talent and his life.

Hawthorne the writer is one of the most individual and recognizable of novelists; hardly a paragraph he wrote could have been written by anyone else. But in spite of the multitude of contemporary witnesses, and of subsequent sleuths bent on finding out his secret, Hawthorne the man remains baffling and not to be finalized—the Sphinx that he wished, or was condemned, to be.

V

'THE NEAR AND THE FAR'

UNLIKE ANY other novel in the field of English fiction, L. H. Myers's tetralogy, *The Near and the Far*, has a place to itself. Nor does it markedly resemble, except in general style and in having a philosophic intention, any of his other works. It comes nearest, perhaps, to *The Orissers*, the first and most considerable of them. Just as in *The Orissers* certain characters are made to illustrate certain illusions and delusions that beset the human mind, so here the conflicting claims of Buddhism, Christianity, Hinduism, and many other creeds and philosophies are embodied in the persons of the story who have embraced their tenets.

But there is one characteristic that *The Near and the Far* shares with *The 'Clio'* and *Strange Glory* as well as with *The Orissers*, and that is the exoticism of its setting. A realistic setting was distasteful to Myers; he wanted to isolate his characters against a background utterly remote from that of everyday life—especially of everyday English life. I remember his telling me that the idea of one of his characters walking down Piccadilly oppressed and frustrated him. Accordingly, much of the scene of *The Orissers* is laid in a distant and almost fabulous district in Wales, the passengers of the *Clio* are becalmed on the Amazon, while the characters in *Strange Glory* enjoy their idyllic romance in a moss-hung bayou of New Orleans.

In *The Near and the Far* he went much further than this in separating his story from the world we live in. To indicate the scope and intention of the book, I cannot do better than quote his own words:

This is not a historical novel, although the action is placed in the time of Akbar the Great Mogul (who was a contemporary of Queen Elizabeth's), nor is it an attempt to portray Oriental modes of living and thinking. I have done what I liked with history and geography as well as with manners and customs. Facts have been used when they were useful, or ignored or distorted when they were inconvenient. Few of my characters bear the names of real people, and of these the only person drawn with any regard for historical truth is the Emperor.

In choosing sixteenth-century India as a setting, my object was to carry the reader out of our familiar world into one where I could—without doing violence to his sense of reality—give prominence to certain chosen aspects of human life and illustrate their significance. It has certainly not been my intention to set aside the social and ethical problems that force themselves upon us at the present time. On the contrary my hope has been that we might view them better from the distant vantage-ground of an imaginary world.

He goes on to say that the writing of the book took him ten years. The first volume, *The Near and the Far* (the nomenclature of the books is rather confusing), was published in 1931; the last, *The Pool of Vishnu*, in 1940.

This is important, for during those years, the troubled years of the 'thirties, Myers's political ideas, in fact most of his ideas, underwent a fundamental change. At the outset he was a patron and amateur of the arts—a very serious-minded one, but without, I think, any settled political convictions; and he emerged to all intents and purposes a Communist.

The change affected his whole outlook. He became very intolerant of any political ideas that differed from his own and hostile to the people who held them. But if it affected his attitude to life it did not affect his way of living, which was that of a rich man, an enlightened hedonist and an aristocrat—all the things of which, as a Communist, he most disapproved. Although he did not believe that a man's political convictions need be reflected in his behaviour, he was never, I think, quite comfortable about the apparent discrepancy between his precepts and his practice, and this may have had something to do with the extremeness of his later views and the violence with which he expressed them. He may have felt that his personal position was vulnerable and that attack was the best means of defence.

To those who had known him in the 'twenties, a fastidious individualist and epicure, ploughing a lonely furrow, possessed of an exquisite wry sense of humour of which he was half-ashamed, and an unequalled gift for entering into the minds and problems of his friends, the change was startling. How had it come about?

As with so many other literary figures of the 'thirties, the rise of Fascism was the cause. Fascism, he felt, must be destroyed. Communism was to be the instrument of its destruction and into Communism he put his whole heart and soul. Half-measures were abhorrent to him. 'Intention must never be adulterated', says the Guru, the holy man, in *The Pool of Vishnu*. 'A terrible purity of intention is demanded of man.'

Although, as I have said, *The Near and the Far* is a work unique in literature, it owed something of its mood and tempo and even of its method to another great novel. This was *The Tale of Genji*, a work which Myers enormously admired. The quality of its sensibility was curiously akin to his own. Love and intrigue, conducted in the most civilized manner possible, those were things which instinctively appealed to him. And its melancholy appealed to him, too. A certain clear, pensive, melancholy was, before he became a Communist, the natural climate of his mind, as it was of Lady Murasaki's.

But she was not a philosopher, she was not interested in ideas as he was. In the first three volumes of *The Near and the Far*, and indeed in the last, though in a rather different way, the ideas are as important as the characters: you might almost say they *are* characters. Rajah Amar, the Buddhist, who is about to renounce the world and become a monk; his wife Sita, the Christian, who is able to love the world in spite of its imperfections; little Prince Jali, their son, whose education in life and suffering is one of the main themes of the book; Ghokal the Brahmin, whose wisdom of thought and speech is almost fatally contradicted by the folly of his life—his mad infatuation for the beautiful, worthless Gunevati; Hari Khan, the amorist; Ambissa and Srilata, those worldly ladies whose delight is in the gossip of the Court: these are persons in the story but they also embody the ideas that animate it: they illustrate aspects of the spiritual life or condemn the absence of it. And it was to affirm the supremacy of the Spirit as the guiding principle of life that Myers wrote his great novel. All the more surprising is it that he should finally have embraced the most materialistic of doctrines—Communism.

Behind and towering above the other personages of the story is the mysterious and gigantic figure of the illiterate Akbar: the Emperor, the dictator, and one might say—for so he almost thought of himself—the god. The gradual build-up of Akbar is extraordinarily impressive, everything we hear whets our curiosity; but when at last we are allowed to see him he is sadly disappointing, almost a buffoon. For by this time Myers's anti-dictator prejudice had taken such a strong hold of him that any ruler, however well-meaning (and on the whole Akbar was well-meaning), had become anathema.

It is not easy to disentangle the principal themes of this tremendous and most complex work. Perhaps the dominant one is Rajah Amar's resolution to abandon his great position and become a monk—a resolution continually frustrated by the personal and political problems that crowd upon him. Only at the end of the third book, and then almost as the result of an accident, does he achieve his desire. Aloof from humanity, as far as circumstances allow him to be, he bears his troubles with Oriental serenity, whereas his son, Jali, and his mentor, Ghokal, are tormented both in flesh and spirit. Myers was himself a hypochondriac and his characters reflect his preoccupation with his health. They are always falling ill. Ghokal is certainly once, and possibly twice, poisoned by his mistress, Gunevati, a girl so utterly vile that one cannot be altogether sorry when she has her tongue cut out. Jali is a neurotic child who sweats and even swoons from fear; but he is also a boy of spirit and never shirks the call of adventure or experience. His spiritual life is developed very early and mainly through the instruction of Ghokal, to whom he is fast bound by ties of reverence and affection. Even *l'homme moyen sensuel* of the book, Hari Khan, Jali's uncle, one of the few characters who acts on impulse and lives for the moment, is a spiritually-minded man.

Very seldom does Myers present emotions, even those of love and hate, in the raw: they are remembered in tranquillity, softened by the author's enfolding sensibility, and dimmed by veils of ambiguity and doubt: for in this book things are seldom what they seem. The characters grope blindly in a thick fog of intrigue and half-knowledge: few of them can fully trust each other: the friend of today may be the enemy of tomorrow. Spies are everywhere.

The action centres in the rivalry of Prince Salim and Prince Daniyal, Akbar's two sons, for the succession. Salim is a man of action and a boor; Daniyal is an aesthete and a pervert and an exceedingly unpleasant man. He is, in fact, an incarnation of wickedness; and the incident where he treads on the head of the white Persian cat is one of the most nauseating in fiction.

(Incidentally, it is inconsistent with what we have been earlier told, that Daniyal could not bear the sight of physical pain.) On the shore of a lake Daniyal sets up 'The Camp', a colony of aesthetes with tastes akin to his own: nameless orgies, we understand, take place there. The Camp is a scandal, a source of unlimited evil, into which the young Jali is drawn. What will happen to it and its master? Will they prevail and spread their poison through Society? The worldlings of the book, the gossips and the Court ladies, all those who want to be in the social swim, are tolerant if not actually admiring of the Camp.

At the end of the third book the Camp's fate is settled and with it Rajah Amar's, and in a sense the story comes to an end. The air has been cleared, the evil purged, and some of the personal problems have been solved. All the same, one could not say that any conclusion had been arrived at, any single, dominant truth demonstrated, or any rule or way of life discovered. The views of Buddhist, Christian and Brahmin remain unreconciled.

Myers was a teacher: he often compared himself to the fox in the fable who, having lost his tail, thought that all the other foxes should lose theirs. He wanted to make converts. But in the first three books of *The Near and the Far* he does not show himself a proselytizer: in the symposium everyone is given a hearing, and we could not easily say on whose side the author is. When he reached the end of the third book, Communism was beginning to take hold of him and in it he thought he saw a solution to the troubles of mankind.

The Pool of Vishnu, though much the longest of the four books, is an epilogue; it is scarcely a continuation, still less a *dénouement*. And if it solves the problems that Myers was setting out to solve, it solves them along different lines from those suggested in the earlier books, and with the help of different characters. It is in fact an independent novel, tacked on to the preceding three.

True, many of the characters we know come into it, and Jali has a large but not very important role as listener and observer. But the protagonist, the Guru, the holy man, is completely new: and new also are his chief disciples: Princess Damayanti and her husband, Mohan. Their love-story—the Princess's efforts to get her rather selfish old father to consent to their marriage— constitutes the chief episode of the book: but its main feature is

the Guru's teaching, his belief in the essential goodness of man
—a belief which no one who had taken to heart the three previous
volumes could easily accept. Where, for instance, was the soul
of goodness in Prince Daniyal or Gunevati? Myers brushes this
aside, and the Guru, who has all the answers, holds the floor.
A man of transparent goodness, if at times a little prosy, he is
also extremely persuasive; but even if one agrees with him one
feels that the issues have now been unduly simplified, and his
yardstick is no adequate measure for the vast prospects that
were opened to us before.

Indeed, in *The Pool of Vishnu*, though it has moments of great
beauty, we leave behind the huge cloudy symbols of a high
romance and emerge into the light of common day. The mystery,
the depth upon depth of imaginative distance, rolls away and
we hear the Guru proclaiming his faith in human nature, and his
dissatisfaction with the present structure of Society. Let that be
changed, and all will be well.

> The bad condition of the world as a whole is, I think, largely due
> to the fact that nearly every highly placed person in it defends what
> is morally wrong in his own particular way of living on the grounds
> that somehow or other those particular conditions contribute to
> the public good.

But is this true? Do highly placed persons in fact use such arguments? And if they do, do not low-placed persons also use them?

The Guru's confident humanism seems to me an inadequate
answer to the problems put forward in the earlier books. It is
too narrow and too obvious to satisfy that vast and various
inquiry. Myers the visionary and mystic is much more impressive than Myers the revolutionary and humanist. By itself *The
Pool of Vishnu* might well seem a remarkable novel; it suffers
from the contrast with the others. And if we feel a little let down
it is because, in the others, we were lifted up into an ampler
aether in which we drew in wonder and awe and reverence with
every breath—an aether which perhaps no other novelist has
been able to create.

VI

THE NOVELS OF C. H. B. KITCHIN

THE NOVELS of Mr. C. H. B. Kitchin are well known
to connoisseurs, but not as well known to the general
public as they ought to be. One reason for this is, I think,
that like some other serious writers, he is also the author of a
number of detective stories—indeed it is by a detective story,
Death of My Aunt, that his name is most widely known; and the
two *genres*, instead of uniting to increase his literary reputation,
have divided and reduced it.

This is a great pity, for no novelist of our time is better
worth our attention. His four detective stories, *Death of My
Aunt*, *Crime at Christmas*, *Death of his Uncle*, and *The Cornish
Fox*, illustrate his qualities and are far from being regulation
detective stories, but they are inevitably limited by the detective
story conventions, and it is with his straight novels that I am
chiefly concerned. Even so I can only indicate a few of their
facets, so many-sided are they.

Two, *Streamers Waving* and *Mr. Balcony*, were written in
the nineteen-twenties; three, *The Sensitive One*, *Olive E* and
Birthday Party in the 'thirties; and after a long interval *The
Auction Sale* appeared in 1949.

Mr. Kitchin is responsive to the changing spirit of the times
and his books reflect it. *Streamers Waving* and *Mr. Balcony* have
a frivolous air, much as L. H. Myers's novel *The 'Clio'* had, or
Mr. Aldous Huxley's *Chrome Yellow*: the same impulse to escape
from the drabness of the war years into an exotic setting is
manifest in them. And equally manifest is the serious intention
underneath. With regard to *Streamers Waving* this needs some
qualification. The only one of Mr. Kitchin's novels to end in
unrelieved disaster, it is also the only one, I think, in which the
story is definitely more important than the ideas conveyed. Miss
Clame is an appealing creation and herself brimful of ideas; but

the only idea her brief career illustrates is the ironical one of a butterfly broken on the wheel—a fate which, in his later books, Mr. Kitchin does not reserve for butterflies. The interest of *Streamers Waving* is primarily a narrative interest: we want to know what will happen to Miss Clame; whereas of comparable interest with the narrative in *Mr. Balcony* is the way Mr. Balcony's ideas are to be worked out. What will come of his singular experiment in self-perversion, his determination to make himself precisely what Nature has not intended him to be? And how will it affect his guests on the yacht? Which is uppermost in him, the bully or the benefactor? He is not the only character in Mr. Kitchin's novels to use his wealth to experiment with other people's lives; Emmanuel Stride in *Olive E* does the same.

Unlike as they are in their underlying ideas, *Streamers Waving* and *Mr. Balcony* have at least two things in common which differentiate them from Mr. Kitchin's later work; they display an element of fantasy sometimes so strong as to overpower actuality, and a glitter of surface and brilliancy of technique that dazzle while they enchant. Fantasy is inherent in Mr. Kitchin's work: all his chief characters are capable of it, living as they do in their minds, and in remembered or anticipated dreads and pleasures; but in these two books—in Miss Clame's despairing yet ecstatic swim down the Thames (one of the highlights of Mr. Kitchin's work), and in Mr. Balcony's culminating experience in the jungle—actuality is sometimes lost sight of, which rarely happens in the later books except in moments of extreme horror, such as Dora's 'coffin' dream in *Birthday Party*.

As to the glitter and the brilliance, we can find a parallel and perhaps an origin for them in the novels of Ronald Firbank, an author whose influence on these early books is easily seen. There is the same exquisite artificiality, the same delight in bright colours and in eccentricity for its own sake, the same naughty innuendoes, the same wish to *épater* the bourgeois, the same glancing, allusive technique, the same shimmer of amusingness. But there the likeness ends; for whereas Ronald Firbank was often silly—indeed it was almost his *raison d'être* as a writer to be so—Mr. Kitchin, even at his most flippant or flamboyant, never is; he may differ from some people in what he thinks is reasonable, but he is determined to have reason on his side.

The Sensitive One might be called a transitional novel. It heralds the gloomy 'thirties; it is the bleakest, grimmest and in a way the saddest of Mr. Kitchin's books, with little or no irradiation of fantasy, and little of the consolation of 'just being alive' which, at one time or another, he allows to most of his characters. It also contains, in old, deaf Mr. Moxhay, tyrannizing over his descendants, one of the few really detestable characters that Mr. Kitchin has ever drawn. Like all his books, it is extremely thickly populated. Yet, closely as the family is knit, it is the least gregarious of Mr. Kitchin's novels, one has the impression that everyone, especially Margaret, is living and moving in isolation.

This interplay of gregariousness and isolation is central to Mr. Kitchin's thought and it becomes increasingly marked in *Olive E* and *Birthday Party*. These reflect, by reaction, the political tendencies of the times. Though not a thoroughgoing reactionary Mr. Kitchin is a passionate individualist, and as such loathes all forms of collectivism, compulsion and state control, whether Communist, Fascist or simply bureaucratic. With these, as enemies of the spirit, he couples Science. In *Olive E*, Emmanuel Stride, a wealthy publicist, acts as an *agent provocateur* in the political world. He is, one might say, brought in as a mouthpiece. Many of his tirades are taken down verbatim by his secretary, Olive Everett, and very funny they are—although, as in Disraeli's novels, with which Mr. Kitchin's have an affinity, they stand out from the fabric of the book, and give a 'stripy' effect.

In *Birthday Party* Mr. Kitchin also seeks to discredit Communism by making Ronald Carlice, heir to Carlice Abbey and a Communist convert, a callow and silly young man. But Ronald is at heart a Communist *malgré lui*; he whistles his doctrines to keep up his courage and his good conceit of himself, while in reality he belongs to the genus of sensitive plants which struggle to keep alive in Mr. Kitchin's garden. I use the metaphor advisedly, for gardens, trees, flowers and Nature generally are essential to Mr. Kitchin's outlook on life; they have an almost mystical value for him. The white hyacinths for whose sake Mr. Balcony kept his room uncomfortably cold recur throughout his novels. For the sake of retaining the salpiglossis Isabel Carlice is prepared to go any lengths. Love of flowers is at the heart of Mr. Kitchin's philosophy, or was, at this time: it crystallizes his longing to 'charge the vast material world with happy thoughts', and it extends to plants less romantic than the hyacinth (aspidistralatry is a leading motif in *Olive E*), and to inanimate objects, to furniture and china, to almost anything, in the material world, which the sensibility can fasten on and call its own. To the collectivizing ideologies of those days (and these) with their insistence on a uniform view of life, to the anodyne of mass feeling and mass thinking, he opposes his belief in the spiritual restorative power of the individual's private response to his material environment:

> Was this how life ought to be lived, passing things and repassing them in a railway carriage, developing affections for the familiar, and building a universe out of two narrow strips of land?

Mr. Kitchin's heroines, then—for he tends to have heroines rather than heroes—Lydia Clame, Gloria Swing, Margaret Moxhay, Olive Everett, Miss Elton of *The Auction Sale*—are diffident, sensitive, fastidious women, solitary souls making their own outlook on life. This is true, but is only half the truth, for with Mr. Kitchin's concern for the experience of the soul in solitude goes an equally lively and profound concern with its experience in society, and it is this duality of outlook which gives his books their astonishing richness of thought and texture. By itself, wrapped in its own microcosm, unaware of the external world, the sensitive soul, the subject of so many introverted novels, may easily become a bore; but with Mr. Kitchin the two sides of experience are shown as complementary, constantly modifying and enriching each other.

Despite his prejudice against collectivism and corporate feeling, each of his novels introduces us to a highly organized and distinct society and, it must be added, a very large one. Beginning a novel by Mr. Kitchin is an experience comparable to, though much more agreeable than, one's first day at school. These milieux are often at different social levels and belong to different income groups (Mr. Kitchin is keenly interested in money; it talks loudly in all his books) but they are carefully studied and differentiated, and their interaction gives him unending opportunities for delicate and satiric social comedy. The crowded canvases he delights in are evidence of his interest (usually an affectionate, if sometimes a sardonic interest) in mere people as opposed to sensitive souls seeking their own salvation in poetical reveries and interior monologues. But opposed is the wrong word. The two elements—the social comedy and the individual experience—are not opposed, they are fused, and from their fusion is generated the warmth and sympathy, the sense of human solidarity, which is always evident in Mr. Kitchin's work.

I have left *The Auction Sale* till last, partly because it is my favourite among Mr. Kitchin's books and also because it forms an eminence from which to view his progress and achievement as a novelist so far. It has much in common with the earlier books. Hanging over it is the shadow of a war and a consequent re-organization of society which Mr. Kitchin believes to be inevitable (in passing, one may note how many of his prophecies have come true). Like his earlier books it insists on the collectivist menace, though happily the unsympathetic Mr. Durrant's work on *The Future of the Personal Emotions* was rejected by his publisher. As they, and even more explicitly than they do, it testifies to the author's delight in beauty, whether in Nature or in Art. As they do it shows how he attains wholeness of vision by contemplating diversity rather than its opposite: 'love grows bright gazing on many truths', and those truths, in his case, are often homely and practical and worldly-wise, and in themselves neither romantic nor beautiful.

But there are also significant changes. In this matter of detail, for instance. 'The universe contains no problems but many details', reflects Miss Clame in *Streamers Waving*, and though later she comes up against plenty of problems, her dictum does to some extent influence her creator, with the result that *Olive E* is a little cluttered up with detail and one cannot always see the wood for the trees. *The Auction Sale* is also full of details—far more than there are lots in the sale—but they all have a further purpose: to remind Miss Elton of the past. Again, the tone of *Streamers Waving* and *Mr. Balcony* is at times metallic and a little harsh, their frivolity a little self-conscious; at times their cleverness obtrudes like an undimmed headlight; and at times the technique, varied and original as it is, has an uncomfortably jerky effect, like a series of small shocks delivered by some exquisite electrical gadget, gilded and bejewelled. The sympathy has a shell or hardness, and the wit an infusion of mannerism to increase its natural flow.

These excesses of virtuosity were faults of youth, and *The*

Auction Sale is entirely free from them. The 'surface' is still 'amusing' and the texture very close, but the book is written in a comparatively low tone and in a mood of acceptance. The technique is still sometimes staccato—and necessarily so, for it is punctuated by the auctioneer's hammer. But when we leave the sale marquee, with its good-natured but callous jokes and greedy acquisitiveness, for the past of which it is the cruel outcome, what a change! We find a softened, legato touch, an elegiac wistfulness, and a richness of reminiscence which never becomes cloying, because of the humour and pathos, the sense of the intrinsic value of tiny, separate happenings, with which it is invested. The time is June—June remembered in September—and Mr. Kitchin, whose sensitiveness to seasonal change is of the keenest, gets the utmost from the contrast. The long motor drive that Mrs. Durrant and Miss Elton take with Mr. Sorenius—the one wholly, the other half in love with him—is among the tenderest and most affecting scenes in modern fiction; and the episode of the 'Trissingham Twins' is as beautiful in itself as it is symbolically apt. The sense of tragedy is rare nowadays; fiction is full of terrible happenings, yet lacking in the sense of loss—personal loss, loss to posterity, beauty and happiness missed—which true tragedy requires. But we find it here, in the untimely death of the child violinist who had promised so much.

We may also note a change in Mr. Kitchin's attitude to external reality. Both Art and Nature are fully represented in *The Auction Sale* and the spiritual solace they provide is constantly invoked; but they are no longer elevated into a religion or even into a philosophy. It is primarily a love-story. The emphasis is on personal relationships, on 'The Pleasures of Love and Retirement'. 'You can't live on a beautiful view', observes a character in *The Cornish Fox*, and is not rebuked for a sentiment which in the earlier books might have been condemned as blasphemy.

Mr. Kitchin is always inquiring into the problem of 'what men live by'. After this advance, or retreat, from a Proustian aestheticism, what next? Miss Elton broods over the text, 'He knoweth thy walking through the great wilderness', and is comforted; while the clergyman's wife suggests that the contemplation of an herbaceous border, endlessly renewed, is a truer analogy of the joys of heaven than 'attending harp-class'. It would be rash to infer that Mr. Kitchin is about to become a religious novelist. Even if we take the view, sometimes put forward, that ethics and religion have nothing to do with each other, we have to admit that the Moral Law receives harsh treatment in his books. 'Moral progress' (roundly declares Miss Clame) 'is self-emancipation from the taboos of the so-called "Moral Law".' But I think there are signs that Mr. Kitchin will explore more fully than he has the intricacies of personal relationships and the feelings of people in love. About the relations of the One with the Many, and of the One with Itself (so to speak) he has always been explicit; but much less explicit about the relations of the One with the Other. In most of his novels the love-interest is either one-sided or, if reciprocal, introduced at the last moment like a *deus ex machina*. But in *The Auction Sale* Mrs. Durrant's happy-unhappy love-affair with Mr. Sorenius is fully shared by both, and its irradiating beauty and humanity are an earnest of what Mr. Kitchin may achieve in this vein.

A word as to his use of English. Few novelists of today write as well as he does, none writes better. Urbane, unmannered, flexible but firm, his prose style reflects the clarity of his mind and can do anything he asks of it—modulate from the trivial to the momentous, from the prosaic to the eloquent, without ever losing the poise and authority of literature.

★

After this essay was finished Mr. Kitchin wrote four more books: *Jumping Joan*, a collection of macabre short stories, and three novels, *The River of Life*, *Ten Pollitt Place*, and *The Book of Life*, which won high praise from the critics but did not, alas, attract the public.

He died in 1967.

VII

IN DEFENCE OF THE SHORT STORY

SHORT STORIES are being eagerly read; they are a regular feature of evening papers, some Sunday papers, and of magazines, reviews and periodicals. Perhaps they have never been so much read as they are now. They are read in book form too, but not so greedily. Why? Why do readers devour them singly on a newsheet, or between paper covers, but only nibble at them when they are collected in a book?

It is partly prejudice, I think, and partly laziness. What is there against short stories as such, or—since people obviously enjoy them singly—against short stories *en masse*? No doubt the economic factor counts. Why bother to buy a collection of stories when for a small sum you can get several newspapers, each with a story thrown in? The novel suffers much less from this form of competition; serialized novels are rare; people who want to read novels must buy, borrow or steal them.

But to return to the prejudice against short stories in book form. Individually, we are told, they don't last long enough for the habitual novel-reader; collectively, they last too long—or rather, they induce a surfeit. A dozen short courses are harder for the mind to digest than one long course. Similarly, in conversation, a single anecdote may be fun to listen to, but who could listen to twelve anecdotes on end? The first few paragraphs of a story demand unusual concentration. 'Starting and stopping' exhausts the reader's attention just as starting and stopping uses up the petrol in a car. Another thing is that a novel grows, or should grow, more interesting as it goes on, whereas short stories, in bulk, are subject to a sort of law of diminishing returns: they decrease in interest, in proportion as one's ability to take them in decreases.

These are some of the reasons why people fight shy of a

collection of short stories, and as I said they are mostly lazy reasons, the reasons of those who read simply for relaxation, to pass the time.

Short stories of purely ephemeral interest never find their way into collections. The chosen few are, it must be admitted, for alert readers. For them, a volume of short stories is at least as good value as a novel. It probably contains more ideas, since each story is based on an idea; it has much greater variety of mood, scene, character and plot, for the author will at any rate try not to repeat himself. And, on the whole, it is better written. Almost anyone, it is said, can write a novel, providing he has interesting material. But it takes an artist to write a short story, just as it takes an artist to relate an anecdote. A short story that isn't a work of art, at some level, would hardly get into print— even if the art is only artfulness, a trick up the writer's sleeve. It has to be tightly constructed, with hardly a word wasted or misplaced. A novel is a portmanteau into which nearly anything can be thrust, but a short story must be stripped to its bare essentials. From the literary standpoint the average volume of short stories is a better bargain than the average novel; better worth buying, better worth keeping.

If this were realized, I think that short stories in book form would be more popular than they are. It is a question of acquiring a taste for them. In spite of the proverb one *can* argue about taste: everybody does, and one result is that tastes change. The fashion for going to picture-galleries has grown enormously of recent years. Pictures are not consecutive; each has to be studied on its own merits and looked at with a fresh eye. This means a strain on the attention, but increasing numbers of people find it pleasurable; they have discovered the secret of enjoying it. Might they not find the same satisfaction in studying a gallery of short stories, if they tried?

A novel appeals in the same way that a portrait does—through the richness of its human content. In the past certain novels achieved the distinction of being *loved*: *The Pickwick Papers* for instance, and *Little Women*. Mr. Pickwick, Mr. Tupman, Mr. Snodgrass and Mr. Winkle were personally dear to the public; so were Meg, Jo, Beth and Amy. More recently, the lovable nature of its hero won a similar distinction for *Good-bye, Mr. Chips*. How, it might be asked, can short stories be loved in the same way, when we have no time to get to know their characters? And yet they have been: Hans Andersen's, for instance, and Kipling's, and O. Henry's and Conan Doyle's. Agatha Christie's detective novels are deservedly popular, but I doubt if they are loved in the same way that the 'Adventures' or the 'Memoirs' of Sherlock Holmes were, and still are. True, the latter had the advantage of one personality running through them; they were short stories·where the same hero recurs. Sherlock Holmes hardly seems a character to inspire affection, yet he did, and so have other characters in short stories, however briefly delineated. Who can forget Hans Andersen's *Mermaid* or the boy and girl in *The Snow Queen?*

But it is not only an author's characters that endear him to the public: it is also a quality in his mind, that appears with greater or less distinctness in everything he writes. Short stories themselves may be discontinuous but the mind behind them is not; in different guises, and in brief samples, it can be relied on to give people something that they want, something recognizable and characteristic: a point of view they sympathize with. One still hears people say, 'That's like something in a story by Maupassant or Tchekov'—showing that those writers created a world that was solid and self-consistent, though it only revealed itself in snapshots.

So a volume of short stories has a continuity—not a continuity of character and plot, but a continuity of viewpoint that serves the same end. This the public at large recognizes and enjoys in the work of Somerset Maugham, H. E. Bates, and some other practitioners of the short story; but it is capricious and suspicious and unenterprising and bestows its favours in a chancy fashion. My contention is that as with picture-galleries, so with collections of short stories—if the public gave them a trial it would find in them a reservoir of varied entertainment that hitherto it has only tapped.

VIII

'LEFT HAND, RIGHT HAND'

THE FOUR volumes of Sir Osbert Sitwell's autobiography together make a work of art for which it is difficult to find an analogy in literature. To begin with, the majority of autobiographies, even if written with art, are not works of art, any more than a man's life-history is. They follow a chronological order and are inspired by a single aim, to trace one man's development. He looks into a mirror and puts down what he sees; it is a continuous close-up, with hardly more background and much less sense of design than the average painted portrait has.

Left Hand, Right Hand is a work of tremendous complexity and subtlety in which the facts of the author's life are only one of many interests. His is the most pervasive figure in the drama of an age which reached its zenith in 1914 and has since traced a downward curve. The four books have been conceived and constructed in such a way as to illustrate this drama, which goes on, and is felt, independently of the author's personal fortunes. This is the outermost circumference of the story; but within it there are many lesser concentric orbits, politics. literature, society, in all of which the author moved and on which he left his mark, before we come to those inner rings which were more strictly personal to him—his beginnings as an author, his experiences as a soldier, his youth, his childhood, his family and his father.

In the intensity of the gaze that he turns upon the past Sir Osbert resembles Proust; à la recherche du temps perdu is a passion with him, and like Proust he can recapture the essential flavour of the act of living. His interest in Time is not metaphysical as Proust's was. Yet Time is more than a frame for his picture, it is integral to his narrative and might almost be counted one of the characters. We are continually aware of it, like a wind

blowing past us. Like Proust he burrows, but he even more
eagerly explores the surface; his curiosity about the forms life
takes, as well as about the human beings who compose it, is
insatiable. Foreign people, places and ways have a limitless
fascination for him. The marvellous attracts him no less than
the known. And he is intensely interested in origins, in genealo-
gies, in the enduring effects of blood and race in making human
beings what they are. And therefore in his own origins and how
he came to be what he is.

The lines of the left hand, it is said, denote the qualities one
is born with, those of the right the characteristics one acquires
for oneself. This dual aspect of his career, and its interaction, is
never far absent from his mind; and it is reinforced by another,
parallel duality, which was thrust upon him by his relations with
his father. Sir George Sitwell had very definite ideas of what he
wanted all his children to be, and not to be; but it was upon his
elder son that he exerted the severest and most constant pressure
of his formidable personality. His influence was used to strengthen Sir Osbert's left-hand characteristics. Its effect was to
strengthen those of his right hand, but this was only brought
about by a continuous struggle which ended when the book
ends, with his father's death.

Sir George was the author's *alter ego*, his *âme damnée*, his
relentless opponent in his struggle for personal and even for
financial independence. And his importance in the autobiography, considered as a work of art, corresponds to his importance in his son's life. He balances and dramatizes it. Largely
thanks to him and his infinite meddlesomeness, it is not a one-
man show, with the inevitable monotony and egotistic preoccupation of a self-portrait extended over four volumes; it is
not a *pas seul*, but a *pas de deux*, a figure capable of endless
variations and unexpected developments.

By reaction, Sir George Sitwell was the chief formative factor
in his son's development. But that is putting it too crudely, for
his son made prodigious efforts to meet his father's wishes, to
understand him, to be amused by him and not to be afraid of him
or angry with him. In the end he succeeded in externalizing his
redoubtable parent, and a figure emerges not indeed so amiable
as Don Quixote or the White Knight in *Alice Through the
Looking-glass*, but touched with the same disarming absurdity
and seen in the same light of transforming fantasy. The tyrant

of Renishaw whose icy good manners disturbed the nervous systems of nearly all with whom he came in close contact, whose ignorance of other people's natures was only matched by his desire to bend them to his will, becomes the rather touching exile of Montegufoni, solitary except for a single friend, still occupied with grandiose schemes of architectural embellishment and extension, still invested with the personal dignity that never forsook him, but no longer an object of awe and dread.

There is no doubt that the conflict between the two widened and deepened Sir Osbert's nature and enriched his work. Reacting against his father's policy of indignant and irritable isolation, of regarding almost everyone he met as wantonly unreasonable, his son instinctively developed the powers of sympathy and understanding with other human beings which continually nourish and irrigate his autobiography. Like Dickens, whom he so much admires, he has a deep though not uncritical affection for human nature; and his sympathies are the wider because he seldom writes as a moralist. When he feels moral indignation it comes out in the form of satire, and he thus avoids the loss of poise and balance which avowed anger produces. He is the master of ridicule of our age, as Pope was of his; but he does not kill his victims, as Pope did; he leaves them with a few shreds of fantasy about them to fight, and be worsted, another day.

The lesson of detachment which he learned from his struggle with his father, and the gift of externalization it brought with it, has borne fruit in the particular quality of his observation. He sees people, as Dickens did, always with the eye of fantasy and often with a touch of poetry. Realism in a sketch or portrait never satisfies him.

But though he rebelled against his father's will he did not rebel indiscriminately against what his father stood for, and he interpreted his inheritance and accepted its practical obligations in a fuller and more traditional sense than his father ever did. Though his aesthetic outlook was inborn, it was not until 1916, with the publication of his first poem in *The Times*, that he decided to be a writer. Until then he was engaged in sampling, and trying to choose from, the multitude of courses open to him. Of these the life of a country gentleman at Renishaw was the most obvious and engaged perhaps his deepest loyalties. The landscape that occurs most often to his mind is the Derbyshire landscape—softened by Claude-like reminiscences of Italy. But his life had many centres, physical, intellectual, and emotional. Scarborough and Whitby imbued him with a passion for the sea, fostering and enriching his imagination just as surely as his schooldays cramped and starved it. London meant the Army and the Tower, and experiences alien, though not unamusing, to his spirit; it also meant Lambeth Palace, and a strong family strain of evangelical piety, difficult for his constitution to absorb. It also meant, as the years went on, the Russian Ballet, the discovery of Bloomsbury and the literary world. Later, it meant fame and influence and the glitter of social life; but the war of 1914–18 had come between, troubling his spirit with a restlessness which could only be appeased in far-off countries—in Pekin and Angkor and Guatemala. The experience he gained from these places was deep-seated; it yielded him a spectrum of impressions but also affected him fundamentally and helped to make him the various-minded, many-feeling'd writer that he is.

What we find, in the autobiography, is the residue of these diverse experiences, perfectly assimilated, recollected with marvellous fidelity, and bathed in the unifying light of an unwearying aesthetic sensibility. Nearly half a century of English life is unrolled before us, and a cross-section of society laid bare in which every vein is auriferous. Often disregarding chronology, Sir Osbert marshals his subject-matter in masses like a painter, placing each section where its effect will be most telling. The effect of unity is further strengthened by his prose, a highly individual medium which he has fashioned for himself, with its long rhythms and inexhaustible variety of pace, cadence and attack. Certainly he has reduced his reminiscences, in all their diversity, to a personal idiom and that a highly aesthetic one; yet the process has not drawn the life and vividness out of them, on the contrary it has lent them a new freshness. For some writers the act of writing is a thing apart from their daily lives, a function independent of their other functions. Sir Osbert Sitwell is fortunate in that he lives what he writes; his thought is an integral part of him, and conveys the whole of him, past and present. As his image of the Scarlet Tree with its branching veins and arteries suggests, he writes from the blood-stream, not from the ink-pot.

What is the secret of the popularity of *Left Hand, Right Hand*? First of all, perhaps, its zest for life, and the immense hospitality of the author's mind, which can simultaneously accommodate, without embarrassment, a king and a cab-driver, and pay almost equal attention to his father and his father's footman. And then it is in the main a happy book. It might easily not have been for Sir Osbert did not have an easy time. His childhood, his schooldays, the disintegration in his home life, the 'running shadow' that threatened to engulf the happiness of the whole family, his father's financial worries which, whether real or imagined, were always being drummed into him, the disturbing contrast, so difficult to adapt himself to, between his father's aloofness and his mother's demonstrativeness—all this must have seemed like chaos. Told by a writer with an impulse to self-pity, what a jeremiad we might have had!

But this is not a hard-luck story, it is a tale of success in the fullest and most honourable meaning of the word—success against odds, odds which continued to be against him even when he had fought his way into the literary arena. This spirit of success he manages to communicate to the reader, who shares its exhilaration.

Sir Osbert has not courted popularity. He makes no secret of the fact that he prefers the past to the present. 'I belonged by birth, education, nature, outlook and period to the pre-war era, a proud citizen of the great free world of 1914, in which comity prevailed.' He dislikes sport, and seldom misses an opportunity of deriding it. He denounces war ('Heroism has never been my favourite virtue'). In the abstract he disapproves of the 'common man', though in practice he generally finds him sympathetic. He takes up minority causes, and the only modern phenomenon that he does insistently champion—modern art—may not endear him to the majority of readers. Yet in spite of all this his work is a 'best-seller'. Major works of art were frequently best-sellers in the nineteenth century, but not in the twentieth.

A popularity achieved in defiance of probability is worth inquiring into. When *Wheels* came out in 1916—an annual collection of modern verse edited by Edith Sitwell—not yet Dame Edith—it aroused hostility in almost every section of the reading public. High-brows and low-brows made common cause against the contributors. 'Conceived in morbid eccentricity and executed in fierce fictitious gloom' was one comment. That Sir Osbert's prose is more traditional than his poetry is undeniable; it is also true that in the autobiography we find a breadth of subject and humanity of outlook more marked than in any of his earlier work. Yet there is the same challenge to the reader's comfortable prejudices, the same determination to make him use his mind and breathe an air which is unfamiliar to him, the same scrupulous adherence to an exacting aesthetic standard. These qualities were not likely to make for popularity but surprisingly they have.

The importance of this can hardly be overestimated, for it means that the ever-widening gap between the high-brow and the low-brow—the gap that was threatening art itself with extinction—has at last been bridged. No longer need we feel that readers are divided into two nations, self-consciously aware of and hostile to each other, for here they have met on common ground. Most of the credit must go to Sir Osbert who has known how to make these incompatibles acceptable to each other, but some is due to the public too, for having learned from the author a lesson in connoisseurship which was all the harder to learn because it involved a certain amount of self-criticism. That a great imaginative writer may now hope to address himself to the many as well as to the few is surely a happy augury for the future of English literature.

IX

EDITH SITWELL

NEARLY EVERY important artist is to some extent an interpreter of his times, he gives the bent and impress of his mind to material that is already there; and this is true of Miss Edith Sitwell. She was in the van of the aesthetic renaissance that started in the First World War. That renaissance was also a reaction: a reaction against 'mud and blood' and against the type of literature, realism or satire, that had been wallowing in mud and blood. The reaction took various forms. The 'Georgian' school of poets turned to nature, landscape and the countryside: Edmund Blunden found in the cricket field, the village green, the country church, and in meticulous observation of birds, trees, flowers and clouds, peace and healing for emotions excoriated by the war. The poetry of John Clare had a noteworthy revival, and

> The lesser missel-thrush that perches
> On the lower boughs of birches

suddenly enjoyed a tremendous vogue.

Miss Sitwell had no part in this movement, indeed she was critical of it. For her, reaction from the war meant recoil from stereotyped emotions expressed in tired language, from the tyranny of the mind over the senses, from dull tones and safety-first tactics. She brought to poetry bright colours, hard shining surfaces, and a general electrification of moribund and sleepy words. The Ballet was then at its height. Miss Sitwell's poems danced a ballet and accepted the ballet's convention, its appeal to the mind through the senses, and its stylized emotion, Possibly this convention owed something to French examples. but as it appeared, fully developed, in English literature, it was the invention of Miss Sitwell and her brothers, for in spite of differences in what they saw, they saw through the same eyes.

In prose, a comparable achievement was Ronald Firbank's. He had the same gift for creating beauty, wit, humour and even pathos by applying a highly stylized point of view to the natural, the humdrum, and the familiar. Seen in the light of his sophistication the great out-of-doors became almost blushingly self-conscious.

Miss Sitwell, though she did not follow the example of the Georgian poets in their way of presenting Nature, was just as much inspired by Nature as they were. 'I was brought up in the country,' she writes in the preface to her *Selected Poems*,

> and mine is a country world. The artificiality of which my poems are accused is such that when I write of emotion I try to strip the passion down to the barest possible expression, a quintessential simplicity. When my poems deal with emotion they are always the most simple and primitive emotions of simple and primitive people . . . I was born by the wildest seas that England knows, and my earliest recollection is of the tides, the wild rush of waves, the sweep onward, heard night and day, so that it seemed the sound of one's own blood.

That was in 1936. To those who are familiar with Miss Sitwell's poems written during the present war it may well seem grotesque that she was ever accused of artificiality. And, in any case, why 'accused'? Why must 'artificial' bear a pejorative meaning? The artificial is only to be avoided if it is a substitute for the real, and not always then. If it is used, as Miss Sitwell used it from the first, as her brothers used it and as Ronald Firbank used it, to heighten the reality of an object or an idea, to surprise it into a new vividness of meaning—then there can be no objection to artificiality. As well object to a lantern on the ground that its light is artificial. What we want is to *see*, and any device that helps towards that is laudable, however artificial it may be.

Perhaps to revive the question of Miss Sitwell's 'artificiality' at this time of day is to flog a dead horse. But even if her early work is artificial, I still think that a new way of looking at things, tending to reveal reality rather than to obscure it, is a merit, not a defect.

A new way of looking at things was one of Miss Sitwell's contributions to the poetry of our day. 'My senses', she says, 'are interchangeable; where the language of one sense is insufficient to convey a meaning, a sensation, I use another.'

All poets have done this, more or less; the difference is that whereas their borrowings are often inadvertent, Miss Sitwell's are nearly always deliberate, an intentional transference of the language of one sense to another. Often they need no explanation: 'furred is the light' refers to misty moonlight; the 'reynard-coloured sun' explains itself, as do the 'cotton-nightcap trees'. And if some of the references are, as Miss Sitwell herself says, too recondite, e.g. 'the Martha-coloured scabious' and the 'Emily-coloured primulas', still they are enriching, even if we are not aware that Miss Sitwell's nursery-maid, Martha, once wore a scabious-coloured gown and that the primula reminded the poet of the bright pink cheeks of country girls, so often christened Emily. Moreover, her linking together of a flower, a colour, and a human being, as though all three were aspects of the same thing, is very characteristic of her philosophy, which is unifying, and intent on discovering the essential likeness in all created things. I shall return to this, for it is a vital principle of her poetry.

Though one of the most individual, Miss Sitwell is one of the least personal of poets, if by personal one means a poet who writes for the sake of self-expression. The word 'I' seldom occurs in her poetry and if it does, there is no weight of egoism behind it. She is the vehicle, not the subject, of her inspiration. More than that, she tells us that many of her early poems—those in *Façade*, for instance, 'are, for the most part, abstract patterns, difficult technical experiments . . . inquiries into the effect on rhythm and on speed, of the use of rhymes, assonances and dissonances, placed outwardly, at different places in the line, in most elaborate patterns . . .'

It is unwise to quarrel with an author's definition of his own work, and if Miss Sitwell says the poems in *Façade* are abstract patterns and technical experiments, then they are. But I submit that they are a good deal besides. At the word experiment in connection with literature (and indeed in connection with science) one's heart sinks; one remembers the brilliant talents—Gertrude Stein's, James Joyce's—that have gone astray in the mazes of word-patterns, forsaking meaning to achieve—what? Certain aesthetic effects perceptible to an ear attuned, but even at their most successful constituting an esoteric game to be enjoyed by the few and even by them only with the help (one suspects) of a good deal of self-deception. The sound-effects

Miss Sitwell analyses so minutely are not, it should be noted, effects that belong exclusively or even mainly to an abstract pattern; her choice and placing of vowels and consonants may be, and no doubt are, deliberate, but as she abundantly shows, they are intended to make clear the meaning of the poem, to hasten its message to the mind, whereas a pattern has only value to the eye and ear. In her *Poet's Note Book* Miss Sitwell observes that 'the poet's mind has become a central sense, interpreting and controlling this and the five senses'. If the mind (*pace* Helvetius) is 'the product of the senses' it cannot be satisfied with the evidence of one of them.

Most readers get from *Façade* meanings more intelligible and articulate and images more precise than any that could be conveyed by a word-pattern and it is inevitable they should, for as Miss Sitwell herself says of these poems,

> Some deal with materialism and the world crumbling into dust, some have as protagonists shadows or ghosts, moving, not in my country world, but in a highly mechanical universe; others have beings moving:
>
> *To the small sound of Time's drum in the heart,*
>
> figures gesticulating against the darkness, from the warmth and light of their little candle-show.

Just so; the poems have a subject, they are about something· In literature a word-pattern must be a means to a meaning, it cannot stand by itself, as it does in a carpet. So that in these poems we have meaning as well as music, sense as well as sound.

Façade was written in 1922, a year when the ordinary observer did not suspect that the world was crumbling to dust, far from it. Most poets are prophets, and Miss Sitwell can claim the gift of prophecy in a special degree.

In this connection one is reminded that though she has written at some length about the technique of her poetry, she has said very little about the ideas underlying it, and about her personal experience as a poet, almost nothing.

We must admire her reticence, the reticence of a craftsman to whom his craft is more important than his own performance in it. Miss Sitwell's enthusiasm is for poetry, not for herself as a poet. Her verses do not unlock her heart. Her attitude towards her poetry has always been strictly professional; hers is

> *The strain seraphically free*
> *From taint of personality.*

But poetry springs from emotion, whether recollected in tranquillity or pouring into the ink that flows from the poet's pen. Anyone reading *Gold Coast Customs* for the first time must be overwhelmed by the emotion it arouses. It acts on the nerves of the mind like a violent irritant; and we ask, from what reservoir of feeling does this spiritual vitriol come? Miss Sitwell herself answers the question in a most illuminating note—one of the few that answers the 'why' of her poetry instead of the 'how'.

'The organization of the poem, of a world where all the natural rhythms of the spirit, of the soil, and of the seasons have broken down, but where a feverish intertwining seething movement, a vain seeking for excitement, still exists, presented considerable difficulties.' She goes on to speak of 'this world of the rich man Judas, brother Cain', where

> man is part ravenous beast of prey, part worm, part ogre, or is but the worm turned vertebrate. It is a world where the light is no longer a reality, but a high ventriloquist sound (so high none knows whence it comes), the octave of the black clotted night—no longer the true and guiltless Light:
>
> > (*Christ that takest away the sin*
> > *Of the world, and the rich man's bone-dead grin*)

This is all I can bring myself to say about the poem except from a technical point of view.

Later she writes:

> Throughout the whole poem I have tried to produce, not so much the record of a world, as the wounded and suffering soul of that world, its living evocation, not its history, and seen through the eyes of a protagonist whose personal tragedy is echoed in that vaster tragedy. Of the other implicit meanings of the poem I am unwilling to speak.

No one could have written *Gold Coast Customs* without suffering. Indeed, the poem *is* suffering, suffering in the raw, suffering that is felt along the nerves like a tooth being pulled out, suffering that the mind has not had time to assimilate. It is almost the only poem of Miss Sitwell's that is aimed primarily at the reader's nerves. It is not her best poem, but it is terribly effective and it marks a turning-point in her poetic development.

It is a kind of watershed dividing the stream of her work into two valleys, one of which, the narrower, is all sunshine, and the other, broad and still broadening out, is the valley with which her war poems have made us familiar, a tremendous landscape embracing many climates, many temperatures from torrid heat to polar cold, in which the features are enormous but less sharply defined, and in which the antitheses are on the grandest possible scale, day and night, summer and winter, life and death.

In the one there is no explicit and comparatively little underlying philosophy. Things perceived through the senses wear their face value, their value to the senses; beauty, in such poems as *The Soldan's Song* and *Most Lovely Shade*, is an invocation from words and sounds and images, almost unrelated to human emotion, saved from abstraction only by the vague pathos, the sense of too much beauty, creating a need it cannot quite satisfy, that we feel in the pictures of Giorgione (Miss Sitwell's romantic mood has much in common with his). These poems are sufficient in themselves; they raise no questions and expect no answers, any more than do those delicate decorative pieces, *Through Gilded Trellises* and *The Governante's Song* and *Lily O'Grady*, that take the ear with the delicate rattle of castanets. We are in a pagoda country, superimposed on an English landscape, guests as it were of an Eastern potentate or a magician whose whim it is to charm and divert us; strange words, pelongs, buchauls, pallampores, woo us with soft sounds; braying words, brocade, promenade, arcade, ambassade, prick us with sharp ones; ingenious rhymes tickle our ears, the lines are short and staccato, and the pace break-neck. And if a hint of suffering creeps in, as it sometimes does:

> *Jane, Jane*
> *Forget the pain*
> *In your heart. Go, work again!*

—it is quickly and discreetly banished. And the mythological personages who haunt these scenes are queens and princesses, rustics and milkmaids, or 'chinoiserie ghosts' whose emotions need never be taken seriously.

Of course the division is not water-tight; some of these earlier poems (the *Four Elegies*, for instance) are as tragic if not with quite the same depth of suffering, as any Miss Sitwell has written. But in the main it holds good. If her high spirits were not so spontaneous (few poets have written poems as cloudless and carefree as some of these) one might be tempted to think them poems of escape, happy images that Miss Sitwell has summoned to keep the others out, forced smiles to hold tears at bay.

As all poetry-lovers know, the later poems, heralded by *Still Falls the Rain*, and *Lullaby* and *Serenade* and *Street Song*, are so different in form and feeling and intention that they might almost be the work of another mind. The lines are long—as long as the rollers that break on that northern shore where Miss Sitwell lived as a child; they are often, though not always, unrhymed; their pulse beats strong but slow, there is a note of yearning in them, and the ache of suffering is never absent. They do not, as did *Gold Coast Customs*, play upon the nerves; their appeal is to the mind and the heart. They are utterly serious, not only as works of art—Miss Sitwell has always been a serious artist—but as criticisms of life. They stand up to the most terrible phenomena of the present day, the atom bomb and concentration camp; they are indeed the only poems of our time that accept the challenge of the war, that look, not unmoved, but undismayed, on 'the flag of blood flying across the world', that recognize, without despairing, 'the ultimate cold within the heart of man'.

At least, I think Miss Sitwell does not despair. She has moods, as other poets have, and it would be idle to pretend that she is not sometimes a pessimist. *The Song of the Cold*, that gives its title to her latest book, is an utterance heavy with doom.

> *Have you too known the cold?*
> *Give me your hand to warm me. I am no more alone.*
> *There was a sun that shone*
> *On all alike, but the cold in the heart of Man*
> *Has slain it. Where is it gone?'*

In *The Two Lovers* she writes:

> *We might tell the blind*
> *The hue of the flower, or the philosopher*
> *What distance is, in the essence of its being—*
> *But not the distance between the hearts of Men.*

We may guess what it must have cost Miss Sitwell emotionally to turn—to be compelled to turn—away from the bright

scene of her poetry's childhood to these lightless limbos of her
later imagining—

> *Where fallen man and the rising ape*
> *And the howling Dark play games*

especially when she remembers that

> *. . . There was a planet dancing in my mind*
> *with a gold seed of Folly . . . long ago . . .*

The poems get much of their power from the fact that she has
written them, one feels, *à contre-cœur*; she does not taste a
luxury in grief, she finds no release in moral indignation; we
feel her whole nature protesting against the company it keeps
—'the Worm, the Ape, the Skeleton, the crouching tiger, and

> *Man's threatening shadow*
> *Red-edged by the sun like Cain'*

—and pining, like Proserpine or Eurydice, for the fields of
spring, in which, until quite lately, she sometimes took a holiday, as witness the ecstatic *How Many Heavens* which soars
like a lark's song above the terrifying charnel noises of *Street
Songs*. Goethe said that you must ask birds and children if you
want to know how strawberries taste. 'In these respects, I for
one am both child and bird', is Miss Sitwell's comment. To
write these poems she has had to put away childish things, and
to renounce the bird-song; yet again and again she returns to
the positive, life-giving symbols of the Sun, the Lion, and the
Rose; opposing the elements in man that make for happiness
and survival to those that are suicidal and destructive. She
believes in the kinship of all created things, one might almost
say, she believes they are identical; and this belief enables her,
as she suggests in her poem, *An Old Woman*, to accept sorrow
and perhaps death without complaining, even with a kind of
rejoicing, when they conform to nature's pattern, to the seasons'
cycle of birth, maturity and decay:

> *Though the dust, the shining racer, overtake me,*
> *I too was a golden woman like those that walk*
> *In the fields of the heavens . . .*

It is (I think) the suspicion that man has somehow cast
himself adrift from the order of Nature, and become like a
cancer in the body of creation, a roving cell blindly bent on

mischief, that disturbs her; the fear that human beings may have
put themselves outside the pale of human compassion. From this
dread she seeks refuge by contemplating the sufferings of Christ:

> *Still falls the rain—*
> *Still falls the Blood from the Starved Man's wounded Side:*
> *He bears in His Heart all wounds . . .*

This is one of the few instances in which Miss Sitwell makes
open avowal of the Christian faith. Christianity may be implicit
in all her thought; it shows again and again in her imagery, in
her preoccupation with the parable of Dives and Lazarus, in her
forbearance and in her compassion. But suffering, as I tried to
point out, is alien to her; she does not accept it as many Christians would do, as an inevitable consequence of the Fall. The
bent of her mind is towards rejoicing, as were Blake's and
Whitman's and Smart's; 'the emeralds are singing on the
grasses', and she would fain sing with them. She is not a long-
faced poet. In a world without Gold Coast Customs, without
total wars, she can find in the mere appearances of things the
same spiritual delight that visited Thomas Traherne when he
looked on the orient and immortal wheat. But now, when

> *The pulse that beats in the heart is changed to the hammer*
> *That sounds in the Potter's Field,*

she feels, perhaps, that things have gone too far, and that
humanity no longer has the power to heal its own wounds. And
it is significant that in the last poem in her latest book, after
recalling the names of poets and scientists who have felt in
themselves the Divine Principle or sought it in creation, she
invokes:

> *. . . One who contracted His Immensity*
> *And shut Himself in the scope of a small flower . . .*

and cries, 'with the voice of Fire',

> *Will he disdain that flower of the world, the heart of Man?*

X

HENRY JAMES

IT WAS in 1897 that Henry James first came to live at Lamb House in Rye. He was fifty-four and had already been more or less settled in England for twenty years. The house offered, so he told his sister-in-law, Mrs. William James, 'the solution of my long unassuaged desire for a calm retreat between May and November'. He took it on a long lease but later bought it, and until he died in 1916 he spent most of his summers and a few of his winters there.

I will try [he told his correspondent] to have a photograph taken of the pleasant little old world town-angle into which its nice old red-bricked front, its high old Georgian doorway and a most delightful little old architectural garden-house, perched alongside of it on its high bricked garden-wall—into which all these features together so happily 'compose'.

Here, at Lamb House, he had his friends to stay, but never more than two at a time. He seems to have been an anxious host, always uneasy about the quality of the food, but no doubt he was glad to return some of the hospitality he had received, for surely no man has ever been more greedily entertained than he was. No less than 108 times, he notes, he had dined out one winter; perhaps the time had come to put a stop to so much social distraction. Soon he gave up his flat in De Vere Gardens, and until 1912, when he took a flat in Carlyle Mansions, a room at the Reform Club was his only perch in London.

Lamb House was therefore the signal for a partial withdrawal from the social round which had meant so much to him, both of strain and pleasure. At Lamb House he could defend his privacy; until three o'clock in the afternoon he was inaccessible. But he did not shut himself up; he was incurably sociable. In Sussex he had literary neighbours, Joseph Conrad and H. G.

Wells; but he also soon made friends with the townspeople of Rye. He attended tea-parties and became a familiar and respected figure. Though knowing little about flowers, he had an excellent gardener, and recorded his surprise and delight when, at a local flower-show, he discovered that a prize had been awarded to 'Mr. James's carnations'. He was also a member of the golf-club. But, though he told someone that he chose Rye as a residence because he liked golfers in plus-fours, he could not give the game itself his blessing. 'A princely expenditure of time', he called it on one occasion; and to E. F. Benson (his successor at Lamb House) he summarized it impressionistically as 'some beflagged jampots, my dear Fred, let into the soil at long but varying distances. A swoop, a swing, a flourish of steel, a dormy.'

In other ways Lamb House might be reckoned as a water-shed in Henry James's career. It intervened between two periods of his literary development: his courtship of the theatre, which ended so disastrously with the failure of *Guy Domville* in 1895, and the third flowering of his genius for fiction—the series of long intricate novels which began in 1901 with *The Sacred Fount*. It coincided with what some may think was the peak of his achievement; with the appearance of two of his best-loved novels, *The Spoils of Poynton* and *What Maisie Knew*; with what is perhaps the most popular of all his stories, *The Turn of the Screw*, and it preceded, by only two or three years, *The Awkward Age*, one of the most dazzling and entertaining of all his novels; a transition-piece between his middle and his later manner, and the last perhaps in which his interest in his characters was at least equal to, if not greater than, his absorption in his theme.

His arrival at Lamb House also marked, according to Mr. Percy Lubbock, what has been held to be an important change in his method of composition. Before, he had only made occasional use of dictation; now it became a habit—not only for his books but sometimes for his letters (he apologizes for their 'Remingtonese'). But how hard it is to arrive at the truth. Mr. Simon Nowell-Smith, whose ingenious and delightful compilation, *The Legend of the Master*, has put every admirer of Henry James in his debt, makes amusing play with the conflicting evidence for when this habit of dictation was begun. Was it in 1885, when James was writing *The Princess Casamassima?* Challenged, the Master seems to have agreed that it was. But he also agreed with another interlocutor, who surmised that the change took place in 1896, when James was at work on *What Maisie Knew*. What are we to make of such discrepancies? One thing seems to emerge—that the habit of dictation cannot be held responsible for the inflation of James's later style, since neither external nor internal evidence can tell us at what point the habit began.

More important, perhaps, for the student of James's literary development is the fact that about this time he ceased to 'go behind' his characters, explaining each from the character's own point of view in the fashion of the great novelists of the past, and left them to explain themselves. If indeed it be a fact. Writing to Mrs. Humphrey Ward in 1899 he says,

> I 'go behind' right and left in 'The Princess Casamassima', 'The Bostonians', 'The Tragic Muse', just as I do the same but singly in 'The American' and 'Maisie', but just as consistently *never at all* (save for a false and limited *appearance*, here and there, of doing it a *little*), in 'The Awkward Age'.

If this is so, and we have it from the horse's mouth, not from a reporter, then the publication of *The Awkward Age* is a vital date not only in the history of Henry James's own development but in the history of English fiction. James may have had few direct imitators but his influence—in this very matter of presenting his characters rather than explaining them—has been enormous, and can be traced in the work of almost every serious novelist of the present day—in Miss Elizabeth Bowen's no less than Miss Compton Burnett's. The modern novelist has renounced 'omniscience'; he does not comment or interpret, he leaves his characters to make their own impression and tell their own tale.

How far this renunciation of a privilege which, as James himself says, was automatically claimed by Dickens, Thackeray, Balzac and Tolstoy was a gain or a loss to fiction as a whole, is much too large a subject to enter into here. That it refines and strengthens the *art* of fiction, most people would agree. That it reduces the scope of the novel, and limits the novelist's interpretation of life, is also probably true. It all depends on whether a novel can be, or ought to be, a perfect work of art.

One sees how Henry James arrived at his theory. It was through his love of the theatre, his passion for drama. Fiction appeared to him to be essentially dramatic: 'dramatize! dramatize!' he would exclaim. Now anything in the nature of an explanation is abhorrent, indeed destructive to drama—as witness the weakening effect of such devices as asides and even soliloquies. Everything must be inferred, nothing must be told. Hence Henry James's dislike of direct statement: 'I never do anything so abject, as to state', he once remarked—or words to that effect. The consequence is that, in his later work, his characters only exist in virtue of their relationship to each other, and to their general predicament, which the conclusion of the novel is to solve. He never completely dehumanized his characters: he had too strong a sense of and respect for personality to do that. But whereas Daisy Miller and Princess Casamassima are persons in their own right—we can think of them apart from their fictional context—the tormented quartet in *The Golden Bowl* are almost like unknown factors in a quadratic equation or lines in a parallelogram of forces, so interdependent are they.

Henry James's later method came to exclude both the lyrical and the epical from fiction—that is one reason why, perhaps, he so amazingly underrated the novels of Thomas Hardy, which are full of both, and Meredith's too. He could endure no relaxation of the dramatic tension—anything that did not contribute to that must be kept out as irrelevant. He was an extremely severe critic of the work of some of his great contemporaries—though on the whole an indulgent one of the generation of novelists that was springing up. Progressively as he grew older did his conviction deepen that he himself was on the right track. The failure of his books to sell did not daunt him; he brushed aside criticism and denounced the thick wits of readers and reviewers when they complained of his obscurity. Nothing in all his writing is more moving than the passage in his private papers, meant for his own eye only, in which he welcomes the return of his genius.

> ... I seem to emerge from these recent bad days—the fruit of blind accident—and the prospect clears and flushes, and my poor blest old Genius pats me so admiringly and lovingly on the back that I turn, I screw round, and bend my lips to passionately, in my gratitude, kiss its hand.

What utter abandonment to passion makes itself felt in that tremendous split infinitive—the only passion, so far as we know, that Henry James gave way to in his life. Only in Emily Brontë's poem to her genius do we find the same unshakeable confidence in inspiration, and the feeling of what it means to whoever has it.

James was not the only novelist whose life was given to his art and who seems to have had no important emotional experience outside it. But surely no novelist has dedicated himself to his art as completely and deliberately as he did. Lamb House was the temple—the shrine in which he worshipped it. There is no doubt that he regarded art as a substitute for life—which was partly why he could not brook in fiction the untidiness and irrelevance of which life is full. Many great novelists, e.g. Tolstoy and Charlotte Brontë, have drawn largely on their own experiences for the material for their books; they have brought in their day-dreams too, making their art a vehicle for self-expression. It was not so in James's case. He may have identified himself to some extent with such young expatriated Americans as Strether and Merton Densher; but the germs of his stories came to him from outside in the form of 'situations', dramatic juxtapositions which had no bearing on his own life, but which he instinctively knew could be developed into a novel. And sometimes he would follow up an idea (as he does in *The Bench of Desolation*) almost without reference to its verisimilitude; he tested it by the canons of art, not by its likeness to life, his own or other people's.

Loneliness, so he told Logan Pearsall Smith, must be the artist's watchword. Inner loneliness, he must have meant, for no artist can ever have had more friends or been more sensitive to the obligations of friendship. Think of his letters, not only of their number and length, but of all the different people they were addressed to, with all of whom he was on the most affectionate terms, of all of whose special circumstances he recollects enough to make the letter not merely an acknowledgment and a signal, but a personal communication. Often they were written in the small hours of the morning. Think of the devotion that all this extra mental effort implied, coming at the end of a hard day's work! And he was as indefatigable a conversationalist as he was a correspondent. His verbal output of sociability must have been as great as Dr. Johnson's.

Yet even in his letters, and in his conversation, we see his artistic conscience at work, correcting, editing, and refining the activities of his social impulse. In all the letters it would be hard to find one carelessly written sentence. He wrote to his friend, yes: but in writing he took care to satisfy that sleepless taskmaster whom it was, for him, more important to propitiate than the recipient of the letter. And so in conversation it was not so much what he said that was important as the way he said it; H. G. Wells's variously reported gibe about an elephant picking up a pea no doubt hit the mark. He talked—not so much to his interlocutor, as to give his interlocutor, and himself, a demonstration in the art of verbal expression. Hence his agonized search for the right word—the word he owed to art, not to his audience—to show that standards not only could but must be kept up.

He was a slave to standards, and not only to artistic but to moral and even to conventional standards. H. G. Wells remarked how, on the hall table of Lamb House,

> lay a number of caps and hats, each with its appropriate gloves and sticks; a tweed cap and a stout stick for the marsh, a soft comfortable deer-stalker if he were to turn aside to the golf-club, a light felt hat and a cane for the morning walk down to the harbour, a grey felt with a black band and a gold headed cane of greater importance if afternoon calling in the town was afoot.

He accepted conventions, and conventional opinion, as an index and criterion of morality. This is most important, because if he was an artist first, he was a moralist second—indeed it would not be fanciful to say that his art was an aspect of his moral sense—so closely was it bound up with his feeling of obligation. In all his stories there is, if not a moral theme, a continual reference to moral judgment, sometimes delicate and almost flippant, as in *What Maisie Knew*; sometimes a trifle ambiguous, as in *The Ambassadors*, sometimes breathing fire and brimstone, as in *The Turn of the Screw*, and as it were the final touchstone of existence, as in *The Golden Bowl*. The rules of morality might be as hard to find and as hard to practise as the rules of art, but they must be found and their workings illustrated. Nor were they to be found in defiance of public opinion. In this James differed from the master of his youth, Nathaniel Hawthorne, who accepted conventional society but questioned its moral judgments. Henry James would never have written a novel which seemed to mitigate the sin of adultery.

Born in New York, educated in Boston, in early life Henry James liked to call himself a cosmopolitan. By nature, and choice, he was intensely critical. Not long before his death, writes Mr. Percy Lubbock, 'he confessed that at last he found himself too much exhausted for the "wear and tear" of discrimination; and the phrase indicates the strain upon him of the mere act of living'. He found the Americans of his time distressingly capable of vulgarity, and the English (especially in aesthetic matters) of stupidity. The English are the only people, he told his sister, 'who can do great things without being clever'. While the Continent, in spite of its attraction for a sophisticated mind, did not fulfil his exacting moral requirements. It was full of dubious noblemen intent on marrying guileless American heiresses. Of the three, though with more than one nostalgic glance at America, he chose England as a place to live in. The purchase of Lamb House was a sign that he had finally thrown in his lot with us, and as time went on he became steadily more English in feeling. The 1914 war accelerated the process of identification. He left Lamb House and took a flat in Chelsea and remained there 'almost uninterruptedly till the end'. In June 1915 he took the step, criticized by some of his American friends, of having himself naturalized an Englishman—though, said Mr. Asquith, who acted as one of his sponsors, 'the bonds of friendship were strained to cracking when I had to subscribe to the proposition that he could both talk and write English'. He threw himself heart and soul into the war, talking to soldiers, interesting himself in Belgian refugees, and helping in every way he could. His faculty of writing, far from being paralysed by happenings so foreign to the natural tenor of his mind, was enormously stimulated. He began a new book of reminiscences; he wrote an introduction to Rupert Brooke's *Letters from America*. Only his creative imagination could not breathe the war atmosphere, and he abandoned *The Ivory Tower* for *The Sense of the Past*.

Just before his death, Edmund Gosse brought him the news that he had been awarded the O.M. Lying with closed eyes he made no sign of having heard, and Gosse tiptoed away, leaving the room to the patient, the nurse, and the light of a single candle. But the moment the door closed James opened his eyes and said, 'Nurse, take away the candle and spare my blushes.' He had paid England the highest compliment he could, and England had returned it.

THE NOVELIST AND HIS MATERIAL

IF THE novelist of today finds himself in a difficult position, it is not so much his fault as the fault of his human material. Perhaps I should not say fault in either case. For one thing, with the weakening of our belief in free-will, the word 'fault' like the word 'ought' has lost much of its strength and meaning: some defect of character or conduct which would once have unhesitatingly been called 'our fault' is now ascribed to causes over which we have no control, or very little. The sense of sin has given way to an undifferentiated, almost impersonal sense of guilt, or it has completely disappeared. And even if the word 'fault' still carried with it the implication of personal responsibility that it once had, I doubt if it can be usefully applied to a situation which is the outcome of so many forces, scientific, economic, and other, the drift of which could not be foreseen.

The nineteenth century was the Golden Age of the novel in most countries, because it was the age of individualism, of hero-worship, of the outstanding figure, the Great Man. The characters in Victorian novels were not only free to be themselves, in the cant phrase, they were encouraged to be, both by the writer and the public; they were appreciated, one might almost say, in proportion as they achieved a unique personality. Besides this, they strove, they aspired for something beyond themselves, for happiness and goodness, it might be, or for money and position, by which they could raise themselves to a higher power. Even when, as in Hardy's works, they are the playthings of Destiny, unable to influence their fate, they are still figures of dignity and grandeur, over life-size, distinguished from their fellows by their misfortunes and their capacity for suffering. Man was the measure of the universe in the Victorian Age, which was hierarchical, almost consciously ranking one

man above another, and according awe and reverence to whoever, in whatever sphere of life, reached the top. The discoveries
of science, the achievements of art, were intimately connected
with the names of the men and women who had made them,
indeed those names were often household words to people who
could not have told for what invention, or discovery, or work
of art they were famous.

*

But ours is a collectivist age, in which the changes and developments that have most affected the lives of human beings have
been brought about by mass movements, linked arms, an almost
glacier-like progress in which each particle moves forward
impacted with the rest. The symbol of our civilization today is
the queue, a formation designed to keep people literally and
figuratively in their places. It utterly forbids the quality of
aspiration—which could only take the form of jumping the
queue—and takes away every kind of moral responsibility
except one: to accept your position and stay there. And this
spirit has spread far beyond people waiting for the bus or to
take their turn at the coffee stall; it has become a sort of touchstone of behaviour: the good citizen is the one who keeps his
place in the queue, and the bad citizen the one who tries to
improve his position at the expense of others. He is a 'spiv' or
a 'fiddler', and may be admired as such, but only covertly, for
he has offended against the principle of 'fairness' which is today
of all others the virtue nearest to the Englishman's heart.

When Lytton Strachey wrote *Eminent Victorians* he did more
than poke a little fun at certain nineteenth-century worthies, he
helped to discredit the idea of eminence itself. Eminence: a
position of superiority to one's fellows, a height from which one
looks down on them scornfully and smugly, a position which,
if fairness means anything, no man has a right to take up. It isn't
so much that we suffer from 'a craven fear of being great' as that
the idea of the 'great man' has lost its appeal (Mr. Lionel
Trilling, in his study of Mr. E. M. Forster, has a significant
passage about Mr. Forster's refusal to accept greatness). And
whereas, in the nineteenth century, great men, acknowledged
as such, abounded, today they could almost be counted on the
fingers of two hands—and most of them are over eighty. The
reverence which used to be their due now goes to film-stars and
athletes, whose eminence, being based on the natural endow-

ments of brawn and good looks (which they cannot, so to speak, help), does not offend the sense of fairness so much as it would if they owed it more obviously to their own exertions.

*

From H. G. Wells onwards novelists have tried to meet the demand for unremarkable, unheroic heroes, and have given us the Little Man and the Common Man and latterly (in saying this I hit at no one, for I have done the same) misfits and wastrels and 'don't care' types and criminals—a gallery of the morally underprivileged—demanding for them sympathy and compassion, on the grounds of 'There but for the Grace of God go I.' But, generally speaking, the novelist has tried to give them a little extra something to make them outstanding in their commonplaceness or criminality—mistakenly, so it seems, for now the public taste is for victims who have no spirit to struggle with whoever or whatever is oppressing them and who make a cult, almost a virtue, of their helplessness, drowning in drink their discontent with the poor figure they are cutting. Reading about them, hearing them or watching them, one may feel (though one shouldn't) a comfortable sense of superiority, or a despair akin to theirs; what one can never feel is an enhancement of the value of life, for they set out to devalue it; and the public, or one section of it, seems to like it that way, and may even prefer a bad performance to a good one. An impresario quoted in *The Times* finds 'a deliberate deification of bad taste—a sort of rebellion of the inarticulate, uninformed, and illiterate', and 'if they [the spectators] find themselves faced with an artist of real talent they feel themselves insulted'. 'They resent him apparently', comments the writer of the article, 'because they are incapable of doing as well.'

If this is so, then the wheel has come full circle since Victorian times, and we needs must love the lowest when we see it, not only in the human material presented to us—there always have been, and always will be, people with *la nostalgie de la boue*—but even in the way it is presented. And this is something new—that the artist should deliberately put his worst foot forward, for fear of arousing envy in the public's breast.

What has this devaluation of the individual come from? Why is it that the faculty of emulation has given way to envy, so that the spectacle of people in any way superior to ourselves is distasteful to us? And why is murder the one subject that never palls?

★

'This world', wrote Horace Walpole, 'is a comedy to those that think, a tragedy to those that feel.' For the novelist today both comedy and tragedy are equally difficult to make convincing as modes of experience. After two world wars, and with the prospect of a third, I do not see how life can be squeezed into the convention of comedy. It is too artificial and it leaves out too much. Jane Austen could do it because she inherited the eighteenth-century belief in sense and reason as presiding over human affairs. Her vision was bounded by Reason, deviations from which, in her characters' behaviour, she saw as laughable. But we cannot; the deviations have been too great; besides, apart from the two wars, there is on every hand a flight from Reason, and an almost shocked recoil from sense. Reason is at a discount; not only have the activities of the subconscious mind, now laid bare, torpedoed it, but the wreckage has been labelled with the pejorative near-synonym 'rationalization', which turns our arguments against us. So it speaks with a cracked voice, and a mere whisper from a power-maniac silences it. 'Let Reason frown on War's unequal game': it still frowns but that is all it can do, and the difference between Dr. Johnson's time and ours is that we no longer even hope that Reason will prevail. Comedy depends on bringing human nature to the test of Reason. If Reason as a touchstone is discredited, comedy cannot exist.

And if you cannot have comedy without Reason, neither can you have tragedy without feeling. No one would say that feeling has disappeared from the human breast, but it takes much more finding than it used to, for its rivals, sensationalism and materialism, have overlaid it. 'Tell me about a good murder, give me my pay-packet, and you can keep your fine feelings.' And the two wars, by giving the emotions more than they could take, acted upon them like a hormone weed-killer; they outgrew their strength and, in the case of many people, perished. Some degree of suffering has perhaps always been inevitable, but only in our age has it been made compulsory. When suffering becomes compulsory the spirit steels itself to ignore it, regarding it as a necessary evil, just as, on a lower plane of feeling, we regard the income-tax as a necessary evil. In the wars we were compelled to regard the loss of friends and relations as a necessary evil and in self-defence grew round ourselves a shell which still keeps feeling out although the need for it is temporarily removed. In the past the tragic hero and heroine were outstanding because of their sufferings; we looked on them with awe and pity as having been singled out to endure what the rest of us escaped; they were exceptions and from that they got their tragic stature. But now that suffering has been made the rule, and is inflicted more effectively by the hand of man than by the hand of God, it no longer commands the respect it used to. Potentially at any rate we are all equal in suffering. To complain of it is as futile as to complain of the human lot, and to imagine that it confers on this or that human being a special distinction that we ought to regard with reverence is impossible to us. 'Why should he be made a fuss of more than I?'

Indiscriminate, compulsory suffering is a great leveller, and has done more, perhaps, than any other single factor to give the human countenance a common look—a rather forced smile, as if it was being photographed. In a recent article in *The Times* entitled 'Is Portraiture Doomed as an Art?' the writer answers his own question with the comment:

> Generalizations, referring both to the trend of social life and the main currents of modern art, would have us think so. They suggest that without necessarily being aware of it we have left behind the Humanist era in which the individual human being was important and arrived at one of those periods of which the past has its examples when the individual is submerged in the community, and human interest in the abstract ideas by which the community is governed.

Afterwards, he qualifies this, I am glad to say, for the novelist is first and foremost a portrait-painter, and if it were true that portraiture is doomed for lack of interest in the individual human countenance, then the novel is doomed, too. But he has said enough to show that its position is precarious.

All art proceeds from feeling, and most of all the novelist's art; if feeling is absent, no amount of mental cross-breeding between abstractions and the problems of technique will take its place as an incentive. They are substitutes, and about as much like the real thing as a self-induced orgasm is like the true act of love. The influence of science is another danger, for many people genuinely believe that if you knew the technique, the formula, for writing a good novel, you could write one. They put the cart before the horse, for each work of art dictates its own technique.

★

And another danger, equally insidious, is the growing disbelief in the possibility of altruism. In the past the middle classes believed in altruism and sometimes practised it.

> *Whence does the finest culture come*
> *If the middle class is not its home?*

inquired Goethe. Today the middle class is being sqeezed out of existence, and it is indeed difficult for anyone observing the political or the social scene to believe there is such a thing as a really disinterested action. Yet art demands altruism as no other activity does; the artist *must* believe that his work is more important than he is; he must be prepared to sacrifice himself to it in order to be reborn in it. The middle classes allowed themselves this indulgence, or claimed this privilege—perhaps because they could afford to; but the *sacro egoismo* of the nationalist and other mass-movements into which we are more and more being drawn forbids it.

The novelist of today has many other difficulties to face. To mention only two: the changes in the structure of society, which are so rapid that any attempt to portray it is out of date before the ink is dry; and the fact that no representative view of even a small section of the community is now complete unless it includes characters who are nervously or mentally unbalanced. But the main danger is lest the individual, snowed under by the mass of suggestions, directions, orders, and ready-made designs for living to which he is exposed, should be submerged and lost in the community, so that his reactions and responses will become automatic and predictable, and protective colouring will make him indistinguishable from the rest. But I cannot help believing that this will not happen, and that an awareness of other people's personalities and their right to be themselves, and of one's dependence, for the fulfilment of one's own personality, on them as individuals—not just fellow-sufferers or fellow-criminals with identical faces—will survive, and with it the novel, which thrives on that belief.

XII

SOME ASPECTS OF
GREGARIOUSNESS

BEFORE TRYING to discuss the vast cloudy subject of gregariousness I feel I should apologise for the way I have treated it. I realised increasingly as I went along that, if dealt with at all, it should have been done by someone with knowledge of biology, of which I have none, and with knowledge of psychology, of which I have only a smattering. My references to both these sciences will, I fear, seem perfunctory, puerile and impertinent. I hope, therefore, it will be regarded as a youthful extravagance, a bundle of prejudices in the shape of a personal record, though wanting those more intimate statements which, I imagine, endear the confessions of Rousseau and St. Augustine to the reader. There are many things delivered rhetorically and which will not endure the rigid test of reason. 'If my thoughts are not your thoughts they are nothing', said Walt Whitman, but I suppose a personal account has some sort of value if only as a warning.

*

The problem of how many peas go to make a heap is as old as the schoolmen, or older: but to compute the number of entities required to constitute a crowd, a task which the law in its hardihood has attempted, would be work for Archimedes and more wisely left for solution to the mystical mathematics of the city of heaven. One is justified in connecting heaven with the idea of a crowd: at once the image of 'unnumbered heads bowed 'neath their aureoles' springs to the mind. Heaven is of course a club with certainly a long waiting-list and possibly a long period of probation; but once admitted to it, the attitude of keeping oneself to oneself must be abandoned. Dean Swift, surely the least companionable of men, recognized the necessity of this:

We are God's chosen few;
All others shall be damned:
There is no place in Heaven for you.
We won't have Heaven crammed.

This is of course writ sarcastic. But it is impossible not to wonder at the misguided policy of hermits, who, in forsaking this world, imagined they were preparing themselves for the conditions of the next. Could it never have occurred to them that, having made a lifetime study of the Heaven in their own breasts, they would experience some discomfort, some dismay, when told to seek it outside? What a revelation to them will be that final 'circumspice', that ultimate renunciation of privacy, that début into everlasting publicity! It is strange that few have quailed before the thought of such an ordeal; that among all the hymn-writers none, and among the poets perhaps only one, has raised a protest against it.

Two paradises 'twere in one
To live in paradise alone

said Marvell, naturally mistrustful of prescribed felicities.

This is, doubtless, not a very valuable digression; but at the same time it is not always sufficiently realized that many people of decent, solitary habits, even misanthropes, obscurely cherish the vision of some ideal crowd; a company with which it would be a delight to mingle, in whose collective sympathy one could bask, in whose glances the questioning and wistful eye would meet an unqualified recognition. But let us consider what crowds are really like, and weigh precisely the effect for good or bad of the association of one person with another. Suppose, as sometimes happens, that a stranger or chronically unobservant person desires to find the way to the general post-office or the town hall. He is naturally diffident about asking for the object of his search is probably close at hand, possibly even in full view. He will not ask at random, for fear his choice should fall on the village idiot or another stranger like himself, and so hold him up to scorn. And scorn from whom? Not from the casual passer-by, alert to sympathize and with his derisive faculties unquickened; but from the group round the village pump who, secure in their mutual support, can indulge their sense of humour to the full. It may be long before the essentially right person appears, and so the man we are considering, who is pressed for time, is faced with an alternative: either to accost a row of young men, freshly disgorged by the cinema and radiating what Rupert Brooke called the 'lovely brutality of youth', or to inquire of a retreating itinerant newsvendor, who will certainly sell his information at the price of an unwanted newspaper. Aristotle has said that the collective wisdom of an assembly is equal to the sum of the wisdom of the units that compose it; but, even supposing our stranger to be aware of this, would he risk exposing himself at a disadvantage (i.e. in a state of ignorance) to the collective ridicule of half a dozen youths who have already, so unerring is the instinct of gregariousness, detected some singularity in his appearance? No: he would ask the newspaper-man, and as likely as not get a civil answer.

However suspicious we may be, and rightly, of strangers, we should not shun one, especially if he is growing old and looks a little dejected. At a certain age most people have a sneaking desire to be pitied; there is hardly anyone in whom the sense of self-assertion is so completely developed he will not at times betray the want of it. If there is such a thing as human solidarity it arises from the wish of every man that such solidarity might exist for it is a common want; a disunion that ceases to be complete only when it is intensely realized.

It is easy to think that we have points of contact with people; that our natures overlap, that our interests coincide. We respond to a word, a look, a gesture: but is that response adequate? In our intimate communious, when we are most sensibly in accord, when consciously and unconsciously we grope towards each other—'we two alone, close-kissed and eloquent of still replies'—even then we are apart. Though our encounter be truly royal, and set in a Field of the Cloth of Gold: we enter the lists blindfolded and 'in mad trance strike with our spirits' knife invulnerable nothings.' No question is ever answered, no glance interpreted aright, there is no gesture whose whole significance we do not miss. 'The soul of another', said Turgenev, surely a foremost authority on relationships between man and man, 'is a dark forest.'

Those who believe in the essential gregariousness of the human race, or those again who put forward the view, so useful to the apologists of government, that man is inconceivable apart from his fellows, that he reaches his highest development through association with them, seem to ignore or to deny the fundamental separateness of individuals. Bosanquet regards our ordinary, trivial moods as those in which we are deaf, not to 'the still sad music of humanity', but to the more immediate utterances of the crowd. We are most truly ourselves when caught in the eddy of some common emotion, when identifying ourselves with that beautiful mirage, the General Will—that prophet, in whose infallibility, provided he is dumb, we are bound to believe, though every word he speaks is admittedly a lie, discrediting him and betraying us. Even Mill and the champions of individual liberty take up a defensive position, contending that except in cases where a man's action is likely to injure the liberty of others, he 'ought' to be allowed to enjoy his freedom and rule his life on lines prescribed by himself. Such an attitude regards the fundamental irreconcilability of men as an end to be attained, rather than a fact to be faced.

To the present writer the maintenance of isolation among men seems to require no defence; it would perhaps be more likely to promote their happiness if this isolation were disguised or even denied. For we live by illusions; and there are lines of thought that are best avoided, 'things that must not be thought on; or they will make us mad'. But to return to Bosanquet's contention that society, whether actual or implied, whether all around us or present merely in thought, deepens our consciousness and vaguely presents itself as a support, a solace, something to hold on to existence by. If one may oppose to a generalization of this kind one's own experience—and generalizations upon man's nature are surely the most fallible of all—I may say that my own impressions, based indeed only on the disputed records of self-examination, contradict this. It would be interesting perhaps to know whether writers who are mentally acclimatized to the idea of mingling with crowds, who represent the millions of Asia by a single spirit and talk of the Parliament of Man, would find actual contact with a crowd so destructive or solvent of their trivial moods, so apt to elevate or to transcend their self-communion, as they would have us believe. It is odd to read in Shelley, in whose poetry the general so far outweighs the personal and the exact, reference to crowds, 'where we are most alone'. It would not, I think, be too much to say that the presence of other people, or even the idea of other people, acts on some minds with a force which does not make, wholly or even partially, for their spiritual comfort or exaltation. Such people measure the extent of their bewilderment and unease by the number of the persons with whom they are confronted. They either become silent under an almost palpable weight of oppression, or they dimly cast about for some innocuous, intelligent remark that represents nothing in their thought, past or present, but is eloquent simply of their inadaptability to mental rearrangement. 'No road' is written large across every avenue of thought; the smallest movement requires an agony of premeditation; the others lose their human characteristics and become objects not exactly of aversion (for a kind of despairing universal charity still clings to the victim's mind), but objects that are meaningless except in so far as they balk and harass and disturb.

However trivial the individual's ordinary moods, it can hardly be contended that gregariousness, or at least one aspect of it, has any other effect but that of replacing them by a kind of inward pandemonium, infinitely distressing and disintegrating to the person affected. It neither exalts nor depresses him: it practically annihilates him. But perhaps it would be urged that these circumstances are not favourable for displaying the saving grace of gregariousness; that its true virtue is exhibited in those more fortunate contacts of a handful of people, for the sake of argument say two, who being gifted with miraculous delicacy of perception, arising from long acquaintance and innate faculties of sympathy, are so precisely in tune with one another, so alert to react to each other's manifestations, that the most sensitive person, not to use a more disagreeable epithet, can enrich his consciousness from the common store, dress his mentality in borrowed plumes and for a few delicious moments cease to be himself in the ecstasy of being part of several others. This, it will be maintained is the essential gregariousness; seeing that it preserves the intellect which the mere mob intoxicates and the group of unsympathetic but cultured persons freezes into inanition, and at the same time dissolves the links of that self-chain, whose odious rattle affrights the individual the moment he is left to himself. Communion of such a kind is the true escape; it is that 'handsome foretaste of heaven' which the mystic and the recluse are supposed to obtain, but only after agonies of self-discipline that unfit them for life among his fellows and make them useless as a social unit.

This is perhaps true; though whether it is an aspect of

gregariousness that would be included in Mr. Trotter's three categories of offensive, defensive and social gregariousness is another question. It is certainly neither offensive nor defensive, nor is it social in any but a limited sense; its virtue lies in its intensity, and any attempt to extend it by indiscriminate admissions changes its character. Perfect accord between individuals is moreover a rare phenomenon, and dependent on outside circumstances. There are few people who, wishing to renew an experience of this sort, have not arranged to reproduce it; but something has gone amiss, some trivial preoccupation creeps in and upsets the balance, conversation becomes forced; candour is suppressed and every person concerned feels tenfold the weight of his chance desires and realizes that his hopes have once more changed their name. There is no friendship, however close, that does not experience these distressing lapses of intimacy: indeed the firmer the tie, the more complete the alienation resulting from its fracture. 'To be wroth with one we love doth work like madness on the brain.'

Moreover, granting for a moment the possibility of so entire a rapprochement between individuals, the immediate, and sometimes lasting, result is a reaction as intense as, and more prolonged than, the exaltation that preceded it; for violent delights have violent ends, and the man who, whether deliberately or not, has given as it were large portions of his consciousness into the keeping of others may one day find himself terribly bereft. This is what underlies Montaigne's remark that we should only 'lend ourselves to our friends', and presumably cultivate a certain suspiciousness and reticence, but when we come to claim the loan we find it transformed or even lost. This self-expenditure is not an uncommon phenomenon; there are persons with a rich capital of consciousness in other people, but who are bankrupt of it themselves. Personality therefore should be carefully husbanded, not poured out indiscriminately, lest in the leaner years one come and say 'I owe you much: you showed me this and that', and you, the giver, no longer possess and scarcely realize the meaning of such gifts.

One is forced to the conclusion that of the two foregoing forms of gregariousness, one consisting of the proximity of what Daisy Ashford would call 'mere people', the other of a real communication between a selected few, neither can be accounted a blessing; the first, however its after-effects may stimulate self-resourcefulness, is exceedingly unpleasant while it lasts; while the second exposes the denuded and unwalled personality to unexpected attacks, 'dangers from the East', as Traherne says, in fact for every satisfaction given or received an acuter and more lasting dissatisfaction. The first is a possibly bracing ordeal: the second a seduction. Neither can be said to be a successful mode of development; for the first leads to repression and the second, too often, to depression. Gregariousness must therefore be indulged in sparingly, and only between adequate periods of solitude or quasi-solitude.

But to the thoroughgoing biologist such an emasculated conception of the function of gregariousness, and so guarded an approbation of it, is worse than heterodoxy: it borders on blasphemy. The Human Race is governed by the Herd Instinct. Evidence of this is the instinct for warmth displayed by men in company with dogs, a relic from the ages when men lived in such close proximity that they derived from each other much of their natural heat. A cat, never having submitted to such contacts, is not averse from sitting in the snow. Biology is a powerful word: and at its rising faded metaphysics, religion, politics, 'shrink like things reproved', and are relegated into the position of 'important influences'. Though we are careful to avoid arguing from analogy, we conclusively establish a parallel between the man and the bee, the major unit or nation and the hive, and long for that ultimate day, that climacteric when we may merge our individualities into a swarm. Mr. Trotter seems quite oblivious of the fact that every mention of the noun herd, which he repeats and almost mouths, must awake in many readers a reaction that loses none of its power when various herd-characteristics are instanced: the 'low growl' of a dog at the approach of a stranger which beautifully illustrates the instinct of its members to put the herd on the watch: the punctilious manœuvres by dogs on their all too frequent encounters; which, as a means of discovering whether the party examined is a foe or friend, Mr. Trotter compares with our hand-shaking, and seems wistfully to desire a return to this directer method. He does not seek to examine the reasons why such words as herd, mob, pack, crowd, flock, bevy, ring unpleasantly in our ears. He does not even, like another champion of gregariousness, lament the fact that the moral development of crowds is some centuries behind that of individuals. It does not occur to him that the herd synonyms in the *Te Deum* have to be bolstered and made respectable by such epithets as 'noble', 'glorious' and 'goodly'; whereas the naked word, divested of such elaborate apparel, is sufficient to convey the opposite connotation. He does not animadvert much upon the morality of crowds (it is outside his sphere); he does not tell us that almost their only method of becoming spontaneously articulate is to shout 'Hurray'; that the most reliable means of inspiring them with a common purpose is to have it written on a gaudy banner floating over their heads, that they are impervious to reason and will kill a man because he bears the name of someone against whom they are momentarily incensed; that they have the highest faculties for destruction, but none for construction; that they will burn a man's house with the same readiness that they will watch a man drown; they are most truly a crowd when drunk; that sadism presides over their conception and satiety decrees their separation. There is little reason for believing that the mentality of crowds has advanced for 2,000 years: the Greek soldiers of the Persian expedition, we are told, shouted collectively '*Thalatta*' on catching sight of the sea: in our day it would be left to an individual to make the discovery and spread it like a rumour, among the gaping troops.

'It moves not my spleen', said Sir Thomas Browne, 'to behold the multitude in their proper humours, that is, of folly and madness, as well knowing that wisdom is not prophan'd unto the vulgar and it is the privilege of a few to be virtuous.' This is surely a charitable view: many writers would have used harder expressions. But it is the crowd, with all its manifestations, that we are asked to accept as the leading principle of our existence, whose decay is in the same breath, deplored and denied, and to which, for our preservation, we are bidden to return.

Man, it is said, is for various reasons gregarious; and in the van of these we have the statement that in solitude he experiences loneliness in degrees varying from discomfort to terror. But always, we are to imagine, his secret wish is to be actually in touch with the herd: to feel its presence on every hand; presumably to seek association with crowds, which offer protection against foes—what foes, we might be inclined to question, had not biological ingenuity arbitrarily identified the herd with the nation. Other groups within this major unit are to be deprecated, as perversions of the herd principle and symptomatic of its decay. At this point the modern biologist joins hands with Rousseau.

But does a man in solitude of necessity feel 'lonely'? We remember that Mrs. Elton, in Jane Austen's *Emma*, had, besides the material and social advantage of riding in a yellow barouche, another and more spiritual possession of which she was equally proud: she was independent of other people, for she had 'resources within herself'. Other people were bidden to realize that they were not necessary to the maintenance of her peace of mind. If it is undeniable from the mere existence of clubs, public houses and other conveniences for assembly, that a part of mankind is gregarious, it does not follow that gregariousness is the principle which is chiefly found to underlie man's actions; it is not necessarily his resource in trouble or his outlet in joy. Man thinks in terms of persons, not of humanity at large. Ideas derive their intensity from the concentration on one thing, not their diffusion over many. Thus it may mean little to us to be told that the population of Vienna is starving; if we cannot indict, neither can we sympathize with a nation or a capital. But directly our attention is focused on the sufferings of an individual, whether presented by a harrowing picture in a newspaper or by the recollection that Freud is a Viennese professor, we are stimulated to subscribe. It is amusing to hear that the Mayor and Corporation of Cheltenham, riding in state on the first tramcar to ascend Cleeve Hill, were thrown out because the brakes went wrong and the tram capsized: but if the Mayor had been a friend of ours and perished in this ignominious fashion we should regard the incident with horror and speak of it with appropriate awe. Personal relationships are the shrine of our deepest feelings. It does not irk us to think that the whole herd of swine ran violently down a steep place and were choked, but many must have felt a secret sympathy for Holman Hunt's scapegoat, with its pink protesting eyes, charged with the sins of the children of Israel. We can cry fiercely with Marvell that 'beasts must be with justice slain' because the wanton huntsmen had slain a nymph's fawn, while we complacently wear beaver on our gloves and osprey in our hats.

Not to labour this point further, but to return to the biological assertion that man is unhappy when left alone, one must, on behalf of oneself and many others, disclaim any such generalization as far as it affects us. We have taken the moralist's precept to heart and are able to be alone. Often indeed, in the society of others we wish almost passionately for solitude; more ardently perhaps than, when alone, we yearn to make 'one of a party'. For solitude, and this is a point some biologists seem to miss, is subjective: it means that certain aspects of outward things, or certain processes of thought have ceased to minister to the content of our consciousness, leaving us adrift and as it were unrelated. Similarly liberty does not consist of the absence of external restraint for very restraint, in drawing against it the conflicting complex of our desires and crystallizing them into something like a purpose, a single aim, affords us a moment of true liberty. Solitude admits of degrees; but in its greatest intensity it is in the nature of a discovery and may well visit a man as it did Richard III, when surrounded by a snoring army. 'I am myself alone: there's none else by', remarked the monarch: but there were thousands by—it was only the silent host with which a man communes throughout his waking hours that had abandoned him.

It would be idle, of course, to contend that the researches of biologists, with the system of comparison and tabulation they entail, may not go far to establish characteristics common to all men and types arising from those characteristics. But that such classifications are at present scarcely more than tentative and liable to constant contradiction in their application to special cases, is generally admitted; there are few who would hazard a prophecy, couched in the most general terms and relating to the future of the largest masses of mankind, of what that future is likely to have in store, still fewer whose prophecies would be remembered with honour, either in their own country or outside it. For young as is the science of applied biology, it has already produced some startling differences of opinion: Mr. Trotter recognizing as the prime instincts of mankind the herd-instinct, sex and nutrition; while Mr. McDougall relegates the herd-instinct to a comparatively unimportant position, deprecates its continuance and foresees its decay; laying greater stress, as the moulders of men's lives, on the instincts of pugnacity, emulation and sympathy. He realizes, as who does not?, that there is a certain element of truth in Hobbes's definition of many emotions as essentially self-regarding and even anti-social. And if 'laughter', in Hobbes's words, 'is nothing else but sudden self-glory', and if we are to agree with La Rochefoucald that 'gratitude is a lively sense of favours to come', and that 'in the misfortunes of our dearest friends there is something not altogether displeasing to us', how can we recognize gregariousness as even in the front rank of the influences or instincts that make us what we are? To argue that men must seek each other's company chiefly in order to gratify their insatiable desire to shine at another's expense, to condole with a rehearsal of misfortunes that secretly delights them, to profess brotherhood while inwardly thanking God they are not as other men are, is to put an extremely sinister interpretation on the meaning of gregariousness, and one to which we should be very unwilling to subscribe. But even as members of a university, as citizens perhaps of a provincial town, as readers of the daily press, we cannot profess ourselves immune from this left-handed gregariousness, this instinct that draws us together for a fuller consciousness and a freer discussion of each other's shortcomings than to give the rein to our aptitude for solidarity.

In endeavouring to estimate the prevalence of gregariousness I have refrained as far as possible from attempting to assess its value as a moral force. Biology is not concerned with ethics, except in so far as it accounts for certain phenomena common to various races of men. But one's attitude, even to a tendency or to an instinct, cannot shape itself entirely on the mere consideration of whether that tendency or instinct is more or less deeply rooted; more or less widely diffused or more or less likely to hold its own in the future. It is not possible to regard it so dispassionately. We must 'attempt the difficult assessment of its due'; and what can be said in favour of the impulse that lures men from the country to the town (for the theory that towns are products of economic motives is no longer accepted), that cheapens the quality of their leisure which, if it no longer demands the butchery of a Roman holiday, is satisfied with spectacles of the smallest possible significance to heart or head; that feeds uncritically upon rumour, that produces a mentality that is admittedly impervious to any ideas except the grossest and causes thousands of deaths by overcrowding. It is not surprising that Mr. Trotter's pious hope for the speedy rehabilitation of the herd-spirit is not shared by sociologists like Wallas, who welcome a partial disintegration and hope to see the herd-instinct—the most fruitful cause of wars—perish of inanition.

For we are not altogether convinced by the dexterous manipulation of analogy which identifies Germany with the aggressive herd-instinct and reserves for England that social gregariousness typified by the bee—that spoiled favourite of moralists, whose activities are always turned inwards and which would shrink from extracting honey from a flower marked out for the use of another hive.

I am far from denying that the herd-instinct exists and has its uses, and they are often sweet: but there seems good reason to dislodge it from the eminent pinnacle to which (to say the truth) it has only lately been restored. History sees the wreck and revival of many reputations; but it will need more than a single pen to sweeten the word herd which for ages has stunk in men's nostrils. *Securus judicat orbis terrarum.* It is not enough to allege that human prejudice against the notion of crowds is a proof of their vitality. Gregariousness, in so far as we are subject to it, is a waning force, if not already spent, and it lacks the universal application its champions claim for it. It is emphatically only one among the things men live by. If existence resolves itself into an alternation between solitude and society, is it more true to say that solitude prepares us for society than that society prepares us for solitude? But, as I have tried to show, neither solitude nor society solely is to be gauged or measured by the absence or proximity of others. The influence exerted on us by our fellows may well be the factor that counts for most; but it is the least reliable; it may provide us with our most admirable, as it certainly occasions our most regrettable moments. Mixing with mankind is apt to be a dangerous experiment, we may obtain from it precisely the response we look for, but sometimes it shows itself more fell than anguish, hunger or the sea.

Humour is partially anti-social, it raises a laugh at the expense of someone, real or imaginary, but too often real and not seldom actually present. Stocks and stones and trees, and, less completely, even animals, cannot well be ridiculed out of our regard. They seldom betray the meaning we have set upon them; they cannot withdraw into themselves, or blow hot and cold upon us. They are out chart and compass: the warm gale and ventilation that humanity inspires may well bring us into pleasant harbours, but it has a trick of casting us on rocks. The aspects, angles, and positions of objects are immensely important to the maintaining of our spiritual equilibrium. We do not easily reconcile ourselves to the removal of a picture or the felling of a tree. The main tendency of modern literature is surely to widen our consciousness by the giving of significance to unconsidered trifles, the spiritualizing of surroundings, whether sordid or beautiful, in fact the strengthening and extension of our capacity for solitude: to borrow the lines of Wordsworth:

> *Ours shall be the breathing balm*
> *And ours the silence and the calm*
> *Of mute insensate things.*

It has been argued that man is conscious of incompleteness, and that this want can best be met by identifying our interests with those of our fellows. In cases where this want takes a practical form, where a nation or group has consciously set before itself an aim, whether for getting better conditions or preventing relapse into worse, the value of gregariousness is apparent; and the phenomenon of a general will directed to the achievement of that end is not inconceivable, although such a will is rarely apparent in any specified act and admittedly needs enlightenment and direction from without: 'it wills the good it does not see'. Even Rousseau, in one sense the most uncompromising exponent of collectivism, had recourse to the expedient of a law-giver, a Solon or a Lycurgas, a man almost incredibly above suspicion, to be the mouthpiece of the General Will. And if we accept Bonsanquet's opinion that the Real Will is something deeper and more ennobling than its manifestations, as revealed in the leading articles of newspapers or the uninstructed comments of the man in the street, that it is a pregnant public opinion that still sways men when their words and actions seem most inconsistent with it, we are still unable to regard it as more than one of the principal mediums in which the human self-consciousness can move and extend itself. In the moments when it is realized, it does us infinite service by providing us with landmarks and rallying-points; but (and I submit this with all humility) there are broad tracts in our existence over which it sheds no light, tracts which seem composed simply of small frictions, of the pretty wrongs that liberty commits, when our every act and thought is marked with and apparently foredoomed to insufficiency and failure. At such times even commonplace acts, such as tying up shoe-laces, become matters of effort, an effort in which we are subtly but quite decisively worsted; our handwriting which, whether we take pride in it or not, is still a rude form of self-expression, presents us constantly with a succession of odious, tortured, grotesque characters, each a standing menace to our peace of mind and a perpetual reminder that we fall short of some proposed excellence. It is true that the effect of drink, the right degree of intoxication, often removes these troublesome, obstinate questionings, and that the sensation of being one of a mob, ready to commit a deed of violence, or to be caught up in a religious ecstasy or to swear that two and two are five, temporarily allays them: but not even the most hardened champion of Bacchus or the herd-instinct would affirm that either of these conditions (in most people at any rate) is normal and does not involve the sacrifice of many qualities that differentiate us from animals. In spite of Montaigne's learned and perverse treatise, and in spite of rationalist, biological, or psychological speculation or inquiry, there is a part of us that owes no homage to the sun.

If it be a fact (as I feel it is) that gregariousness or the herd-instinct is only one of the influences that shape our lives and that, in the words of the Sophist, philosophy is good because it enables the philosopher, supposing all the institutions in the world were abolished, to go on living precisely as before, it is not therefore an argument in favour of *laissez-faire*, administrative nihilism or other political creeds founded upon the theory that liberty consists in being let alone; it does not deny that a discussion, in which people have a certain end constantly before them, produces decisions of a practical wisdom quite unobtainable by an individual. It does not advocate extremes of quietism or stoicism, the attitude that lets the world go by, or that other of Emily Brontë which fiercely apostrophizes the god within one's breast, alternately bewailing and revelling in the torture of mere existence, dreading and welcoming death as a release from the pains of identity.

But it denies the generalization that all men, as such, find solitude unbearable. It is said that the individual's account of himself must be accepted, if at all, with great reservations, that it needs a psycho-analyst, prying into our subconscious, to bring our real selves to light. And it is of course true that moods are transient and our being changes from day to day. These surely are arguments against rash generalizations. But however that may be it seems certain that with many people the desire for solitude is no less potent than the desire to be among others. They deliberately depart from society, are satisfied to be away from it and are conscious of no present wish to return to it. The fact that man dreads solitary confinement, and the boast 'stone walls do not a prison make' is, in the mouths of most, a piece of meaningless rhetoric, does not destroy the natural instinct for periods of segregation. One speaks without experience, but one fancies that the bride and bridegroom are not wholly reluctant to relinquish the wedding-breakfast and shake hands with the guests. Why, if man is fundamentally gregarious, does he study the entire length of a train in order to find what is colloquially called 'a carriage to himself'? And why is travelling by tube regarded as a trial, whereas a solitary journey across country has some of the qualities of a spiritual pilgrimage? We must admit that in many functions where the form of gregariousness is maintained the spirit is lacking, a man attends in the hope of meeting a person or persons he knows, and if this pleasure is not accorded him, the fact that many others were there will not prevent him voting the whole thing a bore and resolving inwardly not to go again.

In spite of the formidable mass of authority on the other side I would venture to assert that a man's 'trivial' moods are more likely to be brought out by society than by solitude; that what is sown in the corruption of gregariousness is reaped in the incorruption of isolation; that solitude is essential for 'that emotion recollected in tranquillity' in which great poetry is conceived. The emulative and sympathetic instincts in man are more powerful because more intense than the gregarious, and they are nurtured by a conscious process of selection, the selection from all possible standards of those few against which a man feels he must measure himself, and from the whole vague sum, just those few persons and objects on whom he feels impelled to expend sympathy and affection. It has been said by a modern writer that a man needs clubs, social organizations, to carry out his hobbies, whereas we know that such absorbing hobbies as—moth hunting or china collecting—have an almost entirely personal appeal: it would afford one small satisfaction to hear that some member of one's society had picked up a cheap Ming vase, or that a unit of some lepidopterists' brotherhood had raised his society to distinction by catching a Purple Emperor. If I am asked whether I am a member of a certain club I feel gratified; but if that feeling is analysed, it may be found to proceed partly from an acute realization of the reflected glory which shines on every member of that august body and not least on me, but also from the fact that the inquirer does not share this jealously guarded privilege, much as he might like to; this uncharitable feeling is of course momentary. But thus we see one of the evils of gregariousness illustrated by this society; for though in its origin it is neither offensive nor defensive nor merely social, it begets in one at least of its members that hubris, that intolerance, that suggestion of a caste apart, which cannot be dissociated from any, even the best, social organization.

We do not therefore think collectively. Who, at the sight of a graveyard, is not struck by the thought of the multiplicity, and not the sum, of death: its reality in relation to each man, woman or child who lies under a tombstone that a pitiful ultimate expression of man's desire to preserve his identity contrives to differ unnecessarily and perhaps even inartistically from the rest? *'Je mourrai seul'*, said Pascal. We are brought back once more to the essential solitude of men in the supreme moments of their lives, and remember how few are our points of contact, how incredibly great is the number of even our articulate thoughts and sensations which are incommunicable, as against the paltry, limited, base-metal currency that we exchange, so grudgingly and suspiciously, with others: always ready to palm off a doubtful coin and husbanding the nobler pieces so carefully that we often cannot find them ourselves.

The utmost importance that could be attached to the gregariousness of many people is that while centred in self they are not unpleased to please; they derive an uncertain fortuitous satisfaction from communion with their fellows, a less intense but more reliable and lasting satisfaction from their relations with inanimate objects, the thoughts and sensations derived from these, and even from animals. If I may be permitted a personal reflection, I would say, with all respect, that I derive more pleasure from a chance encounter with my uncle's cat than I do from an interview, even by appointment and heralded by a domestic, with that animal's master or mistress. We entertain one another, as Montaigne says, with mutual apish tricks,

whereas that familiar and satisfying intercourse is impossible
with many (even the most eminent) human beings, with whom
we stand for ever in the attitude and posture of gladiators,
anxious only to score points or (more commonly) to avoid
having them scored off us.

I am aware that there are occasions when no relation, either
with human beings or with inanimate objects, can recruit or
restore our spent soul-forces, when the things and persons on
whom we have (if the expression may be allowed) lavished ourselves, suddenly appear their unworthy selves, without any
admixture or taint of us—they become indescribably alien and
remote. This condition, which is equivalent, I suppose, to the phase
in the mystic's development termed the 'dark night of the
soul', and, looked at from the medical standpoint, is one of the
surest symptoms of neurasthenia, may fall to the lot of a temperament that is neither wholly absorbed in religious ecstasy
nor warped by mental disease. It marks the final fallibility of the
Wordsworthian doctrine of communion with nature as man's
most reliable anodyne, and has never been better expressed
than in the lines of Christina Rossetti:

> *The irresponsive silence of the land,*
> *The irresponsive sounding of the sea,*
> *Speak both one message of one sense to me:—*

> *'Aloof, aloof, we stand aloof: so stand*
> *Thou too aloof, bound with the flawless band*
> *Of inner solitude; we bind not thee,*
> *But who from thy self-chain shall set thee free?*
> *What heart shall touch thy heart, what hand thy hand?'*

This, as it stands, is definitely a secular or non-mystical experience; it merely shows that in this instance at any rate
nature had betrayed the heart that loved her. Though, like
St. Augustine, *amans amare*, Christina Rossetti, one suspects,
never saw the fulfilment of her tentative and constantly-baffled
experiments in mysticism, she could echo Augustine's cry, 'My
heart is restless till it rest in Thee', but she never passed beyond
her novitiate, she was denied that supreme exaltation for the
true participants of which, we are assured, the glory of the
world is over and the earth in ashes. Gregariousness, religion

and mysticism are as far asunder as the poles; they negative each other, and if the reality of mystical experience is admitted, we must recognize in it one of the most powerful factors in human development.

XIII

REMEMBERING VENICE

ON THE map Venice is pear-shaped, or, to be more exact, the shape of a flat fish; and its course is set in a north-westerly direction towards the mainland. But there is not, I should think, another city in the world where cartography and actuality bear so little relation to each other. Once inside Venice, one's sense of direction sickens from a surfeit of possibilities, and then dies.

I lived there for many years, but I doubt if even now I could find the way from the Piazza to the railway station. Follow the crowd, they say, and the advice is not so foolish as it sounds. On the wettest day there is always a crowd in the streets of Venice, moving slowly towards an objective. Following it will take you to some centre, to the Piazza, to the Rialto bridge, to the Accademia, to the Campo San Polo, to the Campo Santa Margherita; at any rate it will not lead you to a dead end, or to a canal without a pavement, as frequently happens when you strike off on your own. The crowd might even take you to the station, a destination which, if it meant I was leaving Venice, I always viewed with a heavy heart. But then of course you would be going in a gondola, with your luggage piled up behind, and funereally draped in the folds of a black cloth, if you had a private gondola, as I had.

Most Venetians and many visitors who are familiar with Venice look askance at the gondola as a means of getting about the city. It certainly has its drawbacks. On very windy days, which often in Venice means wet days since the *siroccale* nearly always brings rain, only the boldest gondolier will venture forth without a second oar; and though he nearly always knows some friend or connection of his family who will oblige, the lad is not always forthcoming at a moment's notice. And if you persuade him to go by appealing to his pride, or by threatening to find a braver, stronger oarsman, his unwillingness may turn out to be justified; for a gondola is sensitive to a puff of wind, it is a fair-weather craft, and its very ability to turn in its own length and slide round the sharpest bend is a terrible handicap on a windy day. Nor, probably, will the passenger have the slightest idea what it means to the gondolier if his precious craft should sustain a scratch, a bump, a shock even: far better that all the passengers, and indeed the gondolier himself, should fall headlong in the water.

How often, with the *bora* (north wind) blowing, has Giacomo reminded me of the risk of taking the gondola into the Sacco della Misericordia, that northern inlet, suitably facing the cemetery, along one side of which runs the garden of the Palazzo Contarini dal Zaffo, the most enchanted spot in Venice. Do I not remember how Signora D. was so nearly wrecked, attempting the transit on a stormy night? It is, he says, a *punto scabbroso*, though no one would guess this on a calm day—the kind of day on which Guardi has often painted it, looking across to the cemetery with the island of Murano on the left, the colour of a dried rose-leaf.

The *siroccale*, too, nearly always brings a high tide: and at high tide there are certain bridges under which a gondola cannot pass. The Carmine bridge, built low, it is said, to spare the footsteps of an infirm Cardinal, is a notorious offender. This bridge was also a focal point for the traditional fights between the Castellani and the Nicolotti—factions drawn from rival districts in Venice. Inlaid at each of the four corners of the bridge's shallow crown is a marble footprint, showing that there the champions of each faction took their stand ready to throw their adversaries into the water.

The Carmine bridge barred my way into the town, for I lived just round the corner, opposite the church of San Sebastiano where Paolo Veronese is buried; and often have I had to wait while the shining *ferro* of the gondola—the Doge's cap conventionalized in steel—plunged up and down like the head of a restive horse, but always too high for the flat arch of the bridge: and disengaged spectators, who are never lacking in Venice, would offer to lend their weight as ballast to our too buoyant craft, so that it passed under, to the accompaniment of much advice and many grunts. Little as I want to see Venice changed, I have often wished that the Ponte del Carmine could be rebuilt to a more aspiring model.

There are other drawbacks to the gondola. Byron called it
'a coffin clapped in a canoe'; but the coffin part, the *felze*, the
sombre cabin lined with silk and crowned with a row of funereal
pompons, is a luxury from more spacious days which few
gondoliers now possess and still fewer are willing to put on, so
heavy is it, so grievously liable to be stained, scratched or
otherwise blemished. If the weather is bad enough to need the
felze, it is too bad to use the *felze*: that is the argument. And
lastly, Venice is not so completely water-borne as strangers
might think, or as it was before the Austrians filled in so many
of the canals. You cannot always drive up to the door, you may
have to get out in the wet, and walk.

Except for long journeys—and the longest single journey
through the city takes but half an hour—I did not use the
gondola much in Venice. I liked to walk, though the air in the
calli is stagnant, the pavement monotonous and dead under one's
feet, and one sometimes comes back feeling more tired than
exercised. But tired only in body. To the eye and the mind the
streets of Venice are a perpetual refreshment. Ruskin was right
to call his book *The Stones of Venice*. In some moods, though not
in all (for the Venetian climate conduces to nervous irritability
and a critical outlook), every stone seems to have been laid with
love. And not only in places where the builders' handiwork may
have been supposed to catch the eye, but in half-hidden spots
where you have to peer and crane your neck to see it. To palace
and hovel alike the Venetian builders gave of their best,
achieving an effect of harmony out of the most incongruous
jumble of styles and sizes. There is no residential quarter in
Venice. A palace may spring out of a slum, may indeed be a slum,
a tenement inhabited by many families. To be sure, the fringe
of great palaces along both sides of the Grand Canal forms a kind
of aristocracy of buildings, but even these are interspersed with
humbler dwellings; and conversely many of the finest palaces—
the Giovanelli, the Albrizzi, the Mocenigo palace of S. Stae—
are tucked away in side streets, and hemmed in by houses of
no account which prevent their enormous proportions being
properly realized.

Venice is a city built for show; the Italians are intensely
sensitive to appearances, and nearly every house, however
simple, has some artistic merit; but it is a democratic show in
which the magnificence is shared alike by the poor and the rich;

indeed the very word *palazzo*, with its presumptuous ring, is a
late innovation; and such Venetian patricians as still inhabit the
homes their forebears built, invite you formally to *cà loro*—
'their house', not their palace.

In many, perhaps in most, great cities the houses of the rich
seem to look down on their poorer neighbours as a Rolls-Royce
looks down on a Baby Austin: to see them is to think of them in
terms of money. Venice must have cost more to build than any
city of its size in the world: yet that aspect of it need never
strike the beholder unless he is looking for it. A few of the
Renaissance palaces—the Rezzonico, the Papadopoli, the Cà
Pesaro, the Vendramin Calergi, with their audacious fronts,
proclaim in voices which can still be heard the pride and power
of the families that built them; but even in their case grandeur
survives ostentation. Oddly enough on the walls of the Vendramin, one of the least beautiful but not the least sumptuous of
the four, whether in humility or to propitiate Fate, we find
written the words *Non nobis domine*—'Not unto us, O Lord, but
unto Thy name be the praise'—a sentiment hard to connect with
the edifice it adorns, but true of most of the stones of Venice.

But architecture is not the only charm of the streets. All
quarters in Venice are poor quarters, but some are poorer than
others. I lived in a very poor quarter, and my nearest way to the
Piazza lay along a street rightly called the Calle Lunga, for it
seemed interminable. There is a tradition that in the Middle
Ages the people of the neighbouring parish, Archangelo Raf-
faele, were so provincial that they had never been to the Piazza
and did not know the way. (Actually it is some twenty-five
minutes' walk.) One of them, greatly daring, entrusted himself
to a guide but took the precaution to drop a fish (most of the
inhabitants were fishermen) at frequent intervals along the
route to mark the way back. An ingenious plan, but alas it came
to naught, for the cats ate the fish and tradition does not record
whether the traveller ever reached home. The same fate would
await him today: like all the streets of Venice, the Calle Lunga
swarms with cats—thin, furtive creatures belonging to a breed
supposedly imported for its ferocity and rat-catching qualities.
They nose about among the parcels of food humane persons
have put down for them and flee at one's approach. They add to
the movement, if not to the gaiety, imprisoned between those
narrow walls. Above, the washing flaps, cheerfully or despon-

dently, according to one's mood, making a restless pattern of
shade and sunshine.

In Venice the life of the houses overflows into the streets; the
people buy and sell, talk, eat and sometimes sleep there, and
they also walk, but not fast, and if you are in a hurry you must
shoulder your way and shout *'Con permesso!'* ('By your leave').
As a rule, the Venetians show in their faces and bearing everything they feel: the happy look happy and sing an operatic
stave; the sorrowful look utterly woebegone; the strong stride
along as though on air; the infirm creep painfully in the shadow
of the wall, where the human current is weakest; the prosperous
expand with consciousness of wealth; the poor shrink into themselves. They are a most self-expressive people. Only when there
is bad news do they walk about with hard, shut faces—*con muso
duro*—keeping their feelings to themselves.

The Venetian temper is *allegro*, but the Venetian tempo goes
adagio. I never seemed to find time to loiter in the streets,
because the routine into which I had insensibly fallen meant
spending the best part of the day on the lagoon. A friend said,
'You use Venice as a place to work up a sweat in', and he was
partly right; incidentally the climate of Venice is irresistibly
sudorific, especially when the weather is under the influence
of the sirocco, a condition which does not depend entirely on the
direction of the wind.

The lagoons of Venice reach down to Chioggia in the south,
a distance of nineteen miles. I helped to row the gondola there
once, against the tide most of the way, past the Lido, past
Pellestrina, past San Pietro in Volta, the long shingly islands
which divide the lagoon from the Adriatic. Alberoni, some
seven miles out, was the chief gateway into Venice before the
channel round the north end of the Lido was developed. When
Chioggia was in the hands of the Genoese, the Venetians, hoping
their enemies would go aground on the *barena*, the mud flats,
removed the posts that marked the canal. The lagoon is threaded
by these natural channels, some of them visible at low tide,
forlorn brown rivulets running between wide tracts of mud; but
in normal conditions they cannot be distinguished from the
water round them, except, on a calm day, as streaks of darker
blue. The lesser-known canals are called *ghebi*, and their where-
abouts has to be learnt. The course of the more important ones
is marked by posts—*briccole*—set at regular intervals, sometimes

singly, sometimes in clusters like bunches of asparagus. On a
still day when the horizon is hazy these posts seem to climb
into the sky before they curve away out of sight.

I came to know most of the canals within a radius of five miles
of Venice; on the south side that is, the north I knew much less
well, though I went to the islands of Torcello and San Francesco
del Deserto—the one bone-pale and monumental, the other
green and sylvan.

I lived on the south side of the town and the north always
seemed strange to me, and a little sad. What a contrast between
that cheerful bustling thoroughfare, the Zattere, a noisy
symphony in a major key, and the corresponding promenade on
the north, the Fondamente Nuove, a nocturne by Chopin, always
in shadow and with few people on it except a little throng round
the steamer-station, waiting to go to Murano or visit their dead
relations in the cemetery. I used to go that way sometimes,
however, skirting the great indented wall of the Arsenal, its
pink surface blotchy with white salt sweat, and tie up at a post
by the island of Santa Rosa, near its minute white church guarded
by two cypresses—*il duomo*, the cathedral, my gondolier called
it: I always knew the moment when this joke would come.

In spring the voluptuous nightingales shouted from the
thickets all through the heat of the day. After lunch we played a
Venetian card game called *briscola*, a simple digestive game less
exacting than the intellectual, memory-straining *tre-sette*, or
the fascinating but maddening *Gi-la-Greca*, a kind of poker—
the point of which was to lose your temper and show it, otherwise the game lost its savour. Like poker it 'belonged to the
bluffed', and I could generally win: but so ignobly, that all the
zest went out of it. Then, after a siesta, I turned to my book and
he to his newspaper—that newspaper which, with others of its
kidney, has made so much bad blood between our countries.

In the late afternoon we rowed back, straight into the sun,
past the church of the Greci with its white leaning tower, out
into the populous dancing water of the *bacino* (basin), the piazza
of Venetian maritime life, past the Dogana, whose clock grew
more and more unreliable under the strain of the political
situation, up the crescent-shaped Giudecca canal, past the red,
many-windowed Casa del Vento where a breeze always blows,
and home.

My seasons in Venice were the spring, April, May and June,

and the autumn, October and November; they embraced every kind of weather and I have seen the lagoon in most of its moods. Twice I have been ignominiously towed home by a tug; once I was nearly benighted at the island of Sant'Angelo della Polvere, a powder magazine of forbidding aspect. In those days our relations with Italy were friendly and the commandant, by the light of his single candle, telephoned to Venice for a motor-boat. We sat watching the crests of foam racing across the dark waters, and thinking that every moving light was the answer to our summons, but the motor-boat never came, and he sent me back in the garrison's boat, manned by a dozen sailors.

None of the islands, however beautiful to look at, was very hospitable. San Servolo was the men's lunatic asylum, San Clemente the women's; Sacco Sessola, which would have been such a useful port in a storm, only admitted consumptives and their friends. The Isola della Grazia held itself aloof from all but cases of fever; Poveglia, with its lovely campanile, one of my favourite haunts, was reserved for those who had come in contact with such cases. The islands that one could land on—Campana, Poveglia Vecchia, Fisolo—forts in the First World War, clad in verdure but little else, were places no one could want to land on. Partly for that reason I used to frequent the nearest, until superstition, born of a number of unexpected thunderstorms which seemed directed at me personally, made me forgo it. And with increasing political tension, the fortified islands like Campalto grew so sensitive to my proximity that angry shouts greeted my appearance on the skyline.

Yes, the islands were forbidden country, emblems of what all Italy afterwards became. They looked friendly and were not. But the lagoon was always friendly, as were the fishermen who rowed across it, or sailed down the canals in barges or, more grandly, in *bragozze*—big and rather clumsy Adriatic fishing boats—with saffron and russet sails sometimes dyed with the emblem of the family who owned them; it might be a conventional design, or a religious subject, or a horse (*'Che cavallo!'* my gondolier used to exclaim, pityingly, at the sight of this naïve but spirited quadruped).

The boatloads of young people who came out on the afternoons of festas, dressed in white, laughing at their failure to manœuvre their little boats, laughing at each other, laughing at nothing, always enjoying themselves, never rowdy or vulgar or inane, were friendly too. And in the distance lay Venice under the guardianship of its cupolas and campaniles, higher than the water, lower than the sky, resting, if it was a calm day, on its own reflections.

As a rule, the most beautiful view of Venice is the one you have coming back from the Lido when twilight gathering round the setting sun turns the air to violet. But the one I know best, the one which Shelley must have seen when he first approached the city, is from the mainland, from Fusina. There is a moment, which must be watched for and which does not last long, when the declining sun catches the brickwork and turns it to gold; a few minutes later the lagoon changes from dark blue to pale blue, with lilac shadows between the ripples. Sometimes the whole expanse becomes a smoky pink.

At a distance, Venice is dominated by the campanile of St. Mark's, but coming nearer, other towers assert themselves; Madonna dell'Orto, solid and round-topped, rules over one quarter on the north side, San Francesco della Vigna, slender as a pencil, soars over another. The Frari leans this way, San Stefano that; churches are always cropping up in positions which do not seem to belong to them—at a distance, the dome of the Salute can easily be confused with that of the Redentore—and I had lively arguments with my gondolier as to which was which. Our church, San Sebastiano, had a modest but satisfying campanile of red brick, much older than the church itself, with an octagonal upper storey where the bells hung. Like all Venetian bells, they were very vocal at sunset.

Back from the lagoon I stood on my balcony to watch the stream of people passing through the little triangular campo across the canal and directly in front of me. Above them, crowning the marble façade of the church, are the figures of three saints, in the centre San Sebastian, pierced with arrows. I thought that his attitude, which though operatic suggests more physical pain than do most representations of the twice-martyred saint, had no message now for the happy, kindly, easygoing throng who chattered their way beneath him. But during the few years that have passed since I saw him, he has become a symbol of mankind.